Ó MEACHAIR

THE STORY OF A CLAN

Gabrielle Ní Mheachair

Uí Cairin Press
St. Louis, MO, USA
Templemore, Co. Tipperary, Ireland
uicairin@woeltje.org

Copyright © 2014 Gabrielle Ní Mheachair

June 2014:   1st Edition

ISBN-13:   978-0-692-24417-3
ISBN-10:   0692244174

To my children,
Maeve, John, and Éile

Go dtuga Dia neart croí is corp doibh i gconaí.

Contents

Chapter 1: English Monarchs and Their Policies in Ireland

Chapter 2: Highlights of Cinéal Meachair

Chapter 3: Ó Meachair

Chapter 4: Genealogy of J. C. Ó Meachair

Chapter 5: Heraldry

Chapter 6: The Celts in Ireland

Chapter 7: The Political Division of Celtic Ireland

Chapter 8: The Barony of Ikerrin

Chapter 9: Cinál Meachair

Chapter 10: Christianity

Chapter 11: The Vikings

Chapter 12: The Anglo-Normans

Chapter 13: Ó Meachair Castles

Chapter 14: The Flight of the Earls

Chapter 15: Demise of Gaelic Ireland

Chapter 16: Cromwell

Chapter 17: The Wild Geese

Chapter 18: The Penal Laws

Chapter 19: Catholic Emancipation

Chapter 20: The Famine

Chapter 21: The Land Wars

Chapter 22: Éire Saor

Ó Meachair Nicknames

References

Foreword

The story of this book began one summer when my father bemoaned the fact that, other than the oldest and youngest of his thirteen children, all had emigrated. Eleven were scattered throughout the world in such places as Canada, Saudi Arabia, Brazil, Germany, Switzerland, England, and the United States. He lamented the idea that his descendants would have no knowledge of their great ancestry. Together he and I decided to collect everything that was written about the Mahers and compile what we found into a simple history for the family. We also began working on the family genealogy. This small project exploded into a giant undertaking. I found myself knee-deep in papers, articles, photos, letters, family history, books, and so on. My father and I continued collecting for about five years. He died suddenly in 1993. His death spurred me to action.

    The goal of this work is to better acquaint Mahers throughout the world with the role their ancestors played in the dramas of Irish history, from the coming of the Celts to the departure of the British.

    I searched tirelessly for poetry that best captures each era of Irish history. My choices have clarity of meaning, purpose, and style. I beg you to read each one. This poetry adds to the mood and will enhance your understanding.

    I must say that the past twenty years have been quite challenging. However, I am now much better informed about the history of my people.

—Gabrielle Meachair Woeltje, 2014

Acknowledgments

This book has taken more than twenty years to complete. During this time I have worked with hundreds of wonderful people. Unfortunately, it would be impossible to name them individually. Hence, I will venture to name those who have gone above and beyond the call of duty in their efforts to help me. I thank Keith F. Woeltje, my husband, for his support and constant encouragement. He championed this book from the beginning. My children, Maeve, John, and Éile, for their patience while I neglected them to hang out in graveyards, farm yards, libraries, and old castle ruins. My mother, Kathleen Ryan Maher, for her ancient lore. Monsignor Thomas Francis Meagher, formerly of Knocka, Drom, for his encouragement. Mary Maher, Ikerrin Hall, Templemore, for the use of her personal library. Joseph Meyers, Hilton Head, South Carolina, who contributed information on the Mahers and Thomas Francis Maher. Elaine Ryan Sullivan, Australia, for her help in unraveling the mystery of Thomas Francis Meagher's heir. Monsignor Maurice Dooley, PP Loughmore, for his advice and support. Mary Guinan Darmody, Local Studies Department, Tipperary Libraries, Thurles, for her patience and help in locating needed documents. Denis Corcoran, St. Louis, Missouri, for the use of his copies of the Annals of the Four Masters. John Bradshaw, Tipperary Clans Office, for his genuine encouragement and advice. George Willoughby, Thurles, for his photographs and good council. And, finally, to the many families who welcomed me into their homes, who answered my letters and phone calls, and who helped compile several Maher genealogies. I thank you all most sincerely.

My proofreaders deserve a special thank you: Perry M. Arthur, Florida; Joan Bick, St. Louis, Missouri; John Maher, Forest, Templemore; William Hayes, Lisheen Roscrea; Dominic Maher, New York; Ger Riordan, Tipperary; Jim Ryan, Thurles, and Katie Sharp, St. Louis, Missouri.

Note: I have endeavored to be objective in my evaluation of what others have written and what I have written about the Ó Meachair Clan. I beg you to be merciful of my inaccuracies and shortcomings.

Éire

William Drennan (1754–1820)

When Eire first rose from the dark-swelling flood,
God blessed the green island, and saw it was good;
The emerald of Europe, it sparkled and shone,
In the ring of the world, the most precious stone.
In her sun, in her soil, in her station thrice blest,
With her back towards Britain, her face to the west,
Eire stands proudly insular, on her steep shore,
And strikes her high harp 'mid the ocean's deep roar.

But when its soft tones seem to mourn and to weep,
A dark chain of silence is thrown o'er the deep;
At the thought of the past the tears gush from her eyes,
And the pulse of her heart makes her white bosom rise.
O! sons of green Eire, lament o'er the time
When religion was war, and our country a crime;
When man in God's image inverted His plan,
And molded his God in the image of man.

When the interest of state wrought the general woe,
The stranger a friend, and the native foe;
While the mother rejoiced o'er her children oppressed,
And clasped the invader more close to her breast;
When, with Pale for the body and Pale for the soul,
Church and state joined in compact to conquer the whole;
And, as Shannon was stained with Milesian blood,
Eyed each other askance and pronounced it was good.

By the groans that ascend from your fore fathers' grave,
For their country thus left to the brute and the slave,
Drive the demon of Bigotry home to his den,
And where Britain made brutes now let Eire make men.
Let my sons like the leaves of the shamrock unite,
A partition of sects from one footstalk of right,
Give each his full share of the earth and the sky,
Nor fatten the slave where the serpent would die.

Alas! for poor Eire, that some are still seen
Who would dye the grass red from their hatred to Green;
Yet, O! when you're up and they're down, let them live,
Then yield them that mercy which they would not give.
Arm of Eire, be strong! but be gentle as brave!
And, uplifted to strike, be still ready to save!
Let no feeling of vengeance presume to defile
The cause of, or men of, the Emerald Isle.

The cause it is good, and the men they are true,
And the Green shall outlive both the Orange and Blue!
And the triumphs of Eire her daughters shall share,
With the full swelling chest, and the fair flowing hair.
Their bosom heaves high for the worthy and brave,
But no coward shall rest on that soft-swelling wave;
Men of Eire! awake, and make haste to be blest,
Rise - Arch of the Ocean, and Queen of the West!
(Hayes, Gwynn, Ed. pp. 14–15)

Ó Meachair

Maher

Meagher

Meacher

Magher

Mahar

Marr

Maghyr

Megher

Meigher

Ó Maher

Ó Meagher

Ó Meacher

Ó Magher

Mahir

Chapter 1: English Monarchs and Their Policies in Ireland

William the Conqueror (1066–1087)
1066 The Battle of Hastings is fought in October.

1066–1154 Norman Rule in England

William II (Rufus) (1087–1100)

Henry I (Beauclerc) (1100–1135)

Stephen (1135–1154)
1134–1174 Dermot Mac Murrough is King of Leinster.

Henry II (1154–1189)
1155 Pope Adrian IV issues a papal bull, which gives Henry the authority to invade Ireland and bring the Irish Church under Roman control.

1166 Dermot Mac Murrough, King of Leinster, appeals to Henry for help to oppose his enemies in Ireland.

1166–1175 Rory O Connor is the last native High King of Ireland.

1170 Strongbow and the Anglo-Normans arrive to aid Mac Murrough.

1171 Henry invades Ireland and requests the submission of the Irish chieftains. The King of Leinster submits. Henry is accepted as Lord of Ireland.

1171 At the Council of Cashel, the Irish clergy submit to Roman authority.

1177 Prince John is made Lord of Ireland.

1185 Prince John makes his first visit to Ireland.

Theobald Walter is given a grant of lands in Munster. These lands include the ancient territory of the O Meaghers.

Richard I the Lion Heart (1189–1199)
1189 Richard's third Crusade to the Holy Land takes place.

John (1199–1216)
1210 John makes his second visit to Ireland.

1215 John agrees to seal the Magna Carta.

Henry III (1216–1272)

1252 Henry appoints Edward, his oldest son, as Lord of Ireland.

Edward I (1272–1307)

1300 Only King's coinage is to be used in Ireland.

Edward II (1307–1327)
1310 A parliament at Kilkenny bans Irish men from Anglo-Irish monasteries.

Edward III (1327–1377)

1366 The Statutes of Kilkenny are implemented to prevent the assimilation of Anglo-Normans into the Irish culture.

1376 Art Mac Murrough is King of Leinster.

Richard II (1377–1399)

1394 Richard leads an army to conquer Ireland. Art Mac Murrough ambushes Richard's army.

1395 Tadgh Ó Meachair submits to Richard II in Kilkenny.

1399 Richard leads a second army to Ireland.

Henry IV (1399–1413)

Henry V (1413–1422)

1415 Henry defeats the French at the battle of Agincourt.

Henry VI (1422–1461) (1470–1471)

1413 Henry VI is crowned King of France.

1453 The English are driven out of France.

1455 The War of the Roses begins.

1460 Ireland gains parliamentary independence.

Edward IV (1461–1470) (1471–1483)

1477–1513 The Geraldine families come to power in Ireland. Gearóid Mór Fitzgerald is the Earl of Kildare. Edward V (1483)

Richard III (1483–1485)

Henry VII (1485–1509)

1492 Christopher Columbus discovers America.

1494 Poyning's Law declares all Irish laws must be ratified in England.

Henry VIII (1509–1547)

1513–1534 Gearóid Óg Fitzgerald is the popular Irish leader.

1533 Henry annuls his marriage to Catherine of Aragon and marries Anne Boleyn. Henry is excommunicated.

1534 Act of Supremacy declares Henry supreme head of the Church of England.

1536 Anglo-Irish Parliament acknowledges Henry VIII as the King of Ireland and Head of the Church of Ireland. Suppression of the monasteries in Ireland follows.

1539 Giolla na Naomh Ó Meachair submits to Henry VIII.

1541 Henry VIII is declared King of Ireland.

1541 "Surrender and Regrant" is Henry's policy to subdue Ireland.

Edward VI (1547–1153)

1549 The Act of Uniformity in England makes Catholic Mass illegal.

1560 The Act of Uniformity is introduced to Ireland. Schoolmasters must conform to the Church of Ireland or be transported to Barbados. The Act of Supremacy and the Act of Uniformity must be adhered to in order to hold public office in Ireland.

Mary I (1553–1558)

1554 Protestant persecution in England begins.

1557 England declares war on France.

1569–1583 The Desmond Fitzgerald families revolt.

Elizabeth I (1558–1603)

1572 Tadgh Ó Meachair agrees to terms with the Earl of Ormond.

1588 The Spanish Armada is wrecked off the coast of Ireland.

1592 Trinity College is founded.

1594 Hugh O Neill and the Nine Years War commence.

1598 Hugh O Neill and Rory O Donnell defeat the English at Yellow Ford.

1632–1636 The *Annals of the Four Masters* are compiled.

1601 The Battle of Kinsale is lost to Mountjoy.

1603 O Neill, Earl of Tyrone, and O Donnell, Earl of Tyrconnell, surrender.

James I of England and James VI of Scotland (1603–1625)

1607 "Flight of the Earl's": Earls of Tyrone and Tyrconnell flee to the continent.

1608 The Earls'a lands are forfeited to the crown and settled by Protestant settlers from England and Scotland. The Plantation of Ulster begins.

1620 The *Mayflower* sets sail for America.

Charles I (1625–1649)

1627 England and France go to war.

1641 The Ulster rising begins. Gaelic Catholics rebel throughout Ireland.

1642 The Catholic Confederation convenes at Kilkenny.

1642–49 Civil War breaks out in England.

1649 Cromwell is appointed Chairman of the Council of State. Charles is executed. Roman Catholic worship is forbidden.

Cromwell (1649–1660)

1649–50 Cromwell invades Ireland.

1649 Two thirds of Irish lands are confiscated for English men.

1652 Ireland is governed directly from Westminster. An Act for Settling Ireland is drawn up.

1653 Cromwell is the Lord Protector of England. Surveys for the Cromwellian plantation begins.

1654 Dispossessed Irish Catholics must evacuate to Mayo and Galway by May 1.

Charles II (1660–1685)

1662 The Duke of Ormond is appointed Governor of Ireland. The Act of Settlement for Ireland is enacted.

1663 Irish cattle exports and general trade are restricted.

1664–68 Hearth Tax is imposed.

1671 Direct imports from the colonies are forbidden.

1673 The Test Act prevents Catholics from taking public office. Catholic bishops and members of religious houses are banished. Catholic schools are closed.

1685 Charles converts to Catholicism on his deathbed.

James II (1685–1688)

1686 James attempts to restore Catholicism in England.

1688 Declaration of Indulgence suspends all laws against Catholics and Non-Conformants. The English Parliament rejects James. His son-in-law, William of Orange, is invited to restore English Protestant Liberty. James abdicates and flees to France.

William and Mary (1689–1702)

1689 William and Mary become joint sovereigns of England. Catholic forces loyal to James lay siege to Derry. The Williamites win the day.

1690 The Battle of the Boyne is fought. The Williamites win the day.

1691 The Treaty of Limerick is made and broken. "Flight of the Wild Geese": Eleven thousand supporters of the Irish cause go into exile.

Others are convicted of treason. All Members of Parliament must take the Oath of Allegiance to the Crown and the Abjuration Act (denying the supremacy of the Catholic Pope).

1695 Irish Catholics hold 14 percent of the land. An Act of Parliament prohibits the education of Catholics.

1697 The Act of Banishment banishes the Catholic Clergy.

1699 Trade laws restrict the export of Irish wool.

Anne (1702–1714)

1703 Catholics are forbidden to carry arms. Parish priests must register for one parish only.

1703 The Gavelkind Act declares that Catholic farmers must bequeath their property among all of their sons.

1704 Catholics are restricted from land ownership and public offices. The Test Act is enforced.

George I (1714–1727)

1719 England independently makes laws for Ireland.

1727 Catholics cannot vote for Members of Parliament or civil offices.

1728 Act passed to remove franchise in Irish Catholics.

George II (1728–1760)

1760 The common lands in Ireland are closed.

George III (1760–1820)

1762 The Whiteboys organize to protest the closing of the commonages.

1772 The Relief Act allows Catholics to lease bog land.

1775–83 The American War of Independence is fought.

1778 Gardiner's Relief Bill allows Catholics to lease land on longer leases if they take the Oath of Allegiance. The Irish Volunteers organize.

1780 The Test Act is repealed.

1782 Gardiner's Relief Act II allows Catholics who took the Oath of Allegiance in 1778 to purchase land. Religious Penal Laws come to an end. An independent Irish parliament known as Grattan's Parliament is formed.

1783 British recognize American independence.

1789 Owners of reclaimed bog land are exempt from tithes for seven years.

1791 The Society of United Irishmen is founded. Wolfe Tone is among their leaders.

1793 Hobart's Relief Act allows education and professions for Catholics.

1796 The Insurrection Act forbids insurrection and provides for Marshall Law.

1798 The United Irishmen Rebellion is a failure. Wolfe Tone is captured.

1800–1845 The population of Ireland doubles from 4,500,000 to 8,175,124.

1801 Ireland looses its Parliament with the passing of the Act of Union.

1803 Robert Emmet stages a failed revolution. He is captured and executed.

1815 The Corn Laws are passed to protect British agricultural produce from cheaper imports.

George IV (1820–1830)

1822 Irish Constabulary Act appoints magistrates and a county police force.

1823 Daniel O Connell is leader of the Catholic Association.

1824 Complete free trade is allowed.

1828 Daniel O Connell is elected Member of Parliament (MP) for Co. Clare. Being a Catholic, he cannot sit in Parliament.

1829 The Catholic Emancipation Act is passed. Daniel O Connell is the first Irish Catholic Member of Parliament.

William IV (1830–1837)

1831 The National Board of Education is founded.

1832 The Cess Tax (tax for the upkeep of Protestant Church buildings) is abolished.

Victoria (1837–1901)

1838 Direct payment of tithes is abolished, and the landlord is now responsible to pay them.

1838 The Poor Law Act has workhouses built.

1839 The "night of the big wind" causes huge storms and havoc in Ireland.

1842–1848 The Young Ireland Movement is founded.

1846 The Young Irelanders split from O Connell.

1845–1849 The Potato Famine devastates Ireland.

1846 The Corn Laws are repealed.

1847 Black '47 is the worst year of the famine. Soup kitchens are opened.

1848 Thomas Francis Meagher presents the tri-color flag to the people of Ireland. The Young Irelanders stage a failed revolt near Ballingarry, Co. Tipperary.

1849 The Irish Tenant League is founded. The Encumbered Estate Act passes.

1858 James Stephens establishes the Irish Republican Brotherhood (IRB).

1861 The American Civil War begins.

1867 The Fenians stage a failed revolt in Ireland.

1869 The Church Act disestablishes the Church of Ireland.

1870 The Land Act allows for compensation for disturbance. Isaac Butt founds the Home Rule Association.

1872 The Secret Ballot Act is passed.

1875 Charles Stuart Parnell is elected MP for County Meath.

1879–1882 The Land Wars struggles are fought.

1879 There is further threat of famine. Michael Davitt founds the Irish National Land League. There are widespread evictions.

1881 The Land Act II fixes fair rents.

1884 The Gaelic Athletic Association (GAA) is founded in Thurles.

1885 The Ashbourn Land Act provides five million pounds in loans to help tenants buy their land.

1886 The First Irish Home Rule Bill fails to pass in the House of Commons.

1891 The Land Purchase Act provides thirty million pounds in loans to tenants. The Congested District Boards are formed.

1893 The Gaelic League is founded. The Second Irish Home Rule Bill fails to pass the House of Lords.

1896 The Balfour Act provides fifty million pounds in loans to tenants.

1898 The United Irish League is founded. The Local Government Act changes local government from Grand Juries to County Councils.

Edward VII (1901–1910)

1903 Wyndham's Land Purchase Act provides one hundred million pounds in loans to tenants. Twelve million pounds is provided to encourage landlords to sell.

1905 Arthur Griffith founds the Sinn Féin movement.

1907 The Evicted Tenants Act forces landlords to sell.

1909 The first compulsory land purchase is enacted.

George V (1910–1936)

1912 The *Titanic* sinks.

1914 World War I begins.

1915 The IRB is reorganized.

1916 Padraic Pearse goes ahead with the Easter Rising in Dublin.

1917 Sinn Féin and the Irish Volunteers reorganize.

1918–19 There is a general election and a new Dáil is formed.

1920 The six counties in the North vote themselves out of the Irish Union.

1921 A truce is called, and the Anglo-Irish Treaty is presented.

1922 The Anglo-Irish Treaty is approved by Dáil Éireann. The British depart from the twenty-six counties of Ireland. The Irish Free State is established. Northern Ireland is excluded. Civil War ensues.

1923 The Civil War ends.

1923 The Land Act by Saorstát Éireann speeds the transfer of land ownership. A judicial commission fixes land prices.

1926 De Valera founds the Fianna Fáil party. A general election is held in the Free State.

1933 United Ireland (Fine Gael) party is founded under Eoin O Duffy.

1937 The Constitution of Éire replaces the Free State.

George VI (1936–1952)

1949 Ireland becomes a Republic and leaves the British Commonwealth.

Chapter 2: Highlights of Cinéal Meachair

Events in bold print relate to Cinéal Meachair.

AD 200 Provincial kings rule the provinces, and petty kings rule territories. Each chieftain pays allegiance to his overlord. Olioll Ollum is the third-century king of Munster. He is a direct descendant of Eber Finn, the Milesian Celt. Olioll Ollum is the great ancestor of the Cinéal Meachair, who descend from his third son, Cian, King of Ormond.

377–405 Niall of the Nine Hostages is the high king of Ireland. He raids the coasts of England and brings English slaves to Ireland.

C400 Saint Patrick is captured in Scotland and brought to Ireland as a slave from Scotland.

C432 Saint Patrick returns to Ireland as a bishop in an effort to Christianize pagan Ireland.

C470 Saint Patrick comes to Lower Ormond, where Meachar, the Ó Meachair chieftain, and his brothers, Furic and Muinneach, go to meet him. Subsequently the Ó Meachair Clan becomes Christian.

600–700 Ireland flourishes during her golden age of learning, art, illuminated manuscripts, and missionary work abroad.

600–700 The Cinéal Meachair becomes patrons of many monasteries, including Monaincha, Sean Ross, and Corville, Roscrea. The Abbot of Sean Ross performs the inauguration ceremonies of the clan's chieftains. The chieftains and their families are buried at Sean Ross Abbey and Holy Cross Abbey.

795 Vikings attack Ireland and raid the monasteries. Roscrea, the chief town of Cinéal Meachair, is sacked at least three times by the Vikings. The high king's seat is at Tara in County Meath.

852 The Norse occupy Dublin and Waterford. Tensions between the Norse and native Irish chieftains become intolerable.

940–1014 Brian Ború is high king of Ireland. Cinéal Meachair refuses to recognize him as the true king of Ireland. They give their allegiance to Maelseachnaill of Meath, whom Brian had deposed.

1011 At the Battle of Drinan, Co. Dublin, the Norse men are routed. Lorcan Ó Meachair, son of Echtigern, the chieftain, is killed along with many of his clansmen.

1014 Brian Ború is killed at the Battle of Clontarf. However, the Irish win the day and free Ireland from Norse dominance. Hugh the Wounder Ó Meachair leads the Cinéal Meachair into battle at Clontarf.

1169 The Anglo-Normans arrive in Ireland. This is the beginning of English occupation in Ireland.

1197 Rory O Connor is the last native high king of Ireland.

1171 Henry II (1154–1187), the Norman King of England, invades Ireland and demands that the Anglo-Norman lords and the Irish clan chieftains pay homage to him and accept him as their king. The Ó Meachair refuse to submit.

1185 Theobald Walter, the great ancestor of the Butlers of Ormond, is granted five and a half cantreds of Munster. This includes the territory of Éile, which includes the Cinéal Meachair lands in the Barony of Ikerrin.

1212 Theobald Walter fortifies his lands as far north as Roscrea, the oldest town in Cinéal Meachair territory.

1216–72 Henry III appoints Edward, his eldest son, Lord of Ireland.

1280 The Butlers build a castle at Roscrea to fortify their position in the Barony of Ikerrin.

1315 Edmund, Chief Butler of Ireland, is given grants of land, which include the Barony of Ikerrin.

1328 King Edward III is granted James, son of Edmund Chief Butler of Ireland, the title of Earl of Ormond. With this title he is also given large tracts of Tipperary, which include the Barony of Ikerrin.

1366 The Statutes of Kilkenny are enacted. The statutes forbid the Anglo-Normans from intermarrying with the Irish, adopting their language and customs, or following their ancient Brehon laws.

1372 The Ó Meachair, O Brien of Arra, and Mc Conmarre go to battle against the Anglo-Normans.

1377–99 Richard II is king of England. In 1394 he leads an army to conquer rebellious Ireland, but fails. In 1395 he demands that the Irish chieftains submit to his rule. In 1399 Richard returns with a second army to Ireland.

1377 Tadhg Ó Meachair, Captain of his Nation, is killed in battle against the Anglo-Normans.

1395 Tadhg Ó Meachair, son of the above Tadhg, Captain of his Nation, travels to the Dominican Church, Kilkenny and submits to King Richard II. He is given the right to retain the ancient clan lands under English law.

1401 Tadhg Ó Meachair is slain at Loch Carman by the Dublin Danes.

1413 The Ó Meachair, Chief of Ikerrin, dies.

1462 Tadhg Ó Meachair and his confederate troops fight Mac William of Clanrickard. Tadhg's son kills Mac William's son. The Cinéal Meachair wins the day but loses their chieftain during the battle.

1477–1534 The great Anglo-Norman family, the Fitzgeralds of Kildare, rule Ireland. This particular family adopts Irish customs and language despite the Statutes of Kilkenny.

1500–1600 Tipperary earns the reputation of being a most troublesome county.

1536 Henry VIII (1509–1547) declares himself king of Ireland and head of the Church of Ireland. He plots to destroy the Fitzgerald power in Ireland. During this period there is constant plundering and harassment of the Barony of Ikerrin.

1537 Lord Deputy Sir Leonard Grey reports that he has won a battle against Cinéal Meachair of Ikerrin. All are captured and the Ó Meachair is forced to give hostages.

1538 Cinéal Meachair is attacked and held at the castle at Roscrea.

1539 Gilla-na-Naomh Ó Meachair, captain of his nation, submits to Henry VIII in order to keep the clan lands legally under English law. He was tired of the constant harassment and plundering of Ikerrin.

1547 Edward VI (1547–1553) institutes the Act of Uniformity, which makes the Catholic Mass illegal in England. In 1560 the Act of Uniformity is introduced to Ireland.

Late 1500s With relative peace restored in Ikerrin, the Ó Meachair chieftains build castles to defend their territory. The Cinéal Meachair territory is subdivided into minor chieftanships, each with its own tower house. The clan's land is subsequently referred to as Ó Meachair territory or Ikerrin.

1558 Elizabeth I (1558–1603) ascends to the throne. Her personal goal is to subdue Ireland. She divides the land into counties, each with its own sheriff to enforce the law.

1560 A tax or fine of 160 pounds is levied on Ó Meachair territory.

1562 A tax increase of 360 pounds is levied on Ó Meachair territory.

1567 The Earl of Ormond's brothers attack and plunder Ikerrin.

1571 Gillenowe O Meagher is pardoned along with three hundred of his foot soldiers.

1572 Tadhg O Meagher agrees to terms with the Earl of Ormond. He pays one knight's fee in return for full possession of his lands.

1582 The Earl of Ormond plunders Ikerrin, violating the treaty of 1572.

1586 Elizabeth begins to colonize Munster. Ikerrin is excluded because it is considered the property of the Earl of Ormond.

1598 Hugh O Neill, Earl of Tyrone, and Rory O Donnell, Earl of Tirconnell, defeated the English at the Battle of the Yellow Ford.

1599 Keadagh O Meagher, captain of his nation, resides at Boolbawn Castle, Roscrea. He amasses an army of sixty foot-soldiers, thirty horse soldiers, and three hundred men. Sir George Carew, president of Munster, offers a reward for the capture of Keadagh O Meagher, whom he calls a rebel.

1601 The Earl of Ormond wins a surprise attack against O Meagher and O Kennedy. Sixteen O Meagher men are drowned.

1601–02 O Neill of Ulster and his forces camp with O Meagher at Druim Saileach, Roscrea, and Templetuohy. Hugh O Donnell marches his army across the Slieve Bloom Mountains into O Meagher territory. Together these armies march southward to take up arms for Ireland at the Battle of Kinsale. The Battle of Kinsale is the last battle of the Nine Years' War against England. Even with the aid of the Spanish fleet, the Irish lose the battle and the war because of treachery. This marks the end of Gaelic Ireland. Fearing for their lives, the Ulster Earls flee to Europe. Their flight becomes known as "the Flight of the Earls." Their Ulster lands are forfeited to the crown and planted by Protestant settlers from England and Scotland. The O Meaghers march home to fight another day.

1602 Captain Flower burns all of O Meagher's corn and kills some of his men as he plunders Ikerrin.

1603 Thadeus O Meagher of Clonakenny Castle surrender the lands of Clonakenny to the crown hoping that they will be granted to Sir John Davis.

1615 Sir John Davis reassigns the Meagher lands to Thadeus O Meagher. Thadeus dies the same year, leaving John O Meagher of Clonakenny as his heir.

1620 The *Mayflower* sets sail for America.

1641 A confederation of Irish forces is organized in Kilkenny. The O Meachairs join the confederacy.

1642 John O Meagher of Clonakenny Castle is captain of the nation. His son, Colonel Teige Óg O Meagher, of Cloneen Castle, Roscrea, raises a foot regiment and joins Colonel Philip O Dwyer of Dundrum, Baron Theobald Purcell of Loughmore, and others to fight with the confederacy of Irish forces. Colonel Teige Óg O

Meagher and his confederate allies lay siege to Cashel and demand its surrender. O Meagher and his confederate allies also fight against the parliamentary forces and lose. They surrender and make terms. Some of the leaders are exiled, while Tadhg Óg is refused pardon and sentenced to death by hanging.

1649 Cromwell is appointed chairman of the English Council of State in England. Roman Catholic worship is forbidden. In August 1649 Cromwell invades Ireland. Two-thirds of the land of Ireland is confiscated and allocated to English men.

1650 Cromwellian forces enter northwest Tipperary and capture Roscrea Castle. The O Meaghers are routed from their ancient homeland of Ikerrin. Some move west, but many stay behind.

1652 The Irish Confederation surrenders. Forty thousand men and officers are expelled to the continent, where they joined foreign armies. Among them are numerous O Meaghers. This is the first time O Meaghers leave their homeland in great numbers. These O Meaghers keep the "O Meagher" spelling of their name. Teige Óg O Meagher is hanged at Clonmel, County Tipperary. He is the only son of John O Meagher, Clonakenny Castle, and the last O Meagher chieftain.

1652–59 The Act for Settlement Ireland is passed, allowing for Cromwellian surveys to be drawn. These surveys identify the current owners of the land and to whom the land is to be granted. The Civil Survey of 1654, the Census of Ireland 1659, and the Book of Survey and Distribution are also drawn up at this time.

1653 The Act of Satisfaction arranges for the distribution of the confiscated land, including the O Meagher land. The Duke of York, the Duke of Ormond, and Sir Martin Noele get the largest share of Ikerrin; the remainder is divided among English adventurers.

1660–1700 Many O Meagher clan members do not move to Connaught as ordered. Some are worth less than five pounds, which suggests they are common clansmen living on common clanland. Some defiantly refuse to go west and hide in bogs and other desolate places to avoid capture and transportation.

1664–68 The Hearth Tax rolls show that 283 Meaghers are listed as heads of household in 65 parishes in County Tipperary and neighboring counties. This gives testimony to the fact that many Meaghers did not move west.

1660–85 Charles II (1660–1685) institutes a series of laws to restrict and prevent the production and exportation of Irish industry.

1673 Catholic bishops and members of religious houses are banished, and Catholic schools are closed.

1689 William of Orange and his wife Mary become king and queen of England.

1689–91 The Williamite Wars are fought. Many O Meaghers are listed in the various divisions of James's army: Sarsfield's Horse, Butler's Foot, Bagnel's Foot, Oxburg's Foot, Mount Cashel's Foot, and Purcell's Yellow Horse Brigade.

1690 James II of England fights William of Orange at the Battle of the Boyne. William of Orange wins the day.

1690 Captain John O Meagher, the famous Rapparee, is captured and hanged.

1691 The Treaty of Limerick is made and broken. A large number of O Meaghers go into exile. Subsequently they serve in foreign armies, which include the French, Spanish, Prussian, Polish, and Swiss. Meaghers who go into exile with "The Wild Geese" retain the spelling "Meagher." Some even keep the "O."

C1700 After the Williamite War, the Irish race is largely reduced to a tenant nation. They hold one eighth of the land in freehold. The clan system is crushed. Individual families begin using nicknames to distinguish themselves.

1703 The Gavelkind Act stipulates that large Catholic landholders are required to bequeath all their land among their sons. This subdivides Catholic properties over many generations.

1704 The Penal Laws are enforced with grievous penalties. Most of these laws ensure the abolition of civil and religious rights for Catholics. Since the Meaghers re staunchly Catholic, they cannot own or purchase property. They can lease land for thirty-one years, but they continue to be subjected to the whim of the landlord or his agent.

1750 List of Popish Inhabitants is drawn up.

1760 Landlords in Ireland close the common lands. These lands had been set aside from ancient times to provide a place for the poor to graze their animals for free. Many Meagher/Maher families lived on these lands since Cromwellian times. Meagher/Maher families are now forced to find refuge in boglands throughout the Barony. The White Boys, a rebel group, resists the closing of the common lands, but to no avail.

1766 A list of Popish Inhabitants is drawn up of the half Barony of Ikerrin.

1772 A relief act allows Catholics to lease the bogland they had moved to after the closing of the commons in 1760. Many Meagher/Maher families live on the boglands of Ikerrin.

1778 Gardiner's Relief Act is passed. Catholics can lease land on longer leases, sixty-one years instead of thirty-one. The Gavelkind Act, which demands that farmers bequeathed their land among all their sons, is repealed.

1783 The British recognize the independence of America.

1789 Farmers who reclaim bogland are exempt from paying tithes to the Established Church for a period of seven years.

1798 The Rebellion of 1798 occurs. The county sheriff, Judkin Fitzgerald (the Flogger Fitzgerald), had successfully subdued and disarmed north Tipperary before the rising. Carden, the Templemore landlord, invites the Flogger Fitzgerald to his demesne with the express purpose of intimidating his tenants into submission. Martial law is declared in the Barony of Ikerrin. However, in south Tipperary at Slievenamon, Captain John Meagher of Nilemilehouse, leads a failed rising. He is arrested and brutalized by the Flogger Fitzgerald.

1800 The Act of Union is passed. The United Kingdom of England and Ireland is formed. The leading Meagher/Maher families vehemently oppose the act of union.

1800–45 The population of Ireland doubles from almost four to eight million.

1829 The Catholic Emancipation Act is enacted. Catholics can become members of Parliament. Daniel O Connell is the first Catholic MP.

1837–1901 Queen Victoria rules England.

1841 Daniel O Connell holds a "monster" meeting at College Hill, Templemore. College Hill lies at the foot of the Devil's Bit Mountain, the heart of Ó Meachair territory.

1845–49 The Great Famine of 1845–1849 takes place. Many Meaghers die during the famine years. They are mostly young children and infants. Many more emigrate to England, Australia, the United States, and Canada.

1847 "Black '47" is the worst year of the famine. Soup kitchens are established throughout the country.

1848 The Young Irelanders stage a failed revolt at the Commons, Ballingarry, County Tipperary. Thomas Francis Meagher is among the leaders of this revolt.

1848 The British raid Meagher homes at Borrisbeg, Templemore, in search of evidence against Thomas Francis Meagher and his allies. The Borrisbeg Meaghers change their name from Meagher to Maher.

1849 The Encumbered Estate Act benefits landlords who were forced to sell their estates during the famine years.

1858 The Fenian Movement is founded in the United States.

1861–65 The American Civil War is fought between the North and the South.

1864 It is decreed that all births, deaths, and marriages must be recorded. Only random Catholic family records existed before this date.

1869 The Church Act is passed. The Church of Ireland is no longer the established church of Ireland. Catholics are no longer forced to pay tithes to the Anglican Church.

1850–79 There are threats of further famine and widespread evictions of Irish tenants. Many Meaghers/Mahers emigrate to the United States, Canada, England, and Australia. Some of those who go to the United States join the army and fight on opposing sides of the Civil War.

1870 The Land Act is passed. Tenants are compensated for the disturbance.

1872 The Ballot Act was passed. The Irish could now vote by secret ballot.

1879–82 Meaghers/Mahers leave for the United States during these years and join relatives already established there.

1879–1903 Grants are made available to help tenants buy out their farms.

1881 Gladstone's second land act passes. Courts are set up to secure the three Fs: fixity of tenure, fair rent, and freedom of sale.

1885 The Ashbourn Land Act and Land Purchase Act pass. Money is given at low interest rates to help tenants purchase their land.

1896 The Balfour Act is passed. Fifty million pounds are allocated to help tenants purchase their plots from the landlords.

1898 The Local Government Act passes. Grand Juries become County Councils.

1903 The Wyndham Act passes. One hundred million pounds is allocated to tenants for the purchase of their land, while twelve million is allocated to landlords in an effort to encourage them to sell.

1907 The Evicted Tenants Act forces landlords to sell to their tenants. However, in Templemore and Loughmore many tenants fail to buy out their leases because Sir John Carden refuses to sell his estate to the tenants.

1912 The *Titanic* sinks on its way to America.

1916 The Easter Rising in Dublin fails. The leaders are executed and become national martyrs.

1919–21 The Anglo-Irish War is fought.

1921 A truce is called, and the Anglo-Irish Treaty is presented.

1922 The British depart southern Ireland. The Irish Free State is formed; Northern Ireland is excluded.

1923 Land Act of Saorstát na hÉireann passes. This act accelerates the transfer of land from the remaining landlords to their tenants. A judicial commission is set up to fix land prices. Sir John Carden of Templemore finally relents and begins selling his property to the tenants. Many Meaghers/Maher families procure their farms and their nations independence at the same time.

1923–present Several Meaghers/Mahers become involved in local and national politics. They are determined to make their newly independent country a better place for all. Meaghers/Mahers continue to be well represented on committees, boards, and councils throughout Ireland.

Chapter 3: Ó Meachair

This ancient clan has a rich and varied history, which includes tales of saints, scholars, warriors, traitors, fidelities, and treacheries. Any name that spans hundreds of years is certain to be painted and tainted by many noble and ignoble events. The Ó Meachair name is no exception. Ó Meachair is the name of an ancient Irish clan whose homeland was the small barony of Ikerrin in northeast Tipperary. The prolonged policy on the part of the British authorities to subject the Irish, and to destroy their culture, resulted in the widespread dispersal of the old Gaelic clans. It was not until the subsequent Cromwellian confiscations of the mid-seventeenth century, and the granting of their lands to the English planters, that the Ó Meachair Clan was finally dispersed.

Irish names, such as Ó Meachair, are found on every continent. The name Ó Meachair is synonymous with Ireland's plight throughout the past centuries. A more honorable nametag could hardly be worn. The following quote from MacGeoghegan supports the view that Gaelic clans such as the Cinéal Meachair and their descendants are worthy of nobility:

> *A family which has for several centuries kept possession of the same lands, and maintained itself in a certain degree of rank, without contracting any degrading alliance, and of whose ancestors are recorded a long succession of those virtuous actions which attract the attention of mankind—such a family, I say, deserves to be placed in the first class of nobility, and should be considered as such, in every nation in the world ...*
>
> *Though several of those ancient proprietors were deprived of their possessions in the last century, on account of their religious zeal, and their fidelity to their legitimate princes, and consequently have fallen from*

> *that ancient splendor which can only be supported by riches, they are still looked upon in the country in the same light as their ancestors; and provided they can prove the purity of their blood, and regular descent from the chiefs of their house, I see no reason why they should be excluded from the privileges of nobility, any more than others of the same blood, more favored by fortune, and who have persevered their properties... (Mc Geoghegan and Mitchel, 137)*

From about the eighth century, people traced their families from a common ancestor using the appendage *Ua* or *Uí,* which means "descendant of." It was not until about the eleventh century that family names or surnames came into common use. At this time the Christian name of Meachar was adopted as a surname. Surnames were generally taken from a noble or famous ancestor who continued to be remembered and respected within the clan. This noble ancestor's name was then used as the title for the entire clan.

Joseph Casimir (J. C.) O'Meagher's genealogy outlines this development (see Chapter 4, **Genealogy of Joseph Casimir Ó Meagher,** for details). According to J. C. O' Meagher, the Ó Meachair name begins with #98, Meachar son of Aodh. This is the earliest record of the name being used as a Christian name. It is generally accepted, however, that the use of Ó Meachair as a surname did not occur until #107, Meachar son of Moroch.

The name *Meachar* is a genuine Gaelic name. Phonetically it has two syllables: Meach-ar (m` a-char). It is derived from the word *meachar,* meaning "hospitality" or "kindly." It seems that the Ó Meachair Clan took this appendage quite seriously. They were forever proud to be the most hospitable of clans. The following tale proves this.

The Hospitable Clan

In the year 1617, during the reign of James I, Sir George Carew, the President of Munster, decided upon a campaign to demoralize the native Irish chieftains. He hired the well-known poet, Aengus Ó Dalaigh, to help with his plan. Ó Dalaigh was to visit native Irish castles and at an appropriate time satirize his host in front of both guests and clansmen. Aengus began his tour of the many Irish tower houses and publicly satirized each chieftain for his lack of hospitality, food, entertainment, and generosity. It was not long before Aengus became quite unpopular and was forced to travel incognito. When he arrived at the Ó Meachair tower house of Bawnmadrum, Roscrea, the Ó Meachair pretended not to recognize the bard. He treated Ó Dalaigh with the respect due his position as an Irish bard, but he was scorned for his acts of treachery. This infuriated the bard, who went on to satirize the Ó Meachair household.

> *Ó Meagher's men feasted around a great fire,*
>
> *A huge pot hung o'er it, —with blackberries stewing:*
>
> *'T were hard to say which it was—"kitchen" or "byre"—*
>
> *Where Meagher's old cow littered near his "home brewing."*

His cutting words ignited violent anger amid the clansmen, causing a servant to lunge toward the bard and stab him in the neck. All the while he shouted, "The Red Bard should never satirize an Ó Meagher because he did not recognize him." Ó Dalaigh fell to the floor, and with his dying breath he retracted his satire of Ó Meachair and admitted to his treacherous treatment of other Irish Chieftains.

> *All the false judgments that I have passed*
>
> *Upon the chiefs of Munster I forgive;*
>
> *The meager servant of the Grey Ó Meachair*
>
> *Has passed an equivalent judgment on me.*

Aengus Ó Dalaigh, one of Ireland's finest bards, secured for himself an untimely death in an Ó Meachair castle, unaware that his satire tread deeply upon a tradition intimately associated with the ancient name.

Ó Meachair, Meagher, Maher, Marr, Mahar

Like many Irish clans, the Ó Meachairs were eventually forced to anglicize their customs, language, and names. During the 1600s it appears that the name was anglicized to Ó Meagher, Meagher without the Ó, or Magher. Later it was changed to Meaghair, Meagher, Maher, and some of the following variants: Ó Maher, Ó Meagher, Ó Magher, Ó Meacher, Megher, Meigher, Maghyr, Marr, Mahar, and Meacher.

The most commonly spelled variants in the County of Tipperary were Maher and Meagher. The spelling variations are partly the result of English translators' literary skills and the preferences of the clergy who recorded baptisms, deaths, and marriages. The differences also reflect language developments that span centuries of invasion and conquest. Various records seem to confirm that Meagher was the most popular Anglicization until the eighteenth century; and thereafter, Maher became more popular. The latter is now the most common spelling among the descendents of the clan and in the County of Tipperary today.

The earliest written documents relating to the Ó Meachars were written by Irish authors in the Irish language. Here the name is spelled as Meachar, Ní Mheachair, Uí Meachair, and Ó Meachair. Surveys, which were compiled by and written in English after 1640, spell the name as Meagher, with a few Mahers and the very odd Mar, Marr, or Mahar.

It seems that the official spelling of the name from 1640 onward was taken from these surveys. Many names were changed to the English form forever. In subsequent years Maher seems to have transitioned from Meachar to Meagher to Maher, with the latter being the most common variant in Tipperary and Ireland today. The Meagher spelling is more common among the diasporas who emigrated from 1600 to the late 1700s. Some Mahers became Meaghers in honor of Thomas F. Meagher of the "69 Brigade" fame.

Many Irish names carry the prefix Ó, which means that the bearer is a descendent of this family. Ó has also been said to mean "the grandson of," unlike Mac, which means "the son of." During the sixteenth century, attaching either prefix to a name immediately identified the bearer as an Irish patriot or troublemaker, thus drawing negative attention from the English ruling class. Some Irish families dropped these obvious and dangerous identification tags. Also worthy of note is the fact that those Irish who fled with the Earls and later with the Wild Geese maintained the Ó until the latter part of the seventeenth century. These exiles also tended to spell their names Meagher.

Most Irish names are patronymics, which means they come directly from family origins. Meachar is one such name. Other names are either from location, characteristic, or occupation. The latter are most common among English names.

Patronymic: Micheal Ó Meachair (Michael O Meagher . . . "of Meachair")

Location: Éanna Inis (Enda Ennis)

Occupation: Brían De Bhard (Brian Ward . . . "the Bard")

Characteristic: Cíarán Ó Cruimín (Kieran O Cremin . . . "bent or crooked")

Ó Meachair

Meachar is the nominative case of the name. *Uí Meachair* means "the descendants of Ó Meachair."*Cinéal Meachair* means "of the Clan of Ó Meachair." *Ó Meachair* means "the son or grandson of Meachair." A woman married to Ó Meachair is called "Bean Uí Meachair." *Ní Mheachair* means "the daughter of Meachair."

Due to grammar rules, the *Ní* before *Meachair* changes the name to Mheachair by adding the letter *h* after the letter *M*. It is then pronounced *Veachair* with a *v* sound. Note the end spelling *ar* and *air* of Meachar. The addition of the letter *i* puts the noun in the genitive case.

Chapter 4: Genealogy of Joseph Casimir Ó Meagher

Joseph Casimir (J. C.) O'Meagher is the first known individual to undertake a study of the Meaghers of Ikerrin. His book, *Some Historical Notes of the Meaghers of Ikerrin* (New York, 1890), contains a partial genealogy of the Meaghers of Clonan Castle, Roscrea. Joseph Casimir is a direct descendant of this line. His pedigree, as outlined below, includes some of the very early genealogy of the Ó Meachair Clan. Other such pedigrees remain fairly consistent with the one outlined here.

Genealogy of Ó Meachair of Uí Cairin (O Hart, Vol. I)

#85   Olioll Olum was king of Munster in the third century.

#86   Cian, son of Olioll Olum, had another son named Tadg, whose son was Conla, whose son was Forat, whose son was Furic. Furic was one of the three Ó Meachairs who met Saint Patrick. Muinneach and Meachair were the other two.

#87   Conla, son of Cian

#88   Fionnachta, son of Conla

#88   Fionnachta, second son of Conla

#89   Eochaid, son of Fionnachta

#90   Etchon, son of Eochaid

#91   Lugha, son of Etchon

#92   Feach (or Fiacha), son of Lugha

#93   Felim, son of Feach

#94   Doncuan, son of Felim

#95   Lugha (2), son of Doncuan

#96   Fergna, son of Lugha

#97   Aodh, son of Fergna

#98   Meachar, son of Aodh. According to O'Clery, the name Ua-Meachair or Ó Meagher is derived from this Meachar.

#99   Cu-coille, son of Meachar

#100   Ceallach, son of Cu-coille

#101   Meachar (from the Irish word *meach*, meaning "hospitality"), son of Ceallach, hence Ó Meachair.

#102   Dluthach, son of Meachar

#103   Teige Mór, son of Dluthach

#104   Eigneach, son of Teige Mór

#105   Donal, son of Eigneach

#106   Moroch, son of Donal. He was the first to assume the surname Meachair.

#107   Meachar, son of Moroch. O' Clery also referred to him as Murchadh-Óg.

#108   Feach, son of Meachar. He had a brother Eochaidh, which is translated to Kehoe, Keogh, and Mac Keogh in Munster.

#109   Iarin, son of Feach

#110   Donoch, son of Iarin

#111   Murtach, son of Donoch

#112   Melachlin, son of Murtach

#113   Fionn, son of Melachlin

#114   Dermod, son of Fionn

#115   Gilla-na-Naomh, son of Dermod. He had an older brother, Gilbert. This Gilbert was the father of Piers, who was the father of Gilbert, who was the father of Teige Ó Meagher.

#116   Teige, son of Gilla-na-Naomh

#117   "Gilleneuffe (Gilla-na-Neeve) Ó Meagher was the son of Teige. An inquisition taken at Clonmel on the May 30, 1629, found that this Gillaneuffe Ó Meagher on August 30, 1551, executed a deed by which he covenanted to pay John Ó Meagher, of Clonykenny Castle, who was then chief of his name, and father of Colonel Teige Óg Ó Meagher and of Ellen, wife of Doctor Fennell, member of the Supreme Council of Confederation . . . and his heirs a rent of twelve shillings" (O'Meagher, 1890).

#118   Daniel (1508–1576), son of Gilleneuffe Ó Meagher

#119   John (1541–1599), son of Daniel. This John was seized of the lands of Ballybeg, Camlin, Clonyne, Cloughmurle Grange, and Gortvollin, which are situated in the Barony of Ikerrin, and the County of Tipperary, which he held by knight service, and that John Ó Meagher was his son and heir-at-law, of full age and married.

#120   John Ó Meagher (1570–1640), son of John

#121   Thaddeus Ó Meagher (1603–1650), son of John

#122   John Ó Meagher (1635–1705), son of Thaddeus Ó Meagher. This John Ó Meagher and his mother, Anne Ó Meagher, were, on January 30, 1653, ordered by the Commissioners sitting at Clonmel to transplant to Connaught. By an order in Council dated Dublin Castle, December 3, 1655, their petition was referred to the Commissioners of Revenue at Loughrea.

#123   Thaddeus Ó Meagher (1662–1732), son of John

#124   John Ó Meagher (1705–1775), son of Thaddeus

#125   Thaddeus Ó Meagher (1739–811), son of John

#126   John Ó Meagher (1772–1844), son of Thaddeus

#127   Joseph T. Ó Meagher (1803–1832), son of John

#128   John William Ó Meagher (1829–1844), son of Joseph. John William Ó Meagher had a younger brother, Joseph Casimir Ó Meagher, who was born in 1831 and living in Dublin in 1887.

#129   Joseph Dermot Ó Meagher (1864–1884), son of John William Joseph Dermot Ó Meagher was the son of Joseph Casimir, born in 1864; who had four brothers. They were John Kevin, born in 1866;

Donn Casimir (1872–1874); Malachy Marie, born in 1873; Fergal Thaddeus born in 1876; and, a sister, Mary Nuala

Chapter 5: Heraldry

The Milesians, who were regarded as the first Celts to invade Ireland, copied the banner tradition from the Tribes of Israel, who carried banners to distinguish among the twelve tribes. The Milesians' banner was an escutcheon with a dead serpent and a wand. This symbol was reminiscent of Gaedheal Glás, their great ancestor who was stung by a snake and cured. The Milesians continued this tradition until the reign of Ollamh Fola, who lived about seven centuries before the birth of Christ. Born in 680 BC. Ollamh Fola instituted the first "Irish Parliament," which was held at Tara and called *Feis Teamhair,* or the "Festival of Tara." This was a triennial meeting of kings, chieftains, druids, historians, and judges, during which the laws, justice, genealogy, and history of the land were discussed, examined, and sanctioned. The king ordered a coat of arms to be made for the chief of each family. These shields were hung behind the designated seats of each chieftain. Feis Teamhair continued until the arrival of the Anglo-Normans in the twelfth century.

A coat of arms is very difficult to read or interpret. The original may have changed through the generations, depending on which son carried the lineage. Also, individuals often made changes, especially before the introduction of strict laws by Henry V, which limited the issue and use of coats of arms. Years later, Henry VIII hired officials to validate, deny, and record the coats of arms during his reign. The Ó Meachair coat of arms as originally designed was described as follows: "Azure, two lions rampant, combatant or supporting a sword in pale proper: on the base two crescents of the second." Translated, this reads, "Blue, two gold lions attacking facing each other; holding a sword placed vertically, naturally colored; on the base two gold crescents." Above the shield and helmet is the crest "on a green mound, a hawk rising, bellied and hooded, naturally colored, on each wing a gold crescent."

The coat of arms of the Ó Meachair is blue. The color blue refers to loyalty, splendor, and truth. The color yellow/gold, which is used for the lion, sword, and crescents, symbolizes generosity and intellectual superiority. Lions are the most common animals used in heraldry. They are a symbol of kingship, strength, nobility, and agility. On the Ó Meachair shield, the lions are combatant. This is not surprising, as the Ó Meachairs always fought for the right to retain their land. The lion is the king of beasts, but it is not the king of birds. Hence, in order to balance a coat of arms, the eagle, the king of all birds, is often added to the coat of arms as its crest.

The Ó Meachair shield has as its crest a falcon standing ready for flight, belled, and hooded. The falcon stands upon a green mound, which brings the deeply personal issue of land to the shield. The green mound could be interpreted as the Devil's Bit Mountain, which marks the western boundary of Ó Meachair territory, while the falcon represents the abundantly popular gaming bird found on this mountain. The two crescent moons below the lions and on the wing tips of the falcon are symbols used by second sons. Perhaps these crescents refer to the Ó Meachair being a second line of the O Carroll.

The Ó Meachair coat of arms is very similar to that of the O Carroll's. The O Carroll coat of arms also has two lions rampart with a sword and a hawk rising from its helmet. The war cry of the O Carrolls was *"Seabhac Abú,"* or the "Hawk to Victory." This, too, was a battle cry of the Ó Meachairs. Since the Ó Meachair Clan is a descendant line from the O Carrolls, it does not seem unusual that they have a similar coat of arms and war cry.

Figure 5-1 Ó Meachair coat of arms

Ó Meachair Mottoes

Family mottoes varied and did not necessarily belong with the coat of arms. They were usually war cries chanted by a clan in battle. Some may have been related to a clan name or expressed the clan's religious stance or exploits in battle. Some were simply the clan's hopes or aspirations on a particular day. When a new chief was elected, his personal agenda could cause a change in the clan motto. This seems to have been the case with the Ó Meachairs. The following are three different mottoes attributed to the clan: *Deus Protector Noster* ("God Is Our Protector"), *In Periculis Audax* ("Bold in Danger"), and *Toujours Pret* ("Always Ready"). *Deus Protector Noster* seems to be the most popularly accepted motto.

The Truth About Heraldry

Michael Ó Comain's excellent book, *The Poolbeg Book of Irish Heraldry* (Poolbeg, 1991), reveals a long-ignored truth about heraldry. He explains that, in recent times, a thriving business has grown out of the selling of family shields to any bearer of the name or name variant. The purchaser of this shield is often of the opinion that it belongs to the family and is a link to an ancestor or particular clan. The truth of the matter is that shields are not unique to a name or a clan. A shield is unique to an individual.

     In order to obtain a shield, an individual must apply to the Chief Herald of Ireland or England for the honor of holding a shield or heraldic achievement. If the heraldic achievement is granted to the applicant, the Chief Herald then legally records the details. The shield belongs to the applicant, or grantee, and it becomes the hereditary property of his immediate family or bloodline for as long as the direct line should exist. The shield is not the property of anyone who happens to bear the same name as the grantee.

Since heraldic achievements are considered property, one could legally challenge the usurpation of one. However, such lawsuits are unheard of, because few chieftains of the direct bloodline remain to make such a challenge. Those chieftains who do exist are magnanimous enough to ignore the practice. They probably enjoy the idea that their specific ancestors are being venerated all over the world!

> *What they are in effect doing by assuming these derelict arms is assuming the chieftainship of that name, without acceptable proof to substantiate the claim. Although there exists in Gaelic armory a tradition of expressing one's wish to be known as related to a particular, perhaps famous, family, to do so by the use of an undifferenced coat of arms without provable descent most certainly has no legal sanction. Quite apart from any legal considerations, to misappropriate another's arms shows, in the would-be armiger, a scant respect for his true ancestors and though he may not be prosecuted he may well be ridiculed. (O Comain, 31)*

Chapter 6: The Celts in Ireland

What follows is an overview of early Irish history based on mythology.

Noah built the ark to save mankind from the flood.

Japheth was Noah's son.

Fenius the Ancient, the grandson of Japheth, helped with the building of the tower of Babel. He was a great linguist and retained the knowledge of all the languages when they were separated at Babel. He started a school of languages.

Niul, the son of Fenius, was also a language teacher. He went to Egypt and married Scota, the Pharaoh's daughter.

Gaedheal Glás, the son of Niul, lived in Egypt and is responsible for the creation of the Irish language.

Esru was the son of Gaedheal Glás.

Sru was a descendant of Esru. He and his people left Scythia and set out in search of a new home. They eventually made their way to the Mediterranean Sea and sailed to Spain.

Breoghan was a descendant of Sru and the leader of the clan at the time of the discovery of Ireland.

Ith, a son of Breoghan, claimed to have seen a green island to the north of Spain. He set out to find this green land and found Éire.

Bile was the son of Ith.

Milead was the son of Bile. Milead is the most famous of this line in terms of Celtic-Irish history. The Milesian clans (Clan na Míle) are his descendants. Between the years 1700 and 800 BC, Milead's children and some of their uncles sailed to Éire. Eremon, Eber Finn, Eber Donn, Ir, Arann, Colptha, and Amergin are among the historically documented sons who actually survived the voyage to Éire.

Eremon was the oldest son of Milead. He became the first absolute monarch of Éire. The clans and septs that are descendant from him are called the Eremonians.

Eber Finn, another son of Milead, was the second most powerful leader in Éire at the time of their invasion. The clans and septs that descend from him are called the Eberians. The Ó Meachair Clan claims to descend from Eber Finn.

Ir was a younger son whose descendants were called the Irians.

Lughaidh was the son of Ith, Milead's grandfather. He was one of the many uncles who traveled to Ireland with his adventurous nephews. The generations that descend from him are called the Ithians after Ith, his father.

Amergin was a talented harpist and a knowledgeable bard. He became known as Éire's first bard.

      The list reflects the mythical nature of early Irish history and genealogy. One cannot forget that much of Ireland's ancient history has been garnished from the many surviving manuscripts that were written centuries after the actual events occurred. These ancient tales were handed down from generation to generation orally. The druids, the bards, the ollamhs, and family savants were the keepers of this knowledge. Each in turn changed the stories to suit their agenda, audience, and personal storytelling skills. According to Dr. Daithi Ó hOgain:

> *The ultimate origin of the Irish people is put down to Scythia. The people of that area were descendants of Noah's son Japheth; and the first important person among them was Fenius the Ancient, who was one of the leaders of different nationalities who went to build the tower of Babel. Fenius was a great linguist and, when the languages were separated at Babel, he alone retained the knowledge of them all. His grandson was Gaedheal Glas who, we are told, fashioned the Irish language ("Gaedhilg") out of the whole seventy-two tongues then in existence. Gaedheal and his people lived in Egypt (Ó hOgain, 296).*

Dr. Ó hOgain also recounts how Gaedheal was bitten by a poisonous snake while wandering the desert with Moses. Moses cured him with his staff and declared that Gaedheal's descendants would live in a land free from such creatures. When the wound healed, a green scar remained on the skin. As a result Gaedheal was renamed *Gaedheal Glas* or Green Gaedheal .

> *No serpent nor vile venomed thing*
>
> *Can live upon the Gaelic soil,*
>
> *No bard nor stranger since has found*
>
> *A cold repulse from a son of Gaedheal.*
>
> *(Hyde, D. p. 45)*

The Celts in Ireland

In northern Spain, Breoghan built a watchtower to guard against attackers and invaders. His son, Ith, spent many hours surveying the landscape from this tower. He insisted that on a clear day he could see an island to the north and believed it to be their Inis Fail, or "Island of Destiny." With 150 warriors he set sail for the mysterious island. When they arrived in Éire, they quarreled with the natives. Ith was killed. His men retreated to their boats carrying their leader's body back to Spain.

By the time they returned, Ith's grandson, Milead, was the leader of the clan. He was a popular leader, and the people under his protection called themselves the Milesians. Milead himself never set foot in Ireland, but the leading clans of Ireland are insistent upon tracing their ancestry back to his children. Nine brothers and eight nephews took it upon themselves to seek revenge for the brutal murder of Ith. These fierce warriors set sail for Éire with plans to conquer the island and share it among themselves.

Misfortune struck both at sea and on land. Many of Milead's sons were killed. Those who survived, namely Eremon, Amergin, Eber, Ir, and Colptha, defeated the inhabitants of Éire, the Tuatha Dé Danann, in a huge battle at Tailtiú (Teltown, Co. Meath).

The Milesians claimed the island, and from that day forward Ireland was a Celtic land. Eremon and Ir took control of the northern part of Éire. Many generations later, conflict between the Erimonians and the Irians resulted in the latter being pushed farther northward. They were the lesser of the two groups both in strength and in numbers.

Figure 6-1 Poulnabroin Dolmen, an ancient burial site in County Clare

The great clans of Ulster claim descent from Eremon. Eber Finn and Lughaidh, Ith's son, went south. They, too, ended in confrontation. As a result of endless battles, the Ithians (descendants of Lughaidh) were driven farther south and west. Eventually they inhabited the islands off the west coast and the barren areas of western Ireland. The Eberians were the controlling force of southern Éire. They were never quite as powerful as their Erimonian cousins to the north. Most southern clans, including the Ó Meachair Clan, claim descent from Eber Finn.

Much of Ireland's history is a continuation of the conflict between the clans and their territories. Some of these battles were fought between the Erimonian and the Eberians, with the Ithians and Irians choosing allegiance where it most benefited them.

The Milesians

Thomas Moore (1799–1852)

They came from a land beyond the sea,
And now o'er the western main
Set sail, in their good ships, gallantly,
From the sunny land of Spain.
"Oh, where's the Isle we've seen in dreams,
Our destined home or grave?"
Thus sang they as by the morning's beams,
They swept the Atlantic wave.

And lo, where afar o'er ocean shines
A sparkle of radiant green,
As though in that deep lay emerald mines,
Whose light through the wave was seen.
'Tis Inisfail–'tis Inisfail!'
Rings o'er the echoing sea:
While bending to heaven, the warriors hail
That home of the brave and free.

Then turned they unto the eastern wave,
Where now their Day-God's eye
A look of such sunny omen gave
As lighted up sea and sky.
Nor frown was seen through sky or sea,
Nor tear o'er leaf or sod,
When first on their Isle of Destiny
Our great fore fathers trod.
(Fact and Fancy, Senior, p. 20)

Direct Line of Eber Finn 1699 BC

The following list is from John O'Hart's *Irish Pedigrees,* 1892:
Eber Finn (The Great ancestor of the Ó Meachairs)
Five sons, Er, Orba, Feron, Fergna, Conmaol, 1680 BC
Conmaol 12th, High King of Ireland, 1650 BC
Eochaid Faobhar Glas 17th, High King of Ireland, 1492 BC
Eanna Airgthach 21st, High King of Ireland, 1409 BC
Glas
Ros
Rotheacta
Fearard
Cas
Munmoin 25th, High King of Ireland, 1332 BC
Fualdergoid 26th, High King of Ireland, 1327 BC
Cas Cedchaingnigh
Failbhe Iolcorach
Ronnnach
Rotheachta 35th, High King of Ireland, 1030 BC
Eioliomh Ollfhionach 36th, High King of Ireland, 1023 BC
Art Imleach 38th High King of Ireland, 1013 BC
Breas Rioghacta 40th, High King of Ireland, 961 BC
Seidnae Innaridh 43rd, High King of Ireland, 929 BC
Duach Fionn 45th, High King of Ireland, 903 BC
Eanna Dearg 47th, High King of Ireland, 892 BC
Lughaidh Iardhonn 48th, High King of Ireland, 880 BC
Eochaidh Uarceas 50th, High King of Ireland, 855 BC
Lughaidh Lamhdeargh 52nd, High King of Ireland, 838 BC
Art 54th, High King of Ireland, 811 BC
Olioll Fionn 56th, High King of Ireland, 795 BC
Eochaidh 57th, High King of Ireland, 784 BC
Lughaidh Lagha 60th, High King of Ireland, 737 BC
Reacht Righ Dearg 65th, High King of Ireland, 653 BC
Cogthach Caomh
Machcorb 72nd, High King of Ireland, 505 BC

Fearcorb 75th, High King of Ireland, 473 BC
Adhamhra Foltcaoin 78th, High King of Ireland, 417 BC
Niadhseadhaman 83rd, High King of Ireland, 319 BC
Ionadmaor the 87th, High King of Ireland, 218 BC
Lughaidh Luaighne 89th, High King of Ireland, 198 BC
Cairbre Lusgleathan
Duach Dalladh Deadha 91st, High King of Ireland, 168 BC
Duach Dalladh Deadha, last High King of this line BCE
Eochaid Garbh
Muireadach Muchna
Loich Mór Eanna Muncain
Dearg Theine
Dearg
Magha Neid
Eoghan Mór, an ancestor of the Ó Meachair Clan
Olioll Olum, third-century King of Munster

The Tuatha De Danann

Figure 6-2 Crannóg, a Celtic lake dwelling. Re-creation found at the Irish National Heritage Park, Ferrycarrig, County Wexford

The Tuatha De Danann was the ruling race of Ireland before the Milesian invasion. They were descendant from the goddess Danu and were perceived by the invaders as a spiritlike people with magical powers. When the Milesians defeated the Tuatha De Danann at the battle of Tailtiú, the treaty terms demanded either total banishment from the land or submission as a subservient race. The Tuatha De Danann refused to become a subservient race or to leave their idyllic homeland. They are believed to have gone into hiding. They vanished completely. Though they were rarely ever seen again, their presence continues to be strongly felt. Some say that they are the voices on the wind, the music of the night, the mysteries of the land, a magical force within space trapped between both worlds. They are the instruments of fortune or misfortune. Irish mythology strongly hints that the Fairies of Ireland are in fact the Tuatha De Danann still hiding in our midst. As such, they continue to be a controlling influence over the land and its inhabitants.

The Milesian (*Clan na Míle*) invasion of Ireland is but a myth. There were many Celtic invasions that continued through several centuries. All are important to the history of Ireland, because the Celts brought with them a whole new culture that was adopted by all the inhabitants of Ireland and is still a characteristic feature of the country today. The Celts brought their knowledge of iron to Ireland and launched its Iron Age. With these metal advancements came the beautiful Celtic Art, some of which survives today in gold, silver, bronze, paper, and stone artifacts. The Celts also brought the ancient religion of Druidism to Ireland, and the Irish language remains a living legacy of the Celts who came to Ireland in the centuries before the birth of Christ.

The Fairies

William Allingham (1824–1889)

Up the airy mountain,
Down the rushy glen,
We daren't go a-hunting
For fear of little men;
Wee folk, good folk,
Trooping all together;
Green jacket, red cap,
And white owl's feather!

Down along the rocky shore
Some make their home—
They live on crispy pancakes,
Of yellow tide-foam;
Some in the reeds
Of the black mountain lake,
With frogs for their watch dogs,
All night awake.

High on the hilltop
The old King sits;
He is now so old and grey
He's nigh lost his wits.

With a bridge of white mist
Columbkill he crosses,
On his stately journeys
From Slieveleague to Rosses;
Or going up with music
On cold starry nights,
To sup with the Queen
Of the gay Northern Lights.

They stole little Bridget
For seven years long;
When she came down again
Her friends were all gone.
They took her lightly back,
Between the night and the morrow;
They thought that she was fast asleep,
But she was dead with sorrow
They have kept her ever since
Deep within the lake,
On a bed of flag-leaves,
Watching till she wake.

By the craggy hill-side,
Through the mosses bare,
They have planted thorn-trees
For pleasure here and there.
Is any man so daring
As to dig one up in spite,
He shall find their sharpest thorns
In his bed at night.

Up the airy mountain,
Down the rushy glen,
We daren't go a-hunting
For fear of little men;
Wee folk, good folk,
Trooping all together;
Green jacket, red cap,
And white owl's feather!
(McMahon, S. p.184–185)

As the Celts colonized Ireland, they mixed and mingled with the local inhabitants. In truth, the Irish nation of today is a mixture of all the ancient peoples of Ireland plus the Celts and the many subsequent invaders, colonists, and émigrés.

The Celts

Thomas D'Arcy McGee (1825–1868)

Long, long ago, beyond the misty space
   Of twice a thousand years,
In Erin old there dwelt a mighty race,
   Taller than Roman spears;
Like oaks and towers they had a giant grace
   Were fleet as deers,
With wind and waves they made their 'binding place,
   These western shepherd seers.

Their Ocean-God was Manannan Mac Lir,
   Whose angry lips,
In their white foam, full often would enter
   Whole fleets of ships;
Cromah their Day-God, and their Thunderer
   Made morning and eclipse;
Bride was their queen of song, and unto her
   They prayed with fire-touched lips.

Great were their deeds, their passions and their sports;
   With clay and stone
They piled on straight and shore those mystic forts,
   Not yet o'er thrown;
On cairn-crowned hills they held their council-courts;
   While youths alone,
With giant dogs, explored the elk resorts,
   And brought them down.

Of these was Finn, the father of the Bard,
   Whose ancient song
Over the clamor of all change is heard,

Sweet-voiced and strong,
Finn once o'er took Graina, the golden-haired,
   The fleet and young;
From her the lovely, and from him the feared,
   The primal poet sprung.

Ossian! two thousand years of mist and change
   Surround your name-
Thy Fenian heroes now no longer range
   The hills of fame.
The very names of Finn and Gaul sound strange-
   Yet thine the same-
By miscalled lake and desecrated grange-
   Remains, and shall remain!

The Druid's altar and the Druid's creed
   We scarce can trace,
There is not left an undisputed deed
   Of all your race,
Save your majestic song, which hath their speed,
   And strength of grace;
In that sole song, they live and love, and bleed-
   It bears them on through space.

O, inspired giant! Shall we e're behold,
   In our own time,
One fit to speak your spirit world on the world,
   Or seize your rhyme?
One pupil of the past, as mighty souled
   As in the prime,
Were the fond, fair, and beautiful, and bold-
   They of your song sublime!
(McMahon, S., p. 58)

Chapter 7: The Political Division of Celtic Ireland

Ireland was divided among the four sons of Milead, hence the beginning of the four main lineages: the Eremonians, the Eberians, the Ithians, and the Irians. During the reign of Eocha IX (c. AM 3986) the four provinces, as we know them today, were formed with a portion of provience set aside for the king's domain, thus making a fifth province known as Meath. Eocha IX gave the chieftain of each province the title of "king." Within these four provinces there were smaller territories ruled by provincial chieftains who also considered themselves kings. The *Árd Rí* was the recognized high king of all Ireland. The high king of Ireland was not an absolute king. He sought the allegiance of the other provincial and petty kings in times of dispute or battle. These subkings were expected to pay an annual tribute as a symbol of their allegiance. Throughout the history of Ireland there were few absolute high kings to whom all paid homage. Their popularity was usually short lived. Provincial kings each ruled a province: Ulster, Munster, Connaught, or Leinster. Lesser kings or chieftains ruled their individual territories called *Tuatha* or region. A provincial king ruled the province of Munster. Within the province there were subkings who ruled over several petty kingdoms or *tuatha*. Beneath the subkings were petty-kings who ruled over one tuatha or territory.

The Ó Meachair was considered a petty-king. His clan occupied the territory called Uí Cairin, which lies in the northeastern part of the County of Tipperary. It was a small kingdom socially stratified according to Celtic tradition. The chieftain and his family formed the upper layer followed by the various family members of direct bloodline, aka the *derbfine*. Tenants and slaves were the lower level of the social ladder. Many subjects assumed the clan name even though they had no direct blood connection. This ensured protection within the clan system.

Subsequent conquests by the Vikings, Anglo-Normans, and English refined and changed this Celtic system of government.

Clansmen lived within circular earthen enclosures. These ring forts varied in size and fortification depending upon the social hierarchy and number of families that lived within them. The interior of the enclosure was called a *lios*, while the raised earthen bank around it was called a *rath*. Some enclosures had walled surrounds for added protection. The actual dwelling places were mere huts of mud and wattles. In mountainous areas or in the west of Ireland where stone was plentiful the fortification walls and the dwelling huts were often built of stone. The main occupation of the dwellers was cattle rearing. In Celtic Ireland the extent of a man's wealth was based upon the number of cattle he possessed.

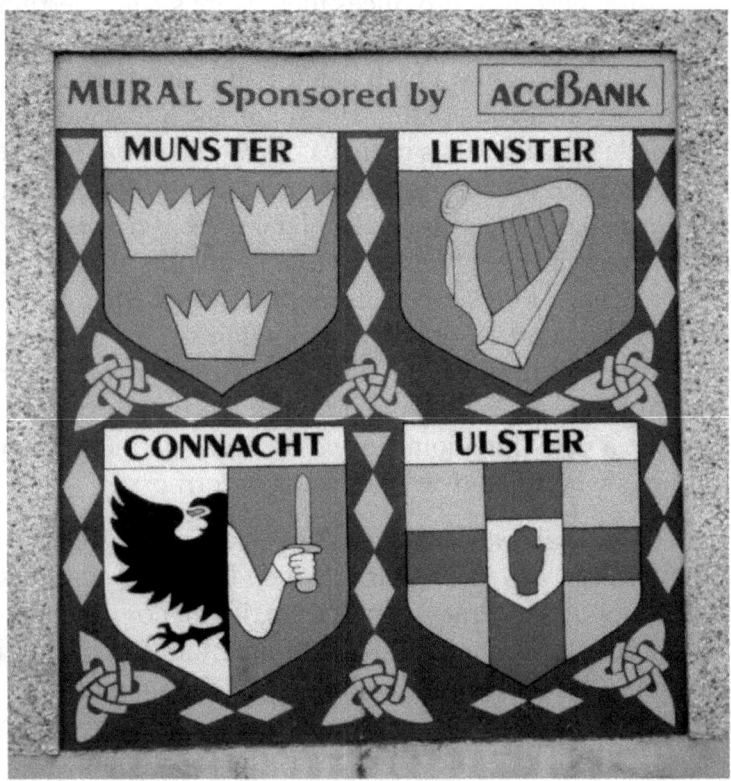

Figure 7-1 Shields of the Four Provinces of Ireland, Semple Stadium, Thurles, County Tipperary

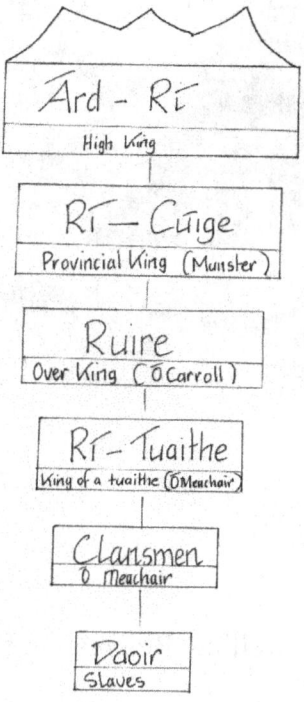

Figure 7-2 The social stratification of Celtic Ireland

Figure 7-3 Celtic Ring Fort Dwelling. Re-creation found at Craggaunowen, County Clare.

Chapter 8: The Barony of Ikerrin

The Ó Meachair Clan, known as the "Cinéal Meachair," was the chieftain tribe of Críoch Uí Cairin, the Barony of Ikerrin. The exact demarcation of the barony only came into being during Anglo-Norman times. Before this period the territory was not clearly defined. *Críoch Uí Cairin* may mean the "land of Kieran." According to one theory this Kieran was Saint Kieran of Seir. The latter was a fifth- or sixth-century saint. However, this theory seems unlikely since the territory name may predate that period. "Críoch Uí Cairin" was anglicized to "Hykerrin" and further anglicized to "Ikerrin," which is the current spelling. The Cineal Meachair showed allegiance to the Ó Meachair chieftain, the Ó Meachair.

Ikerrin is in the northeastern part of the County Tipperary. The latter is considered a fertile midland county. It lies slightly south of central Ireland and is in the province of Munster. Ikerrin was uniquely situated on one of the five ancient routes of Ireland. The Slíghe Dála crossed the northern part of Ikerrin, cutting through the ancient settlement of Roscrea, and then continued northeastward to Tara. This central location made Ikerrin a hive of activity through the centuries. Ó Meachair territory has been touched upon by all the major political, social, historical, and economical events of Ireland's evolution.

Given the status of a barony by the Anglo-Normans, the territory covers an area of 69,805 acres and is divided into 168 townlands with twelve parishes. Two of Ireland's major rivers, the Nore and Suir, rise within the barony. The territory unfolds from the foot of a fascinating mountain called Bearnán Éile, the "Éile's Gap." Due to glacial erosion this nondescript mountain was left with a wide, gaping hole or gap. A wonderful myth explaining its origin follows.

The Devil's Bit Mountain

Once upon a time in the territory of Ikerrin, there lived a noble king called the Ó Meachair. Ó Meachair was a pagan king of noble birth.

Figure 8-1 Éire

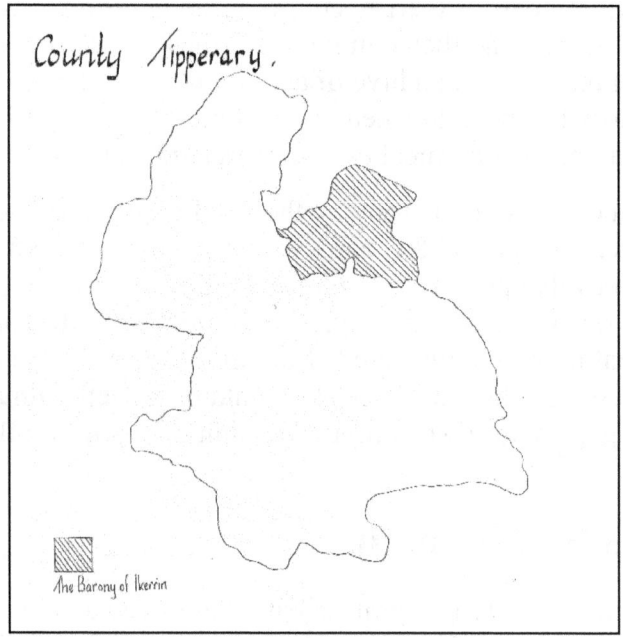

Figure 8-2 County Tipperary

The Barony of Ikerrin

Figure 8-3 The Barony of Ikerrin

He was the son of Forat, son of Conla, son of Tadhy, son of Cian, son of Olioll Olum, the third-century king of Munster. During the fifteenth century a foreigner named Patrick was traveling around Ireland going from one tuatha to another spreading a new philosophy of life. It appeared that Patrick had no immediate plans to visit Ikerrin. When the Ó Meachair heard that Patrick was coming to the neighboring territory of Lower Ormond, he was determined to meet him. With his two brothers, Furic and Muinneach, he made plans to visit Lower Ormond.

The Devil heard the news of Patrick's visit and that the Cinéal Meachair were planning to meet the saintly man. He feared that he would lose his power over Southern Ireland, where Patrick had yet to preach. "If the Cinéal Meachair convert to Christianity it will be the end of me," he said to no one in particular. "I'll have no choice but to quit the land for good. That lad, Patrick, could banish me like he did my snakes. I'll have to prevent the Ó Meachair from going to see him."

The night before their journey, the Devil visited the sleeping Ó Meachair and warned him, "If you as much as step in the direction of that fellow Patrick, I'll rip you, your people, and your land from the face of Ireland and fling you into the ocean." When morning came, Ó Meachair remembered his restless night and the Devil's threats. However, he decided to ignore the warnings and busied himself preparing for the trip.

It was late afternoon when the three brothers arrived at Lower Ormond. A huge crowd had gathered around Patrick, who was already preaching. He intrigued all who were present. Muinneach was the first of the brothers to be baptized, and the others followed suit. During the ceremony Patrick took a great interest in the three brothers and bestowed many blessings upon them. He assured them that their descendants would not only be numerous but noble and great. The Ó Meachair was thrilled. Patrick was also delighted. Having converted a chieftain, he knew that he now had freedom to preach in his territory. He was also confident that having won over the chieftain and his brothers, it was only a matter of time before the rest of the clan would follow suit. With the light of Christ warming their hearts, the Ó Meachair brothers returned to Ikerrin.

Furic, Muinneach, and Meachar were hardly home a day when a horrific storm suddenly swept over the mountain. Omnious clouds blackened the plain beneath, and torrents of rain spilled down upon the land. It was a most unnatural tempest. The Devil, shaped like a vicious dragon, crashed through the darkening clouds. He rose high into the air and hovered directly above the crest of the purple mountain known as Bearnán Éile. His crackling voice cast profanities like javelins upon the startled Cinéal Meachair below. With lightning speed he dropped toward the mountaintop and sank his jagged teeth into the highest point.

He tugged and pulled at the mountain until he managed to rip a huge chunk or rock from the center. Thrashing his tail like a whip, he rose farther into the air before swooping down upon the terrified clansmen below. Soil, stones, rocks, and plants rained down upon the clan. The valley was littered with pieces of the Devil's load. He rose into the clouds and flew up and out over the Ó Meachair territory.

When the Devil realized that he had failed to rip the land of Cinéal Meachair from the face of Ireland, he dropped his heavy load in disgust. It landed right in the middle of the territory of Aengus at Cashel. This huge chunk of rock is called the Rock of Cashel.

Ó Meachair relaxed as he watched the Devil depart. He knew that his territory was safe. They were spared the full wrath of the Devil's anger, because he and his clansmen were now loyal to a force stronger than he. This enchanted mountain was renamed the Devil's Bit. Although the Irish translation remains "Bearnán Éile," for the "gap of Éile."

In the early twentieth century, the people of the Templemore erected a large cement cross (forty-five feet high with two twelve-foot-long arms) on the summit of Bearnán Éile. On Rock Sunday, the third Sunday of July, an annual pilgrimage is made to this monument. In recent years a statue of the Blessed Virgin was erected on Bearnán Éile.

Figure 8-4 The Devil's Bit Mountain

Figure 8-5 The Rock of Cashel

Figure 8-6 The Devil's Bit and the cement cross at its summit

Chapter 9: The Ó Meachair Clan

The Celts arrived in Ireland in tribal units (c. 350 BC). These tribes fought constantly to establish territorial rights in their new country. As a result, there was regular migration throughout the land. When the Uí Neill of Ulster expanded into south Meath, a tribe called Éile was pushed southward toward Munster. This Éile tribe fought its way into north Tipperary and subdued the existing settlers. The territory they claimed and settled was called Éile in honor of the tribe. It is believed that the third-century king of Munster, Olioll Ollum, defined the boundaries of ancient Éile, which comprised all of O Carroll territory. In the late twelfth and early thirteenth century, the Anglo-Normans established what is called modern Éile. The land divisions were called cantreds, which were based on the existing Gaelic territorial divisions. The boundaries of Éile were further defined in the sixteenth century.

Eoghan Eoghanacht Clans Kingdom of Desmond	Cormac Dalcassian or Dal Cais Kingdom of Thomond	Cian Ciannacht Clans Kingdom Of Ormond
Mac Carthy	O Brien	O Carrol
O Sullivan	O Kennedy	O Meagher
O Keefe	O Boland	O Casey
O Callahan	O Kelleher	O Hara
	O Hickey	O Gara
	O Hogan	
	Mac Namara	
	Mac Clancy	

Figure 9-1 The descendant clans of the three sons of Olioll Olum

Throughout the many generations that followed, eight territories and tribal groups developed from the Éile sept. Among them was the Ely O Carroll (Éile Ó Cearbhaill), who were the overlords of the entire Éile territory. Ó Meachair of Ikerrin and O Fogartys of Eliogarty (Éile Ó Fogartach) were among their subsepts. In the thirteenth century the lands of Ikerrin and Eliogarty were detached from Éile and became separate territories. This separation was a direct result of the Anglo-Norman invasion.

There are three theories as to the origin of the name Éile. *The Book of Rights,* edited by O Donovan, claims that the name Éile is from a Celtic tribe that inhabited the territory named after them. Abbe McGeoghegan, in his *History of Ireland,* claims that Éile comes from Éile Ríoghdearg, a descendant of Olioll Olum. Éile Rioghdearg lived in the fourth century and was the eighth descendant of Olioll Ollum and the seventh descendant of his son Cian, the common ancestor of the O Meaghers and O Carrolls. The third theory put forward "in the handwriting of Adam Ó Cianan (O Keenan), a celebrated Irish Antiquarian, the two districts, Eli and Uaithaine (Ely and Owney), were named after two daughters of Eochaid (Eochy), son of Leichta, King of Munster, an ancient law-giver, who lived about the same time of the Incarnation. O Keenan tells us that he copied this account from the book of the great Master, John Ó Dugán, the chief poet of the O Kellys of Hy-Maine, an astronomer, topographer, and historian, who died AD 1372," (J. Gleeson, 20).

Éile was anglicized to Eli or Ely. The name, in its original form, has almost been lost. Fortunately, it still survives in some local place names. Brí Éile is Croghan Hill, County Offaly; Dúrlas Éile is Thurles Town; Bearnán Éile is the Devil's Bit Mountain; and Móin Éile is the bog that sorrounds the monastery of Monaincha, which stretches from County Offaly southward between Counties Tipperary and Kilkenny. Hoping to revive the name, I named my daughter Éile.

It is highly probable that the Éile tribe came from the Leinster area and had a genealogy invented for itself. This genealogy linked the tribe to Tadhg, the grandson of Olioll Olum, affirming Éile as a Munster tribe directly descendant from the third-century king of Munster. If the genealogy was invented, this may explain why the O Meaghers insist on claiming kinship with the O Neills of Ulster, who seem to have been their overlords at one time. (In the absence of any pre-Éile history, this book will continue with the tradition of succession from Olioll Olum, the third-century Munster king.)

The Ó Meachair Clan

The Ó Meachair Clan is one of eight clans that developed within the Éile tribe. This clan was a subsept of the O Carrolls; hence, the O Carrolls were their overlords. The Ó Meachair Clan held lands in south Éile in a territory called Uí Cairin, anglicized as Ikerrin. They claim to be descendants of the third-century king of Munster, Olioll Olum. Olioll Olum was a direct descendant of Eber Finn, one of the early Milesian leaders. When Olioll Olum died, his kingdom was divided among his three sons, Eoghan king of Desmond; Cormac king of Thomond; and Cian king of Ormond. Olioll Olum stipulated that the kingship of Munster should alternate between the heirs of Eoghan of Desmond and Cormac of Thomond. Cian's descendants were excluded from this arrangement. Hence they had no claim on the Munster throne.

The Ó Meachairs claim descent from this third son, Cian. Gilla na Naomh Ó hUidrin wrote a topographical poem in the fifteenth century that described the Leinster's and Munster's leading clans and their territories. Below are the verses that refer to O Carroll and Ó Meachair.

Olioll Olum	Olioll Olum	Olioll Olum
Eoghan	Eoghan	Eoghan
Cormac Cais	Cormac Cais	Cormac Cais
Cian	Cian	Cian
Tadhg, son of Cian	Tadhg, son of Cian	Tadhg, son of Cian
Connla, son of Tadhg	Connla, son of Tadhg	Cormac Galeng, son of Tadhg
Iomcadh Ullach, son of Connla	Fionnachta, son of Connla	O Hara, O Gara, O Flannagan. O Delahunty, O Corcoran, O Casey
Ó Cearbhaill	Ó Meachair	

Figure 9-2 O'Carroll and Ó Meachair lineage according to Keating

O Carroll

Lords to whom great men submit
Are the O Carrolls of the plain of Birr;
Kings of Ely as far as the lofty Slieve Bloom,
The most hospitable land in Erin;
Eight districts and eight Chiefs are ruled
By the Prince of Ely, the land of cattle;
Valiant in enforcing their tributes
Are the troops of the yellow-ringletted hair.

Ó Meachair

Mightily have they filled the land
The Ó Meachairs, the territory of Uí Cairin,
A tribe at the foot of the Bearnán Éile,
It is no shame to celebrate their triumph.

Chapter 10: Christianity

In the fifth century AD, Saint Patrick came to Ireland as a Christian missionary. He was not the first Christian to come in this capacity, yet he became known as "the Apostle of Ireland," because he was the most successful missionary ever to come to the island. Patrick owes his success to the fact that he had lived for several years among the Irish as a slave. During this time he learned their language, traditions, and customs. He also gained valuable insights into the unique mentality and social structure of the Irish society. The Irish had embraced the pagan religion that dated back to Celtic Europe. Conscious of this fact, Patrick chose to super-impose his Christian beliefs upon their Celtic traditions. In so doing he successfully converted many.

By the sixth century, monastic life was flourishing throughout Ireland. Monastic settlements were not merely places of religious worship but also cultural centers of learning. Their syllabi included

Figure 10-1 Monaincha Abbey, Roscrea

lessons on reading, writing, poetry, classical languages, music, law, agriculture, art, and a multitude of handcrafts. Students lived in mud-and-wattle huts outside the monastery walls. It is from such settlements that the clan chieftains gained their extensive education. Several monasteries dotted Ireland at this time. In fact many modern towns grew from these monastic sites.

Christianity and the Ó Meachairs

In 470 AD Saint Patrick came to preach at Lower Ormond, a neighboring territory of Ikerrin. Chapter eight recounts how three sons of the Ó Meachair chieftain went to visit Patrick and agreed to be converted. Patrick was particularly impressed with these noble men and bestowed great blessings upon them.

Muinneach the Great believes
In Patrick before all,
That there might be over his country
Chieftains of his race forever.
Meachair believed,
For he was a true just man
Patrick gave him a lasting blessing-
The companionship of a King.

By the seventh century, Christianity was well established in the barony of Ikerrin. Evidence to prove this is found in the monastic ruins throughout the territory. One of the oldest and most notable monasteries in the territory of Ó Meachair is the monastery at Monaincha, Roscrea. This tiny monastery is located on an island in the bog formerly known as Móin Éile. Monaincha has a wealth of lore, legend, and history attached to it. It was strongly associated with the Ó Meachair Clan. Along with the Devil's Bit Mountain, this is the author's most favorite site in Ó Meachair territory. A visit to the barony of Ikerrin would not be complete without a pilgrimage to both.

Much confusion abounds as to the actual history of Monaincha, probably because it predates many of the historical religious writings. O'Hanlon, in his *Lives of the Saints,* credits Saint Cronan with the founding of the monastery. Others credit St. Canice, while still others claim that Saint Kieran of Sier founded the monastery of Monaincha. It is highly probable that Saint Kieran the Elder found these secluded islands, in the middle of a lake camaflauged by trees, an ideal location for a retreat. Saint Kieran, a contemporary of Saint Patrick, was a great lover of solitude and often sought out remote places to contemplate, fast, and pray. Saint Canice, who continued in the tradition of Saint Kieran, also used the islands of Móin Éile for solitude, prayer, and contemplation.

In the seventh century, while fasting and praying on the island, Saint Canice was inspired to make a copy of the Four Gospels and write a commentary upon them called *Glas Chaining* or the "Commentary of Saint Canice." When asked about the exemplary skill of his work, he replied, "The Son of the Holy Virgin, Himself, inspired me." Sadly, this work of Saint Canice has not survived. Saint Canice is also credited with the founding of the monastery of Aghaboe in County Laois and Kilkenny.

About fourteen hundred years ago, Saint Cronan came to Roscrea, where he visited the island sanctuary of Monaincha. Finding the island too remote, he built his first monastery at Sean Ross in about the year 600 AD. Soon he found Sean Ross to be too remote for his social and hospitable personality. He lamented the fact that the monastery rarely attracted pilgrims or visitors. He established a new, more accessible monastery close to the ancient highway (Slighe Dála) at Roscrea. In 1475 the monks at Monaincha Abbey moved to the Sean Ross Monastery, which became the favored inaugural site of the Ó Meachair chieftains. Years later Sean Ross became the parish church of Corbally. Later still it was incorporated into the Corbally Demesne, while today it remains a majestic ruin on the grounds of Saint Anne's School, Roscrea.

The town of Roscrea grew out of the monastic settlement founded by Saint Cronan on the Slighe Dála. It was at Saint Cronan's Monastery during the late eighth century that the beautifully illustrated manuscript, *The Book of Dimma,* was written. The text is mostly Latin and contains a copy of the Four Gospels. This unique manuscript is housed in the Long Room, Trinity College, Dublin, and is exhibited alongside many other illuminated manuscripts, including the *Book of Kells*.

While the origins of the actual monastery on the island of Monaincha still remain elusive, it is accepted that it was an active place of retreat for a thousand years. Three different monastic movements are associated with this ancient place. Irish Columban Monks lived there from about 600 AD to the eighth century. Their first monastery was probably made of wood and later fortified in stone, particularly after the ravages of the Danes. From the eighth century until the early part of the twelfth century, the Céile Dé, or Culdees monastic reformers, lived here. The Canons Regular of Saint Augustine was the final group to settle here. The Canons came at the latter end of the twelfth century and stayed until Cromwell's soldiers suppressed the monastery in the mid-seventeenth century.

Figure 10-2 Sean Ross Church, Roscrea

Monaincha has a colorful history and a multitude of legends associated with it. Some of the more notable are included here, beginning with its very name. The ancient name for the monastery at Monaincha was Inisnambeo, which translated means "The Island of the Living." It was thought that nothing could die on the island and that the monks who lived there never grew old. It was also thought that any person or animal of the female sex who ventured upon the island would meet with immediate death.

During the Cromwellian invasion (1649–1650), English soldiers failed to gain access to the monastery, so they went to the home of a woman who lived nearby and questioned her about the secret route to the island monastery. The woman was in the process of baking bread and refused to give them any information. They tortured her until she finally relented and divulged the whereabouts of a tin boat and the secret route that would take them directly to the island. As a result of her treachery, the woman and her bread were turned to stone. The weathered stones of both woman and bread are supposed to be in the graveyard at Monaincha.

As the soldiers approached the island, a flurry of monks rushed to their boats with as many of the monastic treasures as they could carry. Other monks hid what remained in the hollows of the trees that surrounded the island. One group of soldiers followed the monks out onto the lake. The other soldiers rounded up the remaining monks and hanged them from low-hanging branches. The monks aboard the boat secured the treasure in a chest and fastened it to a very long chain, letting it fall into the lake. By the time the soldiers reached them, they were empty-handed. These monks were slaughtered, and their bodies were thrown into the muddy depths below them.

In the late 1800s the English planters who owned this property decided to drain the bog. When the land drainage began, the water is said to have roared in fury at the desecration of such a holy place. Legend also states that several human bones were excavated from the bottom of the lake, while holy altar vessels and candlesticks were found hidden in the trees. Another story tells how a tenant farmer found a chain on the lake floor. At night under cover of darkness and fortified with tools, he returned to explore the chain. He failed to locate

Figure 10-3 Twelfth-Century High Cross, Monaincha, Roscrea

the exact spot of his earlier find and returned home empty-handed. In 1903 this property was sold to a William Meagher, who claimed to be a descendant of the original owners, the Meaghers of Ikerrin.

The monasteries at Sean Ross and Monaincha, Roscrea, were strongly associated with the Ó Meachair Clan, who became important patrons and controllers of these monastic settlements and subsequent churches in their territory. A series of documents from the Holy See that deals with the Priory of Monaincha in the fourteenth and fifteenth centuries shows it to be under lay domination by the O Meaghers, who controlled the diocesan revenue (Gleeson, D.F., 47–48):

1413 April 4th, Mandate to archbishop of Cashel and Dermot O Kennedy, canon of Killaloe, to cause Marianus Ó Meachar to be appointed perpetual vicar of Killmomeneg in the diocese of Cashel and to be promoted to Holy Orders and admitted canon of Monaincha, void by the death of Thomas Ó Meachar.

1415 The Papal registers record the following;

Mandate, July 4th, provision to appoint Donald Ó Mechayr who is 24 years old and of the order or St. Augustine, to the priory of St. Mary's, Monaincha, vacant by the death of Dermott Ó Mechayr.

1419 Mandate to the Prior of Saegyrkyerayn (Sier Kieran) in Ossory to assign to Donald, son of the late Donatus Ó Meachayr, layman, canon of the Augustinian priory of St. Mary, Monaincha, in the diocese of Killaloe, the said priory independent and conventual, with cesse and elective value not exceeding 30 marks, void because Donald Ó Meachayr has become a friar minor,

1425 July 18th, Mandate to the prior of St. Mary's Monaincha, to collate and assign to Thady Ó Meachayr, clerk, to be promoted to the perpetual vicarage, value not exceeding 8 marks of Buryne, (Bourney) void because John Ó Meachayr, who is to be removed, held it for more than ten years without having himself ordained priest and without dispensation.

1427 In this year Cornelious Y. Mecayr was rector of Roscrea. (Callanan, 157–158)

William J. Hayes in his article, *The Mahers and their Ikerrin Homeland,* confirms that,

The O' Meaghers promoted other ecclesiastical sites in Ikerrin in the early Christian era also. A possible one of those is in the Ballycrine townland on Carrig Hill near Roscrea, which shows up in an aerial photograph by way of an extensive circular enclosure close to the impressive ring fort named Lisnageeha. Another early ecclesiastical site could have been in Clonakenny, a site, which is thought by some local historians to have been named after Saint Canice whose most notable foundation, was at Aghaboe. There are also signs of an early ecclesiastical enclosure around the old graveyard and church in Rathnaveogue.

Figure 10-4 Doorway of Monaincha Abbey

Hayes also states that sometime in the twelfth century the Ó Meachair Clan gave a grant of lands to a monastic settlement. This land was later given the status of a parish and named Corville. Because the Ó Meachairs were so generous and supportive of the monastic settlements in their territory, they were allowed many rights and privileges. Among them was their right to have their inauguration ceremony and their burials in Sean Ross. Some of the Ó Meachair chieftains were also buried in Holy Cross Abbey in the former territory of the O Fogartys.

The monasteries in the Roscrea area were strategically positioned near the Slíghe Dála and were the main centers of Christianity in Ikerrin. Sean Ross is reputed to have been the place of inauguration for the Ó Meachair chieftains. The Ó Meachair chieftain was not a provincial king, nor was he a subking. He was in fact the lowest form of king, a fourth-degree king. Yet the Ó Meachair was inaugurated as the king of his clan with a mighty ceremony at the ancient monastery of Sean Ross near the ancient town of Roscrea.

The coronation ceremony began with the gathering of the clan on a hill summit. High-ranking members of the clan, the brehons, poets, and historians were all present to witness and record the momentous event. The high-ranking members of the clan were robed in full battle dress. They and their horses wore the colors and pattern of Saint Cronan and his Comarha, or successor. The Abbot of the monastery, the Comarha, welcomed everyone to the coronation. The clan's hereditary historian recounted a brief history of the clan and an account of how this current champion came to be the new chieftain. The laws of Ireland were recited for the Ó Meachair, who was required to swear that he would enforce, uphold, and obey these ancient Irish laws for as long as he remained the chieftain. If he failed in this mandate, the clan could depose him and elect a new chieftain. He was then handed a straight white rod or staff as a symbol of the need to be straight, direct, and honest in all his dealings and to keep his character free of blemish or stain.

Holding his white staff, he turned trice from left to right and trice again from right to left in honor of the Holy Trinity. As he turned he surveyed his kingdom and his people from all compass points. Then he knelt down, allowing the Abbot of Sean Ross to stand at his shoulder and proclaim him the Ó Meachair, king of the clan. The Ó Meachair rose to his feet and stood before his people as the new king of Ikerrin. He stepped forward bareheaded, wearing the colors of Saint Cronan. Finally the clan's men encircled their new chieftain and proclaimed him their chieftain king.

Cúcoigcríche Ó Cléirigh, one of the compilers of *The Annals of the Four Masters,* wrote the following account of the ceremony: "The steed and battledress of every Lord of them belonged to the Comarba of Cronan and of Inchnamber, (Inchnambeo, Monaincha), and these must go trice round him, when proclaiming him Lord; and the comarba should be at his shoulder; and he should rise before the comarba; and that Machair was king of Ely."

The Ikerrin Crown

In 1692 a group of farmers was digging turf on the slopes of the Devil's Bit Mountain. About ten feet into the bog, they unearthed a gold cap. It is commonly accepted that this golden cap was the coronation crown of the Ó Meachair chieftains. It was referred to as the "Ikerrin Crown." In his *Histoire d'Irlande Ancienne et Moderne* (1758), Abeé Mc Geoghegan described the crown as a gold cap weighing about five ounces. He tells how Joseph Comerford purchased this cap in 1692.

Joseph Comerford, a captain in the Earl of Tyrone's regiment of foot, and in the Waterford Regiment of the army of James II, bought the Ikerrin crown and took it with him to his newly purchased estate in France. The Ikerrin crown has not been seen or heard of since. The only evidence of its existence is an illustration at the Royal Irish Academy, Dublin, Ireland.

Figure 10-5 Ó Meachair Coronation Crown

Comerford purchased the estate and town of Anglure, Champainge, France. Subsequently he claimed the title "Marquis d'Anglure." The Marquis d'Anglure died in 1729, leaving no direct male heir. His nephew, Captain Louis Luc de Comerford, inherited the castle and estate. Captain Comerford sold these estates. Hence the Comerford name is no longer associated with this estate.

Much speculation abounds as to the nature and whereabouts of the Ikerrin crown. Some imply the crown was made of bronze and of no value. Others suggest it was made of gold and probably melted down for its value during the Reign of Terror in France. It is also argued that the cap predates the Ó Meachair era and may have no connection to the clan whatsoever. This fact is supported by the absence of any Christian symbols in the decoration, which would suggest that it was probably pre-Christian in origin. However, the Ó Meachair history predates the coming of Saint Patrick!

Ó Meachair Saints

There appears to be three firmly documented saints of Cineal Meachair. *O'Clery's Calendar of the Irish Saints* mentions the feast day of the daughter of Mechair of Ikerrin as September 7. Also mentioned is Dermod, son of Meachair. He was bishop of Toorah, Co. Fermanagh, and his feast day is January 6. The third saint from this clan is mentioned in the biography of Saint Columba written by Saint Adamnan. Machar, one of Saint Columba's disciples, went to preach in Scotland. He founded a monastic settlement near the mouth of the River Don, called the Church of Aberdon (Aberdeen). A gothic church was constructed in 1366 on this site and was called the Cathedral of Saint Machar. Behind this cathedral is a lane where Saint Machar's Cottage was located. Adjacent to this cathedral is a building known as Ó Machar's Poor House. A fourth saint of the Cineal Meachair is mentioned in considerable detail in *Some Historical Notes of the O' Meaghers of Ikerrin* by Joseph Caismir O' Meagher (1890).

According to Joseph Caismir O'Meagher, Thaddeus Ó Meachair was of the royal house of Ó Meachair at Cloyne, Roscrea. This was one of the royal houses of the Ó Meachair Clan. In 1490 Thaddeus was appointed bishop of the dioceses of Cork and Cloyne. (Cloyne is a small town in East Cork and has no connection with Cloyne Castle, Roscrea. The similarity in name is purely coincidental.) Two years after being appointed a bishop, Thaddeus set out on a pilgrimage to Rome with plans to meet Pope Innocent VIII. He traveled across Europe to Switzerland and through the Great Saint Bernard Pass into Italy. Upon reaching Ivrea, Piedmont, Italy, he was exhausted and sought refuge at the Hospice of Saint Anthony, where he died the next day. The following account of the demise of Thaddeus is from the translation of a letter received by Joseph Caismir O' Meagher from Canon Saroglia, chancellor of the Cathedral of Ivrea, in May, 1887. This excerpt was translated from Italian to English.

In 1492 passed to heaven the blessed Thaddeus, and Irish Bishop, concerning whom we hear the following details: He was of the royal stock of O'Meacher, born in the town of Cloyne, (quere Cloyne in Ikerrin), in Ireland, and was probably Bishop of Cork. In the second half of the fifteenth century the lay powers in the country set about depriving the Church of its immunities, and compelled some of its bishops to seek in foreign lands that peace that they could not have in their own country. Amongst them was the Blessed Thaddeus, who set out from Rome, and passed through Ivrea, and on the night of the 24th of October, 1492, was admitted as an unrecognized pilgrim to the Hospice of St. Anthony: he was broken down by the long journey over the great St. Bernard, then covered in snow. On the following night the officials beheld a great light gleaming on the bed where the stranger lay. Being frightened they ran to extinguish it, but to their great surprise they discovered that it was a light that did not burn, and that the pilgrim, breathing an air of paradise, was then dead. Next morning the Governors of the hospice were prayed to relate to Monseigneur Garigliatti the miraculous occurrence, and on going to the hospice and examining the papers found on the person of the deceased pilgrim, they discovered that he was a bishop; they then thought it their duty to provide him with a befitting interment. The bishop with the chapter and clergy, accompanied by all orders of citizens went processionally to the hospice and removed the body of the pilgrim, and caused it to be clad in bishop's dress. The bells of the city were set tolling, and the bishop translated the corpse to the cathedral, where solemn obsequies were held. Remembering the extraordinary light at the time of the decease, and knowing that certain miraculous cures had occurred at that very time, the bishop decided that the corpse should be interred in the cathedral and at the altar of Saint Andrew, where reposed the relics of St. Eusebius, Bishop of Ivrea.

> On the 17 August 1742, Monseigneur Michele Vittorio de Villa caused the sepulcher, where were the bodies of St. Eusebius and the blessed Thaddeus, to be opened, and the body of the latter was found whole, and not decayed, clothed in a violet soutane and rochet, his white beard falling on his breast, and a ring on his finger (O' Meagher, 18–19)

Also preserved in the Cathedral are some Latin verses about Blessed Thaddeus Ó Meagher. An unnamed student from Saint Patrick's College, Maynooth, translated the latter from the original Latin.

Beneath marble tomb, in this the Virgin's shrine,
The bones of many a saint in peace recline here martyred.
Thaddeus there, from Erin's shore he came,
A bishop of Ó Meachair's royal name,
At whose behest were wondrous cures oft made.
We Latins in Genoa now invoke his aid.
Dying, he mourned that not on Irish soil,
Where sped his youth, should close his earthly toil.
Not Ikerrin, not Cloyne, but Ivrea owns,
[For God so willed it!] the saintly bishop's bones.
'Tis meet that they, in marble shrine encased,
Should be within the great cathedral placed.
Like Christ, whose tomb was for another made,
He in Eusebius' cenotaph is laid.
Soon sacred prodigies his power attests,
O ye who hither come, our saint assail,
With prayers and votive gifts;
Nor travelers fail to greet with reverence the holy dead.
Since Christ was born a thousand years have fled,
Four hundred then, and ninety-two beside
Had passed away when St. Thaddeus died.

Catherine Maher Beltrami visited the Cathedral of Ivrea in 1999. She took the photographs of the cathedral, the blessed relics of Saint Thaddeus, and the plaque mounted in his honor (shown on page 97). However, she noticed that while the dates, times, and detailed information on the plaque all concur with the May 1887 letter from Canon Saroglia, chancellor of the Cathedral of Ivrea, to Joseph Caismir O'Meagher (shown on page 94), the name on the plaque does not. The plaque commemorates a Thaddeus McCarthy. Figure 10-6 is a photo of the plaque, followed by a translation from Italian to English by Irma Forlini Beltrami, Montreal, Canada.

CATHEDRAL OF IVREA
AN IRISH BISHOP
Died in Ivrea in 1492

In the urn sitting on the altar are the conserved and respected cremated remains of the Blessed Thaddea McCarthy, an Irish Bishop who died upon his return from Rome, where POPE INNOCENZO VIII, who at first impression, being misinformed, prescribes him a punishment of excommunication, like 'the son of perdition,' consequently, the Pope rescinded and nominates him Bishop of the United Diocese of Cork and Cloyne, and invites all the parishioners to welcome him with reverence and call him a man of 'Richness in Virtue and Wisdom.'

While returning to Ireland to take on the Episcopal responsibilities of his Diocese he dies in Ivrea, the night between the 24-25 October at the age of 37, a humble and unknown pilgrim, poor amongst the poorest in the hospice hospital of 'Vigintiuno' situated next to the Chapel of Saint Antonio, which is always open to the public, and situated on the old road leading to Aosta (road San Giovanni Bosco). The Bishop is described as an admired example of fidelity and of love towards the Church humility and spiritual strength, of evangelistical poverty, of true justice and peace, of believing in God.

The small amphora next to the urn contains a small amount of Irish soil brought over by the Irish pilgrims for the festivities of the 5th centennial celebration, October 25-25, 1992, of the death of the Blessed Bishop.

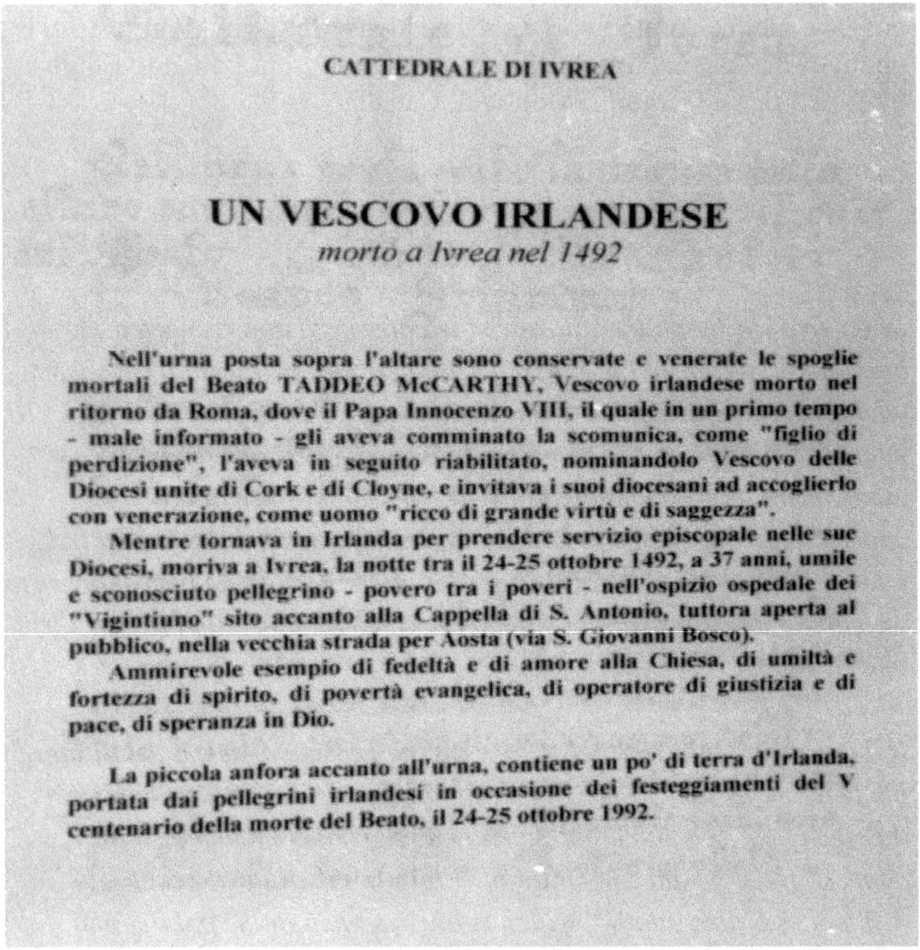

CATTEDRALE DI IVREA

UN VESCOVO IRLANDESE
morto a Ivrea nel 1492

Nell'urna posta sopra l'altare sono conservate e venerate le spoglie mortali del Beato TADDEO McCARTHY, Vescovo irlandese morto nel ritorno da Roma, dove il Papa Innocenzo VIII, il quale in un primo tempo - male informato - gli aveva comminato la scomunica, come "figlio di perdizione", l'aveva in seguito riabilitato, nominandolo Vescovo delle Diocesi unite di Cork e di Cloyne, e invitava i suoi diocesani ad accoglierlo con venerazione, come uomo "ricco di grande virtù e di saggezza".

Mentre tornava in Irlanda per prendere servizio episcopale nelle sue Diocesi, moriva a Ivrea, la notte tra il 24-25 ottobre 1492, a 37 anni, umile e sconosciuto pellegrino - povero tra i poveri - nell'ospizio ospedale dei "Vigintiuno" sito accanto alla Cappella di S. Antonio, tuttora aperta al pubblico, nella vecchia strada per Aosta (via S. Giovanni Bosco).

Ammirevole esempio di fedeltà e di amore alla Chiesa, di umiltà e fortezza di spirito, di povertà evangelica, di operatore di giustizia e di pace, di speranza in Dio.

La piccola anfora accanto all'urna, contiene un po' di terra d'Irlanda, portata dai pellegrini irlandesi in occasione dei festeggiamenti del V centenario della morte del Beato, il 24-25 ottobre 1992.

Figure 10-6 Plaque at the Cathedral of Ivera, Italy (Courtesy of Catherine Maher Beltrami, Vaud, Switzerland)

This plaque commemorates the five hundredth anniversary of the death of Thaddeus McCarthy, who had been appointed Bishop of Cork and Cloyne in 1490 and died at Ivrea in 1492. The details of his death concur almost exactly with those of Ó Meachair. However, Ó Meachair was said to have been on his way to Rome while McCarthy was on his way home from Rome.

The website for the Diocese of Cloyne, County Cork, has a very detailed link that lays a strong claim to these saintly bones. The site tells in great detail how McCarthy was on his way back from Rome, having battled hard to validate his appointment to the Cork and Cloyne Diocese. When Pope Leo XIII declared Thaddeus Blessed on September 14, 1896, the visiting bishops returned to Ireland with relics for the cathedral churches of Cork and Cloyne. Blessed Thaddeus is also honored in a special chapel at Cobh Cathedral, County Cork. In 1992, on the five hundredth anniversary of the death of Blessed Thaddeus, representatives from the Diocese of Cloyne went to Ivrea. It is highly probable that these are the same pilgrims who brought the Irish soil as a gift to their saintly bishop.

According to Canon Gerard Casey of Doneraile, County Cork, author of the Thaddeus McCarthy website,

> *It was the events of his death in Ivrea, Italy, that generated a devotion to him there. In Ireland he seems to have been largely forgotten. It appears that emissaries were sent to Ireland from Ivrea prior to 1892 for the 400th anniversary of his death to research his early story. They found little to go on other than the record of his appointment. At this point the diocese of Cork, Coyne, and Ross reconnected with the story of Thaddeus. The Cathedral of St. Colman at Cobh, Diocese of Cloyne, was under construction and an exquisite chapel was included with the appointment of Thaddeus portrayed in the altar sanctuary, and his name inscribed in the floor mosaic. Beneath the altar lie some of his bone, brought from Ivrea after the commemorations. Some of his relics are also in the*

> *Cathedral at Cork. Presumably that the people of Ivrea were working from the documents he (Thaddeus) had in his possession at his death, and that the Roman records also recorded the man they ordained as Bishop, the first of Ross and then of Cork & Cloyne, I would find it difficult to see how they had the wrong man.*

Having studied the documents presented by Joseph Caismir O Meagher, it seems that Canon Saroglia, chancellor of the Cathedral of Ivrea, got the name wrong when writing to J. C. O Meagher. In his letter he writes of Blessed Thaddeo Maker, born in the Clovinese Castle in Ireland. In Italian the name is spelled *Maker*, in Latin, *O Machair*. Both spellings are similar to *MacCartaig*, Mac Carthy.

Also of note is the fact that at this time in Ireland it would have been highly irregular for a Tipperary man to be appointed to a Cork See in place of an equally qualified Cork man. Church appointments were often clan connected or clan patroned. Also, the mention of Cloyne may have caused some confusion, because it refers to both a Tipperary Castle and a Cork Diocese. However, the evidence strongly suggests that the Ivrea saint is, in fact, Blessed Thaddeus McCarthy.

Hence, the Meachair Clan can claim three documented saints, not four as originally thought. However, it seems unreasonable to suppose that the Heavens are not filled with a multitude of saintly Meaghers who can be described as "admired examples of fidelity and of love towards the Church, of humility and spiritual strength, of evangelistic poverty, of true justice and peace, of believing in God."

Figure 10-7 Relics of Blessed Thaddeus McCarthy at Ivrea, Italy (courtesy of Catherine Maher Beltrami, Vaud, Switzerland)

Figure 10-8 Cathedral of Ivrea, Italy (courtesy of Catherine Maher Beltrami, Vaud, Switzerland)

Chapter 11: The Vikings

Kuno Meyer translated this poem from a St. Gall manuscript written in the ninth century by a monk on the island of Inis Murray off the northwest coast of Ireland.

The Vikings

Translation by Kuno Meyer (1859–1919)

Bitter is the wind tonight,
It tosses the ocean's white hair:
Tonight I fear not
The fierce warriors of Norway
Coursing on the Irish Sea.

Figure 11-1 This is a Viking boat with a monastic round tower in the background. Re-creation found at the Irish National Heritage Park, Ferrycarrig, County Wexford.

Between the eighth and twelfth centuries AD, the Vikings, also known as the Danes or the Norsemen, became a familiar menace within Ireland. The word *Viking* means "sea warrior," and indeed this is exactly what the Vikings were. At first they came solely in search of treasure. However, when they realized how lush Ireland was, they began to have designs upon it and decided to stay.

In the beginning they pillaged and raided along the coastline, making lightning attacks ashore and retreating immediately to their longboats. Later these coastal raids became well-organized inland plundering. In order to venture inland, they built home bases or fortresses at the mouths of Ireland's major rivers, the Liffey, the Shannon, and the Suir. Then they sailed upriver and attacked as they progressed. Their principal targets were the wealthy monastic sites, where they were guaranteed to find an abundance of gold and silver.

The Vikings decided to settle in Ireland. Many became rich merchants and traders. Their powerful leaders began laying claim to land and territories. The native Irish resented this bold usurpation of their land and went to battle against the foreigners. There were successes and losses on both sides. Yet the Vikings continued to grow in strength and organization. At this time Ireland was a divided nation with chieftain fighting chieftain for cattle, land, and kingship. There was no high king strong enough to unite the Irish against the common enemy. Ireland had no national army. Chieftains relied on civilian levies and willing clansmen to support their causes in battle. It was easy for the Vikings to gain a foothold among such a divided people.

In 839 a Viking leader called Turgesius began taking possession of large tracts of land outside Dublin. This infuriated the Irish chieftains, who resented the Dane moving outside the boundaries of his Viking stronghold in Dublin. In 840 Maelsechnaill of Meath became the high king of Ireland. He attacked and captured Dublin three times before finally capturing Turgesis and drowning him in Loch Owel. In the year 1000 Maelsechnaill of Meath joined forces with Brian Boru, the leader of the Dal Cais Sept and king of Munster. Together they had a complete victory over the Vikings in the Pass of Glenmama, County Wicklow. This victory seriously demoralized the Vikings. The Irish became a strong force under the strong and united leadership of Maelsechnaill and Brian.

Brian Boru had grown in power from the king of the Dal Cais Clan in County Clare to king of Munster. His relentless attacks on the Vikings made him extremely popular and powerful. It was Brian's dream to unite Ireland under one leader and expel the foreigner for good. He also wanted to re-create an age of cultural blossoming similar to the time when Ireland was dubbed the "Island of Saints and Scholars." Brian believed himself to be the most capable leader to rid Ireland of the foreign scourge, so he boldly demanded the high kingship from Maelsechnaill. Maelsechnaill called upon his allies to support his refusal but found little support. Brian was both feared and admired by most of the Irish chieftains. In 1002 Maelsechnaill unwillingly submitted to Brian, who confidently declared himself the high king of all of Ireland.

The Ó Meachairs of Ikerrin never recognized Brian Boru's claim to the throne of Munster, much less that of high king. Neither did they support him in battle. Instead they gave their full allegiance to Maelsechnaill of Meath. They considered Brian a usurper, because he was a minor king of the Dal Cais who was not of the traditional lineage entitled to hold high kingship.

Brian and Maelsechnaill remained allies and continued to battle their common enemy, the Vikings. Together they finally crushed the Vikings at the Battle of Clontarf in 1014. Although he was seventy-three years old, Brian led his army to battle. Afterward, he retired to his tent and spent the day in prayer. A retreating Viking found Brian's tent and murdered the high king as he knelt in prayer. It was Good Friday, April 23, 1014. Brian Boru was dead, but the battle was won. Maelsechnaill reassumed the high kingship of Ireland and remained high king until his death in 1022.

The Ó Meachairs were well represented in the battles against the Vikings. In 1012 a historic battle against Sitruic, the Viking leader of Dublin, was fought at Drainen (Drinan) County Dublin. The Vikings slaughtered two hundred of Maelsechnaill's men. Lorcan Ó Meachair, son of Echtigern, the Ó Meachair chieftain, was the clan leader in Maelsechnaill's army. Lorcan and many of his cineal were killed during the battle. Hugh the Wounder was the renowned Ó Meachair leader at the Battle of Clontarf in 1014.

Roscrea's vantage point on the Slíghe Dála provided it with much trade and commerce. It was also famous for its fairs and wealthy monastic sites. The Vikings attacked the town and the surrounding areas at least twice. The Danes first sacked the town in 921. At this time they also raided and carried off hostages from the island monastery of Monaincha. Twenty-one years later another army of Danes marched on Roscrea under the leadership of Olflinn. There was a fair in progress at Roscrea. The townspeople decided to march out to meet the enemy rather than have them plunder and pillage their town. A battle on Carrick Hill ensued, and the Danes were assailed from all sides. An estimated four thousand people were killed at the battle of Carrick Hill, Roscrea. Olfinn, their leader, was also slain. Roscrea, being both a market and monastic site, would have provided plenty of booty for the treasure-seeking Vikings. The Ó Meachairs made every effort to defend their territory against them.

As the years went by, the Viking fortresses developed into the finest trading towns of Ireland. Dublin, Limerick, Waterford, and Wexford were among the earliest Viking settlements. Within these towns the Viking families began to learn the Irish language, adopt the Christian religion, and assume Irish customs. They even intermarried with the Irish. Hostility toward subsequent generations diminished.

From "The Defeat of the Norsemen"

by Sedulius Scottus (c. 848), translated from the Irish

Heavens, oceans, and all earth, rejoice!
And rejoice, O people who blossom in Christ,
Admire the acts of the Lord of thunder
And potent Father.

The vigorous arm of a powerful Father
Has leveled with sudden anger-behold it!
The rebel Northman, foe of the faithful,
Glory to God!

Bale is joined on the open plain,
Brightness of weapons glints in the air,

Warriors' manifold voices shake
The frame of the sky.

Opposing armies shower their spears,
The unhappy Dane counts his wounds,
A mighty army aims and strikes
With showers of iron.

Those who have thirsted through the years
Drink the blood of the raving tyrant
And find a sweetness in sathing their breast
With slaughter of men.

Diggers of pitfalls tumble in;
An overweening tower tumbles;
A swelling enemy host- behold-
Is crushed by Christ.

A people great and powerful humbled,
A cursed mass ground utterly down
-Death's mouth has swallowed and evil stock:
Praise, Christ, to Thee.

Reckon that overthrow of people:
Not counting the humble and lesser kinds
More on that hideous field in blood
Than trice three thousand.

The judge is just, the world's ruler,
Christ the glory of Christian people,
Prince of glory, subduer of evil,
In rule supreme.

A strong tower, salvation's shield,
He worsts the mighty giant in battle,
He whose name exceeds all others
And is blessed.

Avenger of a faithful people,
Who drove the sea in swollen tempest

In Egypt once, on chariots and riders
And whelmed all.
(Kinsella, T., p. 42–44)

Chapter 12: The Anglo-Normans

The famous Battle of Hastings in 1066 marked the beginning of the Norman conquest of England. The Normans were the descendants of Vikings who had settled in the province of Normandy, France. Over a century after the Battle of Hastings, the Anglo-Normans arrived in Ireland. These land-lusting invaders were to have a huge impact upon the culture, government, and people of Ireland.

The irony of the Anglo-Norman invasion of Ireland is that it did not begin as an invasion. An angry, exiled Irish chieftain enticed the Anglo-Normans to Ireland with promises of land, riches, titles, and power. He needed help to reclaim his lands and properties in Ireland. This infamous Irish man, known as Diarmuid MacMurrough, was to alter the fate and face of Ireland for posterity. He is remembered as Diarmuid na nGall (Dermot of the Foreigners.) However, it is highly probable that the Anglo-Normans would have eventually made conquests in Ireland with or without the invitation.

Rory O'Connor was the high king of Ireland in 1166. Diarmuid MacMurrough was the provincial king of Leinster. Both men quarreled incessantly, and Diarmuid refused to accept Rory as high king. As a result of MacMurrough's quarrelsome nature, he was forced into exile and fled to England looking for protection from King Henry II. While Diarmuid was in England, Rory divided his lands among favored Irish chieftains.

MacMurrough arrived in England in 1166 and discovered that Henry II was at Aquitaine, France. MacMurrough set sail for France. By the time he reached Henry, he was no longer looking for a guarantee of protection but for help to raise an army to regain his lands. Henry II gave Diarmuid permission to recruit as much help as he needed among the Lords of England and Wales. These forces included Fitzstephen, Fitzgerald, Walshe, De Burgh, and Richard De Clare, Earl of Pembroke. The latter was better known as Strongbow.

Richard De Clare refused to settle for a grant of land in return for his aid. He demanded the title of king of Leinster on Diarmuid's death and a marriage pact with his daughter, Aoife. Diarmuid agreed to De Clare's demands and promised a marriage to Aoife when he arrived in Ireland. Diarmuid returned to Leinster and lived quietly at the Augustinian Monastery of Ferns, which he himself had founded and endowed. High King Rory O'Connor, unaware of the secret pact with De Clare, reinstated MacMurrough as lord of his lands. MacMurrough accepted Rory as high king and reclaimed his lands, yet he had no intention of maintaining allegiance to Rory. When the Anglo-Normans arrived in Ireland, he turned his back on his own people and led the foreign army against them.

The first Anglo-Normans landed in Ireland at Baginbun near Bannow Bay, County Wexford. A fierce and bloody battle ensued. The Anglo-Normans won the day. "In May, 1169, with a small but efficient body of thirty knights in full armor, sixty horsemen in half armor, and three hundred archers, Fitz Stephen (and his Uncle Herve de Mont Maurice) landed at Bannow, Wexford—and another knight Maurice de Prendergast with a company of about three hundred . . . on receiving the news of their landing, MacMurrough raised a body of five hundred from among his Leinster subjects and joined them. And together they marched against the Danish city of Wexford, which after repulsing two assaults, capitulated to the strange army with its armored horses and horsemen and its wonderfully skilled and disciplined soldiers. MacMurrough bestowed the city upon FitzStephen, and settled nearby lands upon de Prendergast and de Mont Maurice." (MacManus, p. 323)

Richard De Clare, (Strongbow) and his Anglo-Norman allies arrived on August 23, 1170. The following year Diarmuid MacMurrough died. Strongbow succeeded him and became king of Leinster. Shortly thereafter the Anglo-Normans began their conquest of the south and the midlands. Dublin fell into their possession. They eventually gained footholds throughout the entire country. In order to maintain the lands they conquered, they built fortresses in strategic places. Castles were erected beside the major roadways, along the coast, and at the mouths of major rivers. As a result the Anglo-Normans had control of many communication and transport routes running the length and breadth of Ireland.

The early Anglo-Norman castles were built of wood and erected on high natural or artificial mounds. These earthen hills or mounds were called mottes. The wooden fortress was enclosed within a high wall with a bridge that joined it to a huge courtyard. This courtyard was known as a bailey. Here the soldiers and their families lived. This type of castle was known as a motte and bailey castle. The motte and bailey was further secured by a deep ditch, which was filled with water. This moat surrounded the outer walls. It was difficult for anyone to make a successful attack on these fortresses because they had to cross the moat. After the year 1200 the Anglo-Normans fortified their castles by rebuilding in stone. Many of these Anglo-Norman castles are now in ruins scattered throughout Ireland.

The Anglo-Normans had a huge impact on life in Ireland. They built castles. They created towns. They had a different language, customs, laws, and social stratification. It was the latter that had the largest impact on the clans of Ireland. The Anglo-Normans claimed Irish land that had belonged to the clans since the Milesian invasion. They made their claims using fire and sword in the name of Henry II of England. Henry II came to Ireland in 1171 to validate, deny, or affirm these claims. He then demanded the submission of the Irish chieftains. Many Irish submitted, having no experience or understanding of English language or law. As a result, in the years ahead there were many misunderstandings, disagreements, and wars between both factions.

Figure 12-1 Motte at Castletown, County Tipperary

Anglo-Norman Society

Anglo-Norman society differed from Gaelic society. It was stratified as follows: king, barons, nobles, tenants, and slaves. The king of England owned everything and ruled over everything and everyone. His favored barons were granted huge tracts of land in both England and Ireland. These barons retained their lands for as long as they showed unwavering loyalty to the king. Barons ruled over lesser nobles, who were subject to the whims of both baron and king. These subordinate nobles were of either Irish or English birth. Beneath them were the free or untitled tenants, usually of Irish birth. The lowest strata of society were the slaves. Each group on the social ladder paid rent or service to the overlord. They also promised allegiance and loyalty in times of revolt or battle. This system of society was called feudalism.

The Gaelic system was not unlike the feudal system, but it had one major difference: The land belonged to the clan. The clan in turn elected a chieftain who was responsible for its territory and welfare. With the coming of the Anglo-Normans and their feudal system, many Irish clans were legally dispossessed of their ancient homelands. These lands were now considered the property of a foreign king guarded for him by the Anglo-Norman lord. The Anglo-Normans allowed the native Irish to continue living on their ancient clan lands as rent-paying tenants. They were required to promise loyalty and aid to their overlord in times of battle. Within a century the full impact of this system was felt by both Anglo-Norman and Irish alike.

When the Anglo-Norman lords were securely planted in Ireland, Henry II asked Pope Adrian IV (the only English man to sit on the papal throne) to grant him the title of Lord of Ireland. He complained that Ireland had fallen into immoral and sinful practices during the centuries it had battled against the Danes and promised to oversee papal interests in Ireland.

> *Undoubtedly, the centuries of the Danish terror had had disastrous effect upon religion in the island—and the question arises how far had religious Ireland recovered itself in the century and a half since Danish power was broken . . . But Irish defenders say their picture is purposely false. In reply they point to the wonderful work done during this period for the rehabilitation of religion, by the great Primates Cellach, Malachi, and Gelasius; and also the holy St. Lawrence O'Toole, to the synods that were held, to the many beautiful churches and abbeys that were being erected, and to the number of Irish Kings, who, resigning their thrones entered monasteries and devoted themselves to God . . . Holy men devoted to religious life were also flocking abroad to join the noted Irish communities in Germany, that were propagating the faith over Central Europe. (Mac Manus, pp, 319–320)*

The Pope granted Henry II permission to set himself up as lord of Ireland. In October 1171, Henry arrived at Waterford. The Anglo-Norman lords voluntarily submitted to him. They considered themselves loyal subjects of Henry and had no ambitions to separate from him or set themselves up as foreign kings in Ireland. From Waterford, Henry went to Lismore and then to Cashel, County Tipperary, where Domhnall O'Brien, King of Thomond, submitted to him. As he traveled through, Ireland Henry continued to exact the same tribute from other Irish chiefs. The Irish thought little of this submission and felt that an absent king would be no king. There appears to be no record of the Ó Meachair submitting to Henry II. It is highly probable that the Ó Meachair failed to submit to Henry because the Ó Meachair chieftains always took their lead from the northern clans, particularly the O Neills, who did not submit to Henry II.

Statutes of Kilkenny

After many generations, the Anglo-Normans became "more Irish than the Irish themselves." They adopted the Irish language and customs. They even intermarried with the Irish. This greatly disturbed the English monarchs, who wanted their lords to remain totally English and loyal to them. In 1367 the Viceroy of Ireland, Lionel Duke of Clarence and son of King Edward III, summoned a parliament at Kilkenny and passed a series of thirty-nine laws called The Statutes of Kilkenny. These laws were to prevent further assimilation with the native Irish. Henceforth, it was high treason for the Anglo-Normans to use Irish names, speak the Irish language, dress in the Irish manner, play Irish sports, offer patronage to Irish bards, attend Irish social functions or fairs, or intermarry with the Irish people.

It is interesting to note that the Statutes of Kilkenny had little effect on the lives of either the Anglo-Normans or the Irish. To a certain extent, they were ignored. However, the English did use them as an excuse to punish or settle scores when it suited them. This happened with some of the more prominent Anglo-Norman families, most especially the Fitzgeralds of Kildare, who became Ireland's most powerful Anglo-Norman family.

The Butlers of Ormond

The Butlers of Ormond were to have a huge impact on the Ó Meachair clan and Ireland as a whole. The Butlers were a powerful family in both Ireland and England. They were fortunate to enjoy the favor of many English monarchs throughout the centuries. Henry II was responsible for the arrival of this influential family in Ireland. Henry reneged on his promise to the Irish chieftains and began bestowing large tracts of their lands to his favored subjects. In 1177 he granted Thomond (Limerick) to Herbert and William FitzHerbert and Joel de la Pomerai. These men refused the grant, preferring not to go to battle against the Irish to claim it. In June Henry granted the same lands to Philip De Braose. De Braose failed to win his claim from the powerful Donal Mór O Brien, who held these lands until his death in 1194.

In 1185 John, son of Henry II and Lord of Ireland, granted the same lands to Theobald Walter and his uncle, Ranulf de Glanville. Theobald Walter decided to pursue his claim. However, Henry II had previously given this land to Philip De Broase. Walter called on his brother, the Archbishop of Canterbury, to help negotiate with William De Braose, nephew of Philip De Braose, for the return of the estate at a cost of five hundred marks. William De Braose agreed. He gave the lands to Walter by charter delivered at Lincoln in the presence of King John.

Theobald Walter was granted five and a half cantreds of Munster, which included all of the territory of Éile including Ikerrin, the Ó Meachair clan lands. Walter in turn promised the Crown his absolute loyalty and military aid to the extent of his property in times of war. Walter was well connected and highly favored in the royal administration. His father, Hervey Walter, was the hereditary chief butler of England. His brother, Hubert, was the archbishop of Canterbury and, later, Lord Chancellor of England. Walter was also nephew by marriage to Ranulf de Glanville, tutor of Prince John, son of King Henry II. When Theobald Walter accepted the grant of lands in Ireland, he was given the rank of chief butler of Ireland. As such he had the right to almost one tenth of the cargo of all wines imported into Ireland. This right remained with the family until it was restored to the

Figure 12-2 Kilkenny Castle

Crown in 1810. It is from the title of chief butler that the surname Butler comes. The descendants of Theobald Walter were forever known as the Butlers of Ormond. They became a huge dynasty in central Ireland. Kilkenny Castle was the seat of the main Butler line in Ireland.

With his claim validated, Theobald Walter set off immediately to claim the property he had so dearly acquired. He built fortresses at the most important strategic sites and towns in his territory. It is thought that he built his first motte castle at a fording of the river Suir, Durlas Éile. This was later fortified in stone and became known as Thurles Castle, County Tipperary. By the year 1213 he had secured his land grant as far north as Roscrea, the chief town of the Ó Meachairs. Here the Anglo-Normans built a wooden castle and fortified their position on the ancient highway, the Slíghe Dála. Around the year 1281 the wooden castle was replaced by a stone construction. Though the Anglo-Norman castle at Roscrea established Butler dominance in Éile, the Ó Meachairs continued to have undisturbed possession of their ancestral lands.

In the year 1328, James Butler, son of Edmund Butler, Earl of Carrick, married the King's niece, Eleanor de Bohun. Eleanor was the daughter of the Earl of Hereford and Elizabeth, who was the seventh daughter of Edward I. A year after his marriage to Eleanor, James Butler was created Earl of Ormond. At a Parliament held in Northampton, King Edward III elevated him to earl and erected the county of Tipperary to a palatinate in his favor. He was granted royal rights, franchises, and other privileges in Tipperary, which of course included the territory of Ikerrin.

In 1315 Edmund, fifth Chief Butler of Ireland, received a grant of the return of all writs in his Cantred of Ormond, Hyogurty, and Hyocarry (Ikerrin); and in 1328 James, his son and successor, was created Earl of Ormonde by Edward III who granted to this nobleman's son, James, (7th Butler) the royalties, fees, and all other liberties in the County Tipperary, and the royal liberty thus established continued down to the year 1714, when by an Act of the Irish Parliament, 2 George I., it was abolished. (Ó Meagher, p. 16)

For several years the Ó Meachairs and their overlords, the Butlers, managed to maintain a cordial relationship. The Ó Meachairs were recorded as intermarrying with the Butlers and supporting other Anglo-Norman families in battle. On December 23, 1385, Sir Almaric Grace, a Norman baron, petitioned the Kilkenny Parliament for a licence to marry Tibina, the daughter of Meagher of Ikerrin. According to the 1367 Statute of Kilkenny, marriages between the Norman and Irish were considered a treasonable offence. Licences were only available with special permission from the king of England. Edward III was the king at this time, and a license was granted to Sir Almaric. This marriage was testimony to the friendly relationship between Butler and Ó Meachair during this time.

Figure 12-3 Thurles Castle, Thurles

I would not give my Irish wife for all the dames of the Saxon Land:
I would not give my Irish wife for the Queen of France's hand:
For she to me is dearer than castles strong, or lands, or life
An outlaw—so I'm near her, to love till death my Irish wife.
I knew the law forbade the banns
I knew my king abhorred her race
Who never bent before the clans must bow before their ladies' grace.
Take all my forfeited domain I cannot wage with kinsmen strife—
Take knightly gear and noble name, and I will keep my Irish wife.
(MacManus, S., p. 339)

Richard II (1377–1399)

When Richard II became king of England, he decided to confirm the current status and ownership of his lands in Ireland. He discovered that since the visit of Henry II in 1171, the Irish chieftains had regained large quantities of land, and it seemed that the English were at risk of loosing their foothold on Ireland. In 1394 Richard arrived in Ireland with an army of thirty-four thousand men intending to reestablish his rights as lord of Ireland and subdue the rebellious Irish chieftains. Art MacMurrough, King of Leinster, engaged Richard in battle at New Ross. Richard lost the day and decided to move northward toward Dublin, hoping to conquer territories as he went. However, the skillful Art MacMurrough and his army harassed Richard all the way to Dublin, making surprise attacks from the hills and forests. By the time Richard reached Dublin, his army had sustained heavy losses. Richard decided to change his tactics and make a pact with the Irish chieftains with plans to subdue them later. If they submitted to him he would allow them to retain their lands. They did. The O Neills of the north submitted to Richard in 1395. Because they considered themselves kinsmen of the O Neill, the Ó Meachair also submitted to Richard II. In fact seventy-five Irish chieftains submitted in Carlow and Drogheda.

Tadgh Ó Meachair, the clan chieftain, traveled to Kilkenny City to submit to King Richard II on April 16, 1395. The object of his trip was formally to submit to the king and thus retain the lands of Ikerrin. This submission was made in the Dominican Church of Kilkenny. Here in the presence of the king he had to remove his Irish garb, which included his girdle, cap, and mantle. He knelt down and placed his joined hands in the hands of the king, promising to be his liegeman. Since Tadgh Ó Meachair spoke Irish, his submission was made through the chaplain, John Malachy, who acted as an interpreter. Another chieftain translated the prepared English statement for Tadgh, who then repeated the oath of allegiance to the king. He promised that his "nation" of Ikerrin would recognize Richard II as their king and be faithful to him and his heirs. Having accomplished this, Tadgh Ó Meachair could return to his people secure in the knowledge that the clan lands were safe and legally titled according to English law. Little did Tadgh know that this security was but a temporary thing that depended on the whim of the reigning monarch!

When reading of Tadhg's submission, one is tempted to shout, "Traitor!" However, it wasn't until the 1700s that a strong sense of nationalism developed among the Irish. For centuries Ireland was an island of different tribes and clans warring with each other for power and property. There was no unified national pride. Thus, for Ó Meachair to submit to a foreign king was simply to choose the most prudent means of securing the clan lands for posterity. Under English dominion it was vitally important to have a legal title to the territory, and as chieftain of the clan, it was his duty to provide the most stable, secure, and peaceful way of life for his people.

Not all chieftains submitted. Art MacMurrough and English Lord Deputy Roger Mortimer quarreled incessantly. MacMurrough renounced his allegiance to Richard II and went to war against him, killing Mortimer at the Battle of Kells, Ossory. Richard II flew into a rage and returned to Ireland, planning to subdue Art MacMurrough once and for all. He intended to make an example of him for those chiefs who chose not to maintain their allegiance to England. Again, Art skillfully defeated him in battle. Richard sent to England for reinforcements, but they arrived too late. Shortly thereafter Richard was recalled to London, where his cousin, Henry IV, deposed him. Richard was imprisoned in Pontefrac Castle and died a year later. Art MacMurrough continued to fight against the English until his death at New Ross, County Wexford, in 1418. Ironically, Art MacMurrough was a direct descendant of the Diarmuid MacMurrough, who had invited the Anglo-Normans to Ireland in the first place!

In the tradition of Art MacMurrough, the Ó Meachairs, the O Brien of Arra, and the O Carrolls of Éile did not look favorably on the constant usurpation of their land. They renewed their resistance against the Anglo-Norman and made every effort to oust the invader. In 1372 Ó Meaghair, O Brien, and McConmarre were at arms against the Anglo-Normans. In 1401 the *Annals of Lough Cé* recorded a great slaughter at Wexford against the Danes of Dublin. A great many men under the leadership of Tadhg Ó Meachair were slain at this battle. In 1462 a record is made in the *Annals of the Four Masters* that states that Mac William de Burgh (Burke) of Clanrickard marched upon the Barony of Ikerrin. Tadhg Ó Meachair and his confederate troops fought back against him. Ó Meachair's son killed William de Burgh, the son of Mac William. Though the Ó Meachairs claimed the day, Tadhg, the Ó Meachair chieftain, was killed.

Throughout the next century, 1400 to 1500, the English kings were engaged in the War of the Roses. The House of Lancaster vied with the House of York for the right to rule England. This internal strife left the English too preoccupied to be much involved in Irish affairs. It was during this period that the Anglo-Norman family known as the Geraldines came to power. They were the Fitzgeralds of Kildare and the Fitzgeralds of Desmond. Though originally Norman, they had by this time become totally integrated. They considered themselves Irish. Their language and customs were Irish, and they were loyal to Ireland and the Irish people.

Henry VIII (1509–1547)

When Henry VIII became king, he grew to resent the power and popularity of the Irish Geraldines. His greatest fear was that he would lose his hold on Ireland if this family continued to grow in strength and popularity. Hence, he did his utmost to depose and ruin the family. After years of petty squabbles, he succeeded in accusing the Geraldines of treason, their crime being "favoring the Irish people over the English." One by one the great earls were arrested until finally, in 1537, Silken Thomas, the last of the great Geraldines, was executed at Tyburn, England. A son, Gerald, was smuggled out of Ireland in 1541. He was sent to the Court of Florence, where he grew to manhood. The power of the Geraldines had been crushed. This brought an end to Anglo-Norman and Gaelic dominance in Ireland. Henry VIII would now rule Ireland with Englishmen from England.

In 1526 Henry VIII appointed the Duke of Norfolk with four thousand light horses to take the land of the McMurrough, O Byrne, and O Connor. He also stated that the lands of Melaughlin, O Molmoye, O Doyne, O Dymsye, O More, and O Meagher would be dearly won. As each territory was conquered, the land was to be let in freeholds of four pence an acre. When this was done, Henry VIII could continue to expand his hold on Ireland.

Figure 12-4 Roscrea Castle

The Act of Supremacy was enacted in 1534. This act proclaimed Henry VIII supreme head of the Church of England in England. By 1536 a similar law was passed for Ireland, making Henry supreme head of the Church of England in Ireland. Following this law was the widespread suppression and closure of monasteries in Ireland and England. In 1541 Henry VIII had himself declared king of Ireland. This was the first time an English monarch claimed full kingship of Ireland, setting the precedent for successive kings and queens of England to claim the same title and right.

Henry appointed Sir Leonard Grey lord deputy of Ireland. A year later, in 1536, Lord Grey reported to the king that he had managed to win a battle in O Meagher territory and that all were taken prisoner. O Meagher was forced to deliver hostages. In 1538 Grey again reported that he was successful in gaining the submission of the O Meaghers.

> *The Ó Meachairs were not amenable to control at all times. In 1537 the deputy Lord Leonard Grey reported having won a battle in Ó Meachair's country, taken the gentleman owner and all who were there prisoners, and Ó Meachair was forced to deliver hostages. Like the O'Carrolls, when the time suited them the Ó Meachairs were ready to submit to terms. (Feargananim O'Carroll submitted to Henry VIII on June 12, 1538.) In 1539 an indenture between the king and Gilla-na-Naomh Ó Meachair, captain of his nation, bound him and his heirs and successors to pay to the king twelve pence annually for every carucate within Ikerrin; and to supply the kings men when required twenty horsemen, forty galloglasses well armed, and victuals for forty days at his own cost; and to make sufficient open road through his country for the easy passage of the kings wagons and warlike instruments. (Brewer and Bullen, Volume I, p. 125)*

Henry VIII decided that subduing Ireland was greatly adding to his already excessive expenditures. He simply had to devise a more economical method to subdue these stubborn Irish rebels.

> *The final consummation of the new policy was that Henry was to take the title of King of Ireland, to which general approval was to be secured. His agent in this was first Lord Leonard Grey (1536–1540) and then Sir Anthony St. Leger for the rest of the reign...Henry preferred the conciliation method, one based on the wish not to spend money on Ireland, and expressed in his phrase, 'sober ways, politic drifts, and amiable persuasions. (Curtis, p. 167)*

Henry's new plan to conquer Ireland was commonly called the Surrender and Regrant Policy. It cost little and caused no bloodshed. The king's agent, Lord Deputy Sir Anthony St. Leger (1540–1548) had the responsibility of encouraging the Irish lords to submit to Henry VIII under the condition of Surrender and Regrant. The Irish chieftain would submit his land to the crown. Henry would then regrant the land to the chieftain under the feudal system. In effect the Irish chieftain was forsaking his Gaelic status in order to accept a lesser title under a foreign king. The chieftain was now a tenant on his clan lands. Henry had the power to evict him on a whim. As for the common clansmen, they had no rights and no identity. Some powerful chieftains were even given an English title along with the regrant of the land.

In 1539 Gilla-na-Naomh, the Ó Meachair chieftain, submitted to Henry VIII. He agreed to accept Henry as his king and overlord. There were terms on both sides. Ó Meachair wanted his rights legally defined in the presence of the king's lord deputy, Leonard Grey, whereby none could argue his right to the land of Ikerrin. The king for his part had a list of demands. Ó Meachair had to pay tribute annually to him. When the king's army or representatives were in the area of Ikerrin, Ó Meachair was obliged to offer the assistance of his army for three days. Ó Meachair was to improve the state of roadways in his territory, allowing adequate passageway through the area for royal troops.

It must be noted that the Ó Meachair's submission to Lord Grey in 1539 was very early in contrast to most of the other Irish chieftains who did not submit until the time of Sir Anthony St. Leger. Usually the Ó Meachairs took their lead from the northern chieftains, the O Neills and the O Donnells. However, the O Donnells waited until August 1541 before submitting, and it was not until December 1541 that Con Bacach O Neill submitted to St. Leger and in 1542 was given the title Earl of Tyrone. The O Donnells waited until the reign of James I to be granted their title Earl of Tyrconnell. These two clans were considered the royal clans of Ireland. They set the example for all. Why then did the Ó Meachair choose to submit to Henry VIII without waiting for a lead from the O Neills? There are many possible reasons for their speedy submission.

Perhaps it was because of Sir Leonard Grey's constant harassment and plundering of Ó Meachair territory that Gilla-na-Naomh submitted to Henry. Or perhaps he took his lead from his kinsmen and neighbors, the O Carrolls of Ely. Feargananim O Carroll, the captain of his nation, submitted to Henry VIII in 1538. (However, years later his son, Teige O Carroll, rebelled. In 1552 he made terms and consented to submit under the title Earl of Éile.) Perhaps the Ó Meachair was too closely linked to his English overlords, the Butlers. In the past they had intermarried with various members of the Butler family. Perhaps this complex relationship between Ó Meachair, Butler, and the king put pressure on the Ó Meachair to submit. It is also probable that the Ó Meachair may have been influenced by the Anglo-Norman tradition of primogeniture.

According to Gaelic tradition, Irish chieftains held the land for their lifetimes. They were not guaranteed that any of their children would replace them. All those who belonged to the *deirbfine,* immediate bloodline of the chieftain, were eligible to contest for the chieftainship. This included father, son, brother, grandson, nephew, grandnephew, and even cousin, hence the Irish obsession with genealogy and family pedigrees. The most able and popular man among the deirbfine would be chosen as leader. No one with any physical blemish could contend for kingship. These ancient rules led to terrible rivalry among siblings, relatives, and clans and even among kings. The Anglo-Normans favored the tradition of primogeniture, where land and property always passed to the oldest son or nearest male blood relative. This guaranteed the continuance of property and power within one family. Perhaps the Ó Meachair chieftain found the Anglo-Norman tradition of primogeniture more attractive.

With relative peace restored in the Barony of Ikerrin, the Ó Meachairs set their minds to things other than fighting. They outlined their territory with stone defenses called tower houses or castles. It was not long before the Barony of Ikerrin had its own collection of Ó Meachair castles.

Chapter 13: Ó Meachair Castles

The late-sixteenth century was a time of relative peace and tranquility in the territory of Ikerrin. The Ó Meachairs began building castles to fortify their lands. These buildings are called castles, but they are in fact tower houses. Built entirely of stone, they provided fortification for the chieftain and his family. The castles built by the Irish chieftains were square or rectangular in shape. They were neither as elaborate nor as large as many of the castles built by the Anglo-Normans. Their main function was defense and not luxurious living. Yet, for the chieftains they were a source of pride and power.

Their ruins are probably the most common sentinels of the past in Ireland today. Very little is known about these castles, which explains the scant information on those listed below. Most are cited in the surveys from the 1600s. At that time they were already in a "severe state of disrepair." H. G. Leask, an authority of Irish castles suggests that,

> *For the most part minor castles find no place in historic record. All must have a history, be it no more than the story of their inhabitants, but of few is there much known. Indeed, it is not too much to say that those castles, which survive in more or less good condition today, do so because their histories have been uneventful, or that many which have disappeared or now lie in shapeless ruin have an unhappy record. (Leask, p. 76)*

According to Stout, the Ó Meachair castles were very similar in design. There were some individual differences, but most were either square or rectangular, the latter being the most common. The castles, including watchtowers, were predominantly built of sandstone and then grouted. Limestone was used for the surrounds of windows, doors, and fireplaces. The fireplaces were generally found in upper-level rooms. In most cases the castles had four stories separated by wooden or stone floors. The floor plans are also fairly similar. Some had murder holes that overlooked the main door, which in turn led into a ground-floor chamber. This main chamber opened to the spiral stairs, which coiled upward to each level. Above were the many floors and assortment of rooms.

Between 1649 and 1650, the Cromwellian invasion managed to dispossess most of the Ó Meachairs from their ancient landholdings and castles. Though many of the clansmen remained as tenants to the new overlords, the chieftains were sent west, their lands and castles granted to adventurers, soldiers, and friends of Cromwell. The days of the Irish chieftain and his castle were over.

"Statistics concerning castles tell us that there were twenty-seven castles in the Ikerrin Barony in 1641 and twenty of these belonged to the O Meaghers." (Hewson, p. 20) The following accounts describe some of the more famous Ó Meachair castles in the Barony of Ikerrin. Those that have survived are in different stages of dilapidation.

Ballinamoe Castle (The Cattle Townland)

The castle of Ballinamoe is hard to find because it is well hidden down a long lane off the Templemore-Dunkerrin Road. It sits peculiarly behind and to the right of what appears to be a new house. Because it is covered in foliage, it is well camouflaged. From this castle there is a great view of the surrounding hills. Only two crumbling walls remain and form the gable for a modern-day farm shed. There is a tall chimneystack that extends to the height of the tallest wall. It opens on the ground floor to a wide fireplace. On subsequent floors the fireplaces are considerably smaller. Though clad in ivy and other creepers, this ruin is quite impressive.

> *It is built of split sandstone, which is randomly coursed. It contains a stone chimneystack, which starts at ground level and serves three simple lintelled fireplaces on the first, second, and third floors. The north wall of the ground floor runs for a distance of 16.75 m and is lit by three single light windows with splayed ingoings. There are two openings with splayed sides in the north wall, which may be the original. The east end of the north wall is defended by a musket hole. (Stout, pp. 127–128)*

"The old Castle of Ballinamoe in 1624 was owned by Thadeus O Meagher . . ." (O'Meagher, p. 120) In 1641 the castle and lands were listed as having been granted to Sir John Davys, attorney general. According to the Civil Survey of 1654, Daniell, Gullerneaffe, and William Mc Egan were the owners of Ballinamoe.

Figure 13-1 Ballinamoe Castle

> *The said Daniell Mc Egan, Gullerneaffe mac Egan and William Mac Egan proprietors of one twelfth part colpe of the said lands in fee by descent from their ancestors as we are informed. These lands are not cleerely devided between the said proprietors whereby it may be distinctly bounded. There is upon the said lands of Ballynamoe a stumpe of a castle and the lands all wast. (Simmington, Vol. I, p. 16)*

Patrick Doughan of Lisduff, Dunkerrin, County Tipperary, recalled a story from his childhood related to Ballinamoe Castle. On a Sunday morning when Patrick was only seven years old, he went hunting rabbits, accompanied by his two little dogs. When he was about three hundred yards from Ballinamoe Castle, he spied a funny-looking pile of pebbles sitting on a rock. Upon closer examination, he discovered that they were old coins. He assumed that they should have been gold and that perhaps time had worn the gold away, leaving only tin coins. Patrick gathered the coins as best he could and stuffed them into his pockets. On his way home he met two elderly neighbors. Excitedly, he showed them his find. They reacted with horror and ordered him to dispose of the coins immediately. They insisted the coins would bring nothing but bad luck. Patrick was terrified by the elderly ladies' reaction and threw the whole lot into the woods nearby. When he got home he recounted his adventure to his father. As luck would have it, he had missed a few coins in the corners of his pockets. His father gave the coins to a man who knew what was best for them! They were never seen again. Patrick went on to say that there was a story of a robbery at the castle where the thieves carried away so much loot that they were forced to drop it as they tried to outrun their pursuers. Perhaps Patrick had found some of the robber's loot!

Ballyknockan Moated Site (Little Hill Townland)

There is a moated site at Ballyknockan, which suggests that there was once a castle on this site. If that is the case, this may be one of the castles that belonged to William O Meagher, who also owned Drummin Castle. Ballyknockan is situated very close to the castles at TullowMacJames, Drummin, and Lisdaleen. "The Castle of Ballyknockan was owned in 1641 by William O Meagher, and figured in Petty's map." (O'Meagher, p.122) "Nothing remains of this rectangular earthwork recorded on the OS first edition. It was located on a slight rise, sloping to the east. There are limited views from this location towards the east." (Stout, pp. 122,129).

Ballyknockan Church

In close proximity to this moated site are the ruins of a small church. It is highly probable that this church belonged to the castle at Ballyknockan. Many O Meagher castles had private churches within walking distance. Some of these churches had graveyards attached, but most did not, because O Meagher chieftains and their families were usually buried elsewhere. However, it is not unreasonable to suggest that the graveyards could have been attached at a later date.

> *This site is marked as 'church' (site of) on the second edition of the 6' OS sheet. It is situated south west of the village of Templetuohy and close to the destroyed moated site of Ballyknockan...On the irregular portion of the bedrock remaining there survives a section of mortar built wall, all that remains of the above mentioned church. (Stout, p. 100)*

Barnane Castle (The Gap Castle)

This castle was built and owned by the Ó Meachairs who held lands at Barnane and the surrounding area at the foot of the Devil's Bit Mountain in fee by descent from their ancestors. It appears that O Meaghers were still the overlords of this area in the early 1600s. Dermot McTeige Ó Meachair owned the castle in 1604. Over the following years, a debt of seventy pounds was placed on the premises. Dermot Mac Teige Ó Meachair died in 1618. His sons Philip and Cornelius were the inheritors of the property and the debt. Cornelius made a new agreement with the creditors in 1619. When Cornelius died in 1622, Guillenanaomh Ó Meachair, the seven-year-old son of Cornelius, and his Uncle Philip were held responsible for the seventy-pound debt. They could not occupy the castle until they paid the debt. As a result of this debt, Theobald Butler of Killoskehane came into possession of the property. He is listed as having bought the castle from Dermot Mac Teige Ó Meachair.

> *There upon the said lands of Barnane one castle inhabited yet wanting repayre and several thatch cabins inhabited... the said lands of Barnane are not clearly divided between the said proprietor whereby each proprietor's portion may be set forth by meares and bounds...The said Theobald Butler of Killoskehane proprietor of the one foure and fiftieth part colpe in fee from his father who purchased the same from one Donogh McTeige Magher of Barnane gentleman many years past as we are informed. (Simmington, Vol. I, p. 24)*

Barnane Castle, originally built and owned by the Ó Meachair, was sold to Butler of Killoskehane as a result of an unpaid debt. The Down Survey of 1655–1658 show that the lands, castle, and town of Barnane were subsequently confiscated and granted to a William Bulkeley. Bulkeley sold the castle and lands to Richard Moore in 1682. Robert Stephen Moore, son of Richard, leased the castle to Jonathan Carden in 1701. "Though Jonathan leased Barnane on 17

Figure 13-2 Barnane Castle (courtesy of the National Library of Ireland)

June 1701 he had already been living there for some time. The lease granted by Robert Steven Moore, was of the castle, town and lands of Barnane." (Carden Barnane, p. 8) Thus began the Barnane Carden Dynasty from 1701–1932; Jonathan (1674–1703), John III (1699–1771), John IV (1731–1789), John Carden "Killing Jack" (1772–1822), John Rutter Carden "Woodcock" (1811–1866), Andrew Carden (1815–1876), and Andrew Murray "Captain Carden" (1853–1932). After the death of Andrew Carden in 1867, the Barnane mansion fell into disrepair and was demolished sometime during the 1940s.

Since there is no trace of the original Ó Meachair castle, much speculation abounds as to its exact location. Many were of the opinion that Carden had incorporated the Ó Meachair castle into his manor home. This theory has been proven unlikely.

> *At one time it was thought that part of the ancient castle was incorporated into the mansion built about 1855 as the tower which is so prominent in all the photographs… However, closer examination of the layout of the buildings shown in the 1840 Ordinance Survey suggest that no tower was incorporated into the mansion at that date. (Carden, Barnane, p. 8)*

It is now believed that the ancient castle was near the graveyard, which is situated close to an ancient church. This is highly probable because of the tradition of Ó Meachair castles having private chapels close by. Arthur Carden seems to concur.

> *There is a now a possible alternative site near the ancient church further down the hill to the south suggested by the fact that the 1723 estate map shows a big building in this vicinity and refers to an adjoining parcel of land as 'Kurtils of Castle' … there is some logic in the idea that castle and church might have been closely associated." (Carden, Barnane, p. 252)*

Barnane Church

Although nothing remains of the castle, the dilapidated ruins of the church are still visible. "The old church now a complete ruin is situated at the foot of the gap in the demesne of Barnane . . ." (O'Meagher, p. 118). " . . . It is a featureless ruin, its northwest and two gables being nearly destroyed. It can be ascertained from what remains that it was fifty-three feet in length and twenty-four feet in breath. The fragment of the walls remaining are three feet one inch in thickness and built in a rude style . . ." (O'Donovan, Vol. II, p. 226)

It is probable that Barnane Church belonged with the castle. Many Cardens of the Barnane line are buried in this graveyard, and their markers are clearly visible today.

Figure 13-3 Barnane Graveyard and Church (courtesy of Arthur Carden)

Bawnmadrum Castle (Cattle Fortress on the Hill)

Bawnmadrum Castle was built and owned by the Ó Meachairs. While little remains of this castle today, its history gives testimony to its greatness at one time. It is situated off the main road between Roscrea and Templemore. It is very hard to find because it is well hidden by the high hedges skirting the curving, narrow roads that lead to it. The fields around this castle are strewn with ancient mounds and other sentinels of the past. This castle was built on a high rise of ground with a beautiful view across Monaincha Bog. It was a square castle with a walled courtyard or bawn. Two gables of the original bawn remain.

> *On the top of a drom or ridge in the town land of Bawnmadrum which means the Cattle Fortress on the Ridge, about a mile east of Boulabaun there is another castle, but its bawn only remains…The castle or keep stood at the southeast end, where its foundations are distinctly traceable. Tradition ascribes the erection of this castle to O Carroll, although it is located in the Ikerrin territory of O Meagher. (O'Donovan, Vol. II, p. 3)*
>
> *Thomas Magher Bollybane Esqr. Irish Papist…The said Thomas O'Magher proprietor in fee by descent from his ancestors. Upon ye said lands of Bollybane there is an old castle out of repayre and Modromy (Bawnmadrum) the walls of an old bawne and noe other improvements. (Simmington, Vol. I, p. 9)*

Thomas O'Magher, owner of the castle in 1654, was evicted from the property at the time of the Cromwellian invasion.

According to Joseph Caismir O'Meagher, this castle lies about five miles south of Roscrea. "Upon this hill the Ó Meachair built an impressive fortress called Moydrum Castle. At one time it was the chief seat of the Ó Meachairs. It was here that O Donnell rested twenty days while awaiting O Neill's army before marching south to the Battle of Kinsale." (O'Meagher, p. 118) This castle is best remembered for its dramatic murder of 1617.

> *The castle of Bawnmadrum owned by Thomas O Meagher in 1639 is figured on Petty's Map in 1685 …here Angus O Daly, while enjoying the hospitality of O Meagher was skeaned to the heart by an attendant and died bemoaning the fate he so richly deserved and too late repenting the biter satires he had uttered against the clans and chiefs of Munster…(O'Meagher, p. 118)*

Bawnmadrum Castle was the seat of the Ó Meachair chieftaincy in the early 1600s. Very little remains of the original castle.

Figure 13-4 Bawnmadrum Castle, Roscrea

A portion of the bawn wall is all that remains at Bawnmadrum today, nestled as it is on a prominent ridge affording limited views of the higher ground to the north, and low-lying pasture land merging with bog to the south. A square uneven area is,

> *Enclosed by walls circa 10m high to the east and north with definite traces of its foundation to the west, and all but obliterated in the south. The basal portion of the east section of wall has been badly defaced… A short section of wall continues outward from the eastern terminal at an angle of 120 degrees. It is possible that this wall supported a staircase, which gave access to a parapet, traces of which are visible 4m above the present ground level on the north section of wall. A deep recess at the western terminal of this gap in the north wall gives access to a musket hole. (Stout, pp. 128–129)*

Boggaun Graveyard

Bawnmadrum and Boolabaun are neighboring castles. "There is a small burial ground called Boggaun about one mile equidistant from the castles of Bawnmadrum and Boulybawn but no sign of a church . . ." (O'Meagher, p. 118) This graveyard is said to have belonged to a church, which was attached to the site many years ago. There seems to be no archeological evidence to prove the existence of such a church.

Boolabaun Castle (White Pasture)

O'Donovan describes Boolabaun Castle as it was in the 1840s:

> *In the town land of Boulabaun in this parish there is a square castle, measuring on the outside 33 feet from east to west, and 30 feet from north to south. It has a round-topped doorway on the east side; a spiral staircase extends to the top in a round tower in the northwest corner. This third floor over the ground one rested on a stone arch, still remaining: and there is another floor over it; all making a height of about 55 feet; but the castle was certainly much higher originally. This pointed and ornamented building was lighted by fourteen windows; of which some are pointed and ornamented and some are quadrangular; all small and constructed of chiseled limestone. The doorway and corner stones are of chiseled limestone; but the rest of the walls are built of hammered red grit well grouted. They are 7 feet in thickness. (O'Donovan, Vol. II, p. 3).*

Today this castle is thickly dressed in ivy and lies about a mile to the east of Bawnmadrum Castle. Boolabaun is one of the few Ó Meachair castles that is relatively well preserved. It is a square castle with four floors. The ground floor roof is still relatively intact. A huge crack has formed in the main wall and is extending upward.

This impressive ruin adjoins modern outbuildings on a north facing hill...It is built of loosely bonded roughly faced masonry with fine limestone quoins. The walls are battered to the first floor, noticeably larger blocks being used at the base... The building is of four stories including an attic which has a vaulted ceiling...The interior consists of two main divisions. To the left of the entrance a short hallway through an arched chamfered opening leads onto a spiral stone stairs occupying one corner of the building and rising to the topmost floor... A barred vaulted roof covers both the turret and main portion of the tower house." (Stout, pp. 129–130)

Figure 13-5 Boolabaun Castle, Roscrea

In 1604 this castle belonged to Keidagh Ó Meachair, son of John O Meagher. Keidagh Ó Meachair of Boolabaun joined with rebels and took part in a rebellion against the crown. "The said Donell Mc Conor O Meagher and John O Meagher with one Keadagh O Meagher formerly of Boolybane entered into rebellion with divers others and that Donell O Meagher in said rebellion died, August 1, 1600. John O Meagher also died on July 1 1602." (Callanan, p. 163) *The Patent Rolls of James I* tells how Keidagh O Maher of Bolebane was given a general pardon on October 14, 1604. This pardon was given after the Battle of Kinsale. His property fell to "Thomas Magher Bollybane Esqr. Irish Papist . . . The said Thomas O Magher proprietor is fee by descent from his ancestors. Upon ye said lands of Bollybane there is an old castle out of repayre and Modromy the walls of an old bawne and noe other improvements." (Simmington, Vol.I, pp. 4,9). "The castle at Boulybawn was owned by Thomas O Meagher in 1639 . . . The stone floor of the top story was then intact but the parapet was wantonly wrecked by so-called athletes long ago . . ." (O'Meagher, p. 118) This Thomas also had lands at the neighboring Bawnmadrum. An inquisition in 1632 in Clonmel shows that the property of Thomas Ó Meachair of Bollibane was confiscated and occupied by Walter Walsh of Castlehale. Thomas was reinstated some twenty years later.

Castleiney Castle (Owney's Castle)

This castle is situated in the parish of Castleiney.

> *Sir John Morres of Knockagh Baronett Irish Papist… Caslteleyny half a clope… The said Sir John Morres proprietor of the said lands in fee by decent from his ancestors as we are informed. There is upon said lands a stumpe of an old castle without repayre and some thatcht cabins. The said land is wholly waste without improvement. (Simmington, Vol. I, p. 25)*

Figure 13-6 Castleiney Castle, Castleiney

Castleiney Castle was built for an O Meagher princess. In 1380 Sir Harve De Montmorenci built this castle for his wife, Owney O Meagher, the daughter of the O Meagher chieftain. Sir Harve called this castle Castle Owney in honor of his lovely wife.

> *Castleleiny, near Templemore, in the parish of Templeree, was built by Sir Herve De Montmorenci, ancestor of Sir John Morris of Knockagh, and was owned by the latter in 1641 . . . Monsieur De La Ponce stated, on the authority of the Montmorenci family, that Hervé de Montmorenci married in 1380 Owny daughter of O'Meagher of Templemore, Dynast of Ikerrin, and in compliment to his wife erected a castle, which he called Castle Owny, since corrupted into Casteleiny." (O'Meagher, p. 122–124)*

A huge fragment of this castle remains. It is situated on a high mound in the center of a large field. The view of the Devil's Bit Mountain from this castle is stunning.

> *The ruins compromise a stone gate tower situated on a natural platform enjoying a central viewing position…The gate tower consisted basically of two symmetrical towers which, are connected by a flanking wall containing a segmental arched opening which is, at present, blocked up…The east tower is entered through a lintelled opening in the eastern end of the south wall which opens onto a hallway lit by a single light window which is badly defaced and another window on the north wall…The first floor landing is lit by a single window with splayed ingoings…The second floor is entered from the same staircase. It has been obliterated except for the north wall… The east side of the gate tower is badly disturbed… However there are traces of a stairwell in the southern corner which probably gave access to the upper floors which have since been destroyed…(Stout, pp. 121–122)*

Clonakenny Castle (Saint Canice's Meadow)

Clonakenny Castle was the principal Ó Meachair stronghold in the early seventeenth century. It sits on a slight hillock overlooking the village of Clonakenny. This castle was built and owned by the Ó Meachair chieftains. It was once a large rectangular castle with a square tower attached. All that remains of its former glory is a lonely, ivy-clad gable wall standing as a sad sentinel reminiscent of former greatness.

> *A tower attached to its southeast corner, and is incorporated into a roughly rectangular bawn wall entered from the southeast. The interior of this bawn accommodates more recent farm buildings and out-offices. The bawn is defended by musket holes in its northwest corner and at the entrance. The northern portion of the tower is built of split stone, randomly coursed masonry, and has an external batter. Ashlar blocks are used to form the quoins." (Stout, p. 130)*

According to *The Patent Rolls of James I*, "On March 11th, 1605, the castle, town, and lands were in the tenure of Teighe O'Magher, were granted to Sir John Davys." (Griffith, p. 286) An inquisition at Clonmel dated April 20, 1624, shows that Thady O Meagher owned Clonakenny Castle and townland. At the time of his death in August 1625, John O Meagher (1595–1666) was twenty years old and married. He inherited the property.

The Civil Survey shows that the above John O Magher still held this castle in 1654. John O Meagher of Clonakenny was at this time the "Captain of His Nation." He was one of the largest landholders in County Tipperary and held much land in common for the clan, along with private properties of his own.

> *John Magher of Clonenakeany Esqr., Irish Papist...The said John Magher proprietor in fee by descent from his ancestors, as we are informed. Upon the said lands of Clonenakeany stands a castle out of repayre the ruins of a mill and upon the lands of Old castle a stumpe of a castle and ye lands all wast... (Simmington, Vol. I, p. 7)*

Cromwell's forces stripped John of his wealth and banished him and his family to Connaught in the year 1655. The transplantation certificate of John O Meagher of Clonakenny states: "1653, Feb'y 24, No. 326: John O' Meagher of Clonakenny, in the County of Tipperary, on the 30th of Jan'y, 1653, 12 persons, ¾ of an acre of winter corne, 2 cowes, 5 garrons, 15 sheepe, fower goats, 2 swine." (O'Meagher, p. 92)

According to the will of John O Meagher of Clonakenny, dated November 29, 1666, his property was left to the widow of his son, Teige Óg O Meagher, and to his daughter, Ellen. Teige Óg married Joan Butler, the daughter of Lord Ikerrin, who was of Butler stock. Teige was hanged in Clonmel in 1652, leaving no immediate heir. His castle at Cloneen (Cloyne) went to Roger O Meagher, who was in turn evicted by Cromwell. Ellen, the daughter of John O Meagher of Clonakenny, married Doctor Gerard Fennell, who was a Fennell of Ballygriffin, Golden, in south Tipperary. Doctor Fennell was a physician to the Ormond family and a member of the Supreme Council of the Confederation. Ellen Meagher Fennell was evicted by Cromwell and ordered to Connaught. Her husband was granted lands in Connaught on her behalf. Ellen died in 1681 and is buried in one of the side chapels of Holy Cross Abbey, Thurles, County Tipperary.

> *In 1645 Lord Castlehaven, one of the Confederate leaders, with a strong force attacked O Meagher's castle at Clonakenny which was garrisoned by the Parliamentarians. He reports that, 'I sent to the adjacent villages and got together crows of iron, pix axes, and whatever else could be found and fell a-storming of the castle and took it in three to four hours, leaving in it a garrison of 100 men.' Later the castle was retaken by the parliamentarians. (Callanan, p. 171)*
>
> *During the uprisings of the 1640s Teige Óg Ó Meachair was the Chieftain of Clonakenny, and he joined the Confederates and served in a regiment of O'Dwyer's Brigade. On March 23rd, 1652 this Brigade surrendered and many of its members including O'Dwyer were pardoned and exiled to the Low Countries. Colonel Teige Ó Meachair was not granted pardon and on December 8th, 1652, he was tried at Clonmel for alleged murders, and on the evidence of one woman, Ellice Jeanes, he was found guilty and executed. (Hewson, p. 18)*

Ellice Jeane's testimony was taken in 1642 at the time of the outrage. Her testimony makes no charge against Teige Ó Meachair. However, ten years later Teige was sentenced to death based on her testimony.

Local folklore tells how noble Teige Ó Meachair rode on his magnificent black horse to the gallows where he was to be executed. After Teige's death, the horse found its way back to Clonakenny. Here it roamed undisturbed for the rest of its days and kept the memory of brave Teige Ó Meachair alive in the parish for many years. Upon the death of the faithful steed, one expected that Teige would soon be forgotten. Not so! The ghost of his steed continues to charge the roads of Clonakenny.

Another ghost story that relates to this castle tells that when the arch of Clonakenny Castle is repaired or built upon, the wall immediately topples to the ground and a horsedrawn carriage drives through. Needless to say, few people go to the trouble of rebuilding crumbling castles. Hence, this ghost hasn't been seen or heard from in

Figure 13-7 Clonakenny Castle

recent years. Hidden in the Red Bog of Clonakenny are the treasures and, possibly, the entire wealth of John O Meagher of Clonakenny. When Cromwell's Parliamentary forces were making progress toward Clonakenny Castle, the chieftain ordered his servant to take the family treasures and hide them. When the soldiers found no treasure among the plundered goods of O Meagher, they plundered the village and neighboring homes. They found O Meagher's servant coming out of the Red Bog empty-handed. Apparently he had already disposed of the O Meagher treasure. It has yet to be recovered from the Red Bog.

Figure 13-8 Castle Road, Clonakenny

Clonakenny Castle Chapel

The small chapel adjacent to Clonakenny Castle is accepted locally as the private Catholic chapel of the Ó Meachairs. There is no graveyard attached. This arrangement would fit with the tradition that the Ó Meachairs were buried at the great monastic sites and not in local graveyards. Nestled in the middle of a lush pasture, this little chapel looks directly across at the castle. It is built of brownish sandstone and cemented with lime and sand mortar. The outside walls are built of cut limestone. A considerable amount of the ruin still remains.

Figure 13-9 Clonakenny Castle Chapel

> *The dilapidated ruins of Clonbough castle are located on a slight rise amidst low-lying pastureland due east of St. Anne's church in the parish of Killavinogue. It has probably been in a ruinous state since the middle of the seventeenth century. The building survives to two stories...The north east corner has been demolished... It was originally entered from the north west corner*

> *of the west wall. There are traces of a segmental arch with splayed ingoings. Only the southern face of the doorway remains. There is a single light window with splayed ingoings in the south wall… There are remains of a doorway. There are remnants of two walls running off the southeast corner of the building. They may indicate the original position of a corner turret here although there is no evidence for the usual stairwell. (Stout, pp. 130–131)*
>
> *Piers Lord Viscount Ikerine Irish Papist…Dromeard and a moyty of Clonebough one half colpe… The said Piers Lord Viscount Ikerine proprietor in fee by descent from his ancestors as we are informed… There is upon the said lands of Clonebough a stumpe of a castle without repayre. The said lands is wast without any improvement. (Simmington, Vol. I, p. 20)*

Clonbough/Clonboo Castle (Cow's Meadow)

This Ó Meachair castle was built and owned by the Ó Meachairs in the parish of Killavinoge. It is also close to the castle at TullowMacJames. This castle is very difficult to find. It is located down a long lane that winds through a private farm.

Saint Anne's Church at Clonbough

> *This little chapel is thickly clad in green. The tiny window gives testimony to its being a small chapel. It is difficult to ascertain how much of the chapel remains beneath the thick green foliage that almost smothers the ruins. "The remains of Saint Anne's Church are located on a slight rise due east of Clonbough Castle in the parish of Killavinogue…" (Stout, p. 101)*

> *"In the townsland of Clonbuagh is a square castle, and nearby are the ruins of a small church called Saint Anne's, said to have belonged to the castle, and not more than three centuries old. In its little graveyard only stillborn children are buried."* (O'Meagher, p. 119)

Figure 13-10 Clonbough Castle (Clonboo), Clonmore

Figure 13-11 Saint Anne's Church, Clonbough, Clonmore

Clonan/Cloneen/Cloyne Castle (Little Meadow)

This castle, built and owned by the Ó Meachairs, was once a large square castle in the parish of Corbally, Roscrea. It sat in the middle a sloping field on a slight rise of ground with magnificent views of the town of Roscrea and the surrounding countryside. What remains today is a large corner chunk of castle that stands alone on the edge of a pasture field. "The castle of Clonyne, in the parish was of considerable extent and built by an O'Meagher, chief of Ikerrin. It is figured on Vallencey's and Petty's maps and the site is picturesque anbeautiful." (O'Meagher, pp. 119, 124) In 1641 this castle was probably still inhabited. "Upon the said lands of Grange there is a castle in repayre and some cabins." (Simmington, Vol. I, p. 12). "By 1840 all that remained of this castle was a fragment of a square tower and a portion of a cattle wall attached to it." (O'Donovan, Vol. II, p. 3).

> *The ruins are located in an elevated position amidst undulating pastureland affording an extensive view of the surrounding countryside. The western portion of the tower which remains is built of roughly faced randomly coursed masonry... There are traces of two single light windows with splayed ingoings in the west wall... There is a musket loop in the southwest corner. This corner of the tower appears to have been inserted into an earlier thicker wall, which is made up of loosely bonded, split limestone blocks. (Stout, p. 131)*
>
> *An inquisition taken at Clonmel on May 16th 1629 shows that John O'Meagher of Cloyne was seized in fee for the townlands of Clonane, Grange, Cloghnuule, Gortvellin, Camlene and Ballybeg in the Barony of Ikerrin. That John O'Meagher his son and heir of full age and married. That an annual rent was payable out of the premises to John O'Meagher of Clonakenny as shown by a deed given on August 12, 1551 and made by Gillenenffe O'Meagher, grandfather of John senior and Daniel O'Meagher." (Callanan, p. 166)*

Figure 13-12 Clonan Castle, Roscrea

"Grange, also near Roscrea belonged to Gilleneeve O Meagher in 1551, it is on Petty's map." (O'Meagher, 119) The proprietor of this castle in 1654 was Roger Maher, who was the son of John, who was the son of John, who had it in fee by descent from his ancestors. Roger was heir to this castle after the death of Teige Óg Ó Meachair, who was hanged in Clonmel on the inconclusive testimony of Ellice Jeanes in 1652. "Roger Maher of Clonyny Irish Papist . . . There is in Clonyny one castle in repayre in this parish . . . The said Roger Maher proprietor in fee by descent from his ancestors." (Simmington, Vol. I, p. 29) Rogers' heir, John, was a minor child when he inherited the castle and the lands at Cloyne. This property was confiscated. John and his mother, Anne O Meagher, were ordered to evacuate west to Connaught. Seventy-five others accompanied Anne and John on their westward journey. Later they made an unsuccessful bid to reclaim their lands, which had been divided among Cromwell's adventurers.

Clonmore (Large Meadow)

Below is the only information the author could find on a castle at Clonmore. Clonboo Castle could be one and the same as this castle, but there is no evidence to prove such a case. Joseph Casmir includes a castle at Clonmore in his list. "The castle of Clonmore in Templeree, was owned by Donogh and Tiege O Meagher in 1641. It is figured on Vallencey's map." (O'Meagher, p. 124) "There is upon the parcel called Clonmore being of the said cope of Moclonmore the ruins of a large stone house." (Simmington, p. 21) Donogh O Magher owned this property. It could well be the castle referred to by O Meagher.

Crannagh Castle

The castle that now stands at Crannagh in the parish of Castleiney is the only inhabited round tower house in the Barony of Ikerrin. Much controversy abounds as to the original builders and owners. The O Meaghers claim it as theirs.

> *There is in said parish... and one castle out of all reparye in Crannagh... The said John Purcell of Crannagh and William Magher of Ballyknockan Irish Papists . . . Crannagh, Ballyknockane, Garrymore, part of Dromune part of Listiline one colpe... The said John Purcell proprietor in fee by descent from his ancestors of half a colpe and one eight of a colpe... The said William Magher proprietor in fee by descent from his ancestors of one forth and one eight part colpe. Upon said lands stands the ruines of an old castle and a stumpe of a castle but noe other improvement. (Simmington, Vol. I, p. 29)*

"The Castle of Crannagh was held in trust for William O Meagher of Ballyknockan, by Lord Ikerrin and John Purcell in the same year." (O'Meagher, p. 122) John Purcell was dispossessed of the castle and lands at Cranagh, and his property was granted to Cromwellian adventurer William Heather. Joseph Lloyd of Wales married the daughter of Heather and came into the property some time after 1670. In 1768 his great grandson, John Lloyd, who was then living in the tower house, erected a Georgian mansion and attached it to the tower house.

The tower house, at present undergoing restoration, is attached to a Georgian house in the grounds of Cranagh estate. It is built of split stone randomly coursed masonry with walls battered to the first level. The building is of three storeys capped by a cone shaped, multi hipped roof erected in Victorian times. Access to the ground floor is through a pointed doorway in the south face of the tower. The arch comprises two cut limestone blocks, which are chamfered externally." (Stout, pp. 132–133)

This Georgian house was destroyed by fire in 1996. Only the original tower house remains.

Figure 13-13 Crannagh Castle, Castleiney

Drummin Castle (Little Ridge)

This Ó Meachair's castle was built in the center of a flat field with a clear view across the countryside to the neighboring castle of Lisdaleen. "In 1840 the vaulted roof of the ground floor was visible." (O'Donovan, Vol. III). "A short section of masonry is all that remains of this castle today. It is located in the center of a lowlying field amidst undulating terrain. It would have enjoyed an unrestricted view of the castle at Lisdaleen, to its east and Tullow castle to the North." (Stout, p. 134) The field in which this castle stood is still known as the CastleField. A William O'Meagher, who also owned castles at Crannagh, Ballyknockan, Lisdallan, and Templetuohy once, owned Drummin Castle. This William died without heirs, and his lands and castles reverted to the overlord, the Earl of Ormond. "The castle at Drummin is nearly destroyed, only the first floor remaining and was also held in trust for the proprietor of Ballyknockan by Lord Ikerrin and John Purcell in 1641." (O'Meagher, p. 122)

Glenbeha Castle (Glen of the Beech Trees)

Very little is known about this castle. It was built on a slight hill with a clear view of the surrounding area near Camblin, Roscrea. Nothing remains of this castle save a mound in the field. Like Drummin Castle, this grassy mound is probably the remains of the old walls that outline where the bawn and castle used to stand. "There is a reference to a castle situated on a hillock in the townland of Glenbeha, in the Ordinance Survey letters of 1840. This was believed to have been built by an O Maher." (O'Donovan, Vol. III) "The Castle of Glenbaha, on a tullan or hillock, was also built by O Meagher; but, in 1641, Edward Butler of Clare, and Richard Butler of Ballinakill, were recorded as owners." (O'Meagher, p. 119)

Killoskehane Castle (Skehane's Church)

Killoskehane Castle was originally built and inhabited by the O Meaghers. "Killoskehane contains 2,541 acres, and signifies the Church of O Skehan, but there are no church ruins, and those of the old castle are incorporated in a new building. It is figured on Petty's Map." (O'Meagher, p. 120) Theobald Butler was in possession of the castle before the rebellion of 1641. He inherited the property from his father, who had purchased it from the O Meaghers some years before.

> *Theobald Butler of Killoskehane Esqr. Irish Papist... Killoskehane one-sixth part of a colpe... the said Theobald Butler proprietor thereof in fee from his father who purchased ye same from the several inheritors There of many years before ye rebellion as we are informed. There is upon the said lands a castle a stone house in repayre and ye rouines of a decayed mill a garden and several cabins there runs a little brook near the house. (Simmington, Vol. I, p. 23)*

Theobald Butler was condemned to death by hanging at Cashel in November 1652. He was convicted along with O Dwyer of Dundrum, under whom Teige Óg Ó Meachair had served during the war of 1641. Teige was also condemned to death by hanging.

In the seventeenth century Killoskehane was owned by Stephen Moore of Kilworth, Co Cork, and perhaps, like Barnane previously by Richard Moore, presumably his father . . . The castle, town and lands of Killoskehane and Lisnegatt, contain-ing 1,461 acres, was leased on 17th June 1701 by Stephen Moore to James Willington for 197 pounds per annum. They held it, leasehold, for 164 years." (Carden, Barnane, p. 342)

James Willington was married to Mary Carden, aunt of Jonathan Carden of Barnane Castle. In fact this castle and lands were leased on the same day that Jonathan Carden leased his Barnane estate. The Killoskehane estate had been in the Willington family for about 150 years when the lease was transferred to John Rutter Carden in 1855. John Rutter Carden was now proprietor of both the Barnane and Killoskehane estates. He began extensive renovations of the castle.

> *Perhaps having over extended himself financially, he agreed to sell the entire 1,304 acres including the castle to Col. Albert Fytche… Unfortunately, John Rutter Carden died within days of signing the above agreement and it was left to his brother Andrew to complete the work and the terms of the agreement. (Carden, Barnane, p. 344)*

Figure 13-14 This picture of Killoskehane Castle, Barname, handed to Arthur Carden by Nancy Murphy is believed to have come from a brochure prepared by Mr. and Mrs. Brown, the then owners, when they were operating the castle as a hotel. (Photo courtesy of Arthur Carden.)

Fytche died, and his son sold the property to John Martin of County Down in 1874. The property has since changed hands regularly. Martin sold the property to Miss Barry, who held it from 1906 to 1919. Miss Barry sold the property to Tom Costigan, who used it as a vacation home from 1919 to 1977. Stanley Brown purchased the property in 1977 and opened it to the public as a hotel. In 1990 Tony and Lavinia Broomall purchased the property. "Today the tower home adjoins the north east end of a Victorian Mansion on the grounds of Killoskehane Castle . . . This building survives to three stories and has been re-roofed to incorporate it into the later building." (Stout, p. 134)

Kiltillane Castle (Saint Sileáin)

Kiltillane Castle is more commonly known as the Black Castle. Its ruins are situated on the bank of a small lake in Templemore's town park.

> *The Castle of Kiltillane and church ruins are within the demesne of Templemore Priory… Near the lake are the ruins of Kiltillane Castle, which was most extensive, and built by O'Meagher, chief of Ikerrin. The present entrance to the demesne is by the original gateway of the castle, which is of considerable height but of rather rude architecture." (O'Meagher, p. 119,122)*

Tradition states that the Ó Meachairs built this castle. Historians dispute this and say that it was a Butler castle. It seems probable that either story could be true. The castle is in the Barony of Elifogarty, but on the boundary of the Barony of Ikerrin and at the foot of the Devil's Bit Mountain, which is staunchly Ó Meachair territory. When John Carden came to Templemore in 1698, he leased this castle from the Butlers of Ormond, who were the owners at that time.

> *James Earl of Ormond… The Mannor, Castle, Town and lands of Tamplemore contained two colpes… The said Earl of Ormond proprietor in fee by descent, as wee are informed. There is on the said lands a castle and the walls of a stone house out of repair and a grinding Mill in repair with some cabins and the walls of a parish Church." (Simmington, Vol. I, pp. 78–79)*

In 1740, while still occupied by the Carden family, this castle was accidentally burned, and the Carden family went to live in their newly built Priory just across the field from this castle.

A huge portion of this castle remains. It is partially covered in green foliage and sits majestically on the banks of a sleepy lake. There is a magnificent view of the Devil's Bit Mountain and the surrounding area from this castle. The arched gate spans a road that leads into a wooded area. Directly across the lake is a church ruin known as the Old Church.

Figure 13-15 Kiltillane Castle, Templemore Town Park, also known as the Black Castle (view from the lake)

Figure 13-16 Kiltillane Castle, Templemore Town Park, also known as the Black Castle (view toward the lake)

The Old Church/An Teampall Mór

Templemore town takes its name from this church, An Teampall Mór, "the big church." The town is built on the townland of Kiltillane or Cill tSileáin. Local tradition claims that the original church was that of Saint Sileán, known as Cill tSileáin, "the church of Saint Sileán." "There is some evidence both documentary and archeologically that the church site in the town park was an ecclesiastical center from at least the early thirteenth century. It was the parish church of Corkatenny or Corcateny sponsored by the Norman colonizers of the area, and dedicated to the Blessed Virgin Mary." (Hayes, Old Church, p. 4) During the fifteenth century Saint Mary's was renovated and extended resulting in the name change, An Teampall Mór. Henceforth, the townland and town were called Templemore. "A main section of the nave of the church was restored for Protestant Service probably around the early decades of the eighteenth century under the auspices of the Carden's, the landlords, who purchased the old manor of Templemore around 1700." (Hayes, Old Church, p. 4)

Figure 13-17 The Old Church (Saint Síleáin's Church), Templemore

Judging from the pattern that we have seen of the O Meaghers having built their castles within walking distance of small chapels, it would not be unreasonable to suggest that perhaps at one time this church could have belonged to, or been patroned by, the O Meagher inhabitants of Kiltillane Castle, as referred to by J. C. O'Meagher (1890).

Knockballymeagher Castle (O Meagher's Hill Town)

The following is O Donovan's account of the state of Knockballymeagher in the 1840. He also mentions the curious round tower, which is all that remains of the ancient castle today. "This castle was

Figure 13-18 Knockballymeagher Tower

situated in the parish of Knock, Roscrea. The place is now known as Rockforest. Only part of a round tower remains. These round towers were sometimes added to residences as places of security." (O'Donovan, Vol. II, p. 3) The townland is littered with standing stones known as the Standing Stones of Timoney. They are a fascinating sight and could well be described as a stone forest or "rock forest." It is not surprising then that the area is more commonly called Rockforest. This castle witnessed many battles during the 1641 rebellion. The parliamentarians constantly ambushed the site. At one point British soldiers garrisoned it. On another occasion the Confederate Irish Forces kidnapped the planter owner and took him all the way to Connaught. Cromwellian forces also attacked this fortress. Local folklore tells how John O Meagher, the then-owner of Knockballymeagher, made an assassination attempt on Cromwell. As a result he had to flee the country. His lands and castles at Knockballymeagher and Slanestown were confiscated.

> *James Earl of Ormond, John Magher of Clonenakeny Esqr. Irish Papist… Knockballymagher, Knockroe, and Spaddirnigh one quarter of a colpe… The said James Earl of Ormond and John Magher proprietors of the said lands moytively in fee by descent from their ancestors as wee are informed. Upon the said lands of Knockballymagher stand the walls of a stone house. The said lands is wast without improvement. (Simmington, Volume I, p. 13)*

When the Ó Meachairs were evicted from this castle by the Cromwellian forces, the castle reverted to the full ownership of the Earl of Ormond. In 1702 the Earl of Ormond had financial problems and sold the castle and lands to James Hutchinson, a Cromwellian soldier. Hutchinson incorporated the castle into a large mansion, which he built on the site. Then he changed the name from Knockballymeagher to Rockforest. He lived there until the early nineteenth century. The property passed to a Captain Gibson, who was the High Sheriff for County Tipperary in 1878. He was also the resident magistrate for many years. Gibson held much property in the area and was a rather popular landlord. In 1907 the land was parceled into smaller farms and sold. The manor house was destroyed by fire in 1922. A recent visit to the site of Rockforest House showed that the castle and manor home had been demolished without a trace. Several walls and outhouses of the manor house remain intact, and there is a curious round tower on the site. Perhaps this is the same castle as the one mentioned by O'Donovan in 1840.

Lisdaleen Castle (Fort of Two . . .)

This Ó Meachair castle lies in the area of Templetuohy within view of Drummin Castle. "Nothing remains of this castle today except for a few mounds of grass covered masonry. It is located on flat terrain in sight of the castle at Drummin and Tullow." (Stout, p. 134) "The castle of Lisdalleen near Templetuohy, was held in 1641 by Lord Ikerrin and John Purcell as trustees for William O Meagher of Ballyknockane." (O'Meagher, p. 122)

Figure 13-19 Lisdaleen Castle, Templetuohy

Parkmore Castle (Big Field)

This castle was located on Carrick Hill, south of Roscrea. Tradition states that Parkmore Castle was built and, at one time, owned by the Ó Meachairs. Cromwell banished the inhabitants, and the land was confisgated. There is no trace of this castle today.

> *The said Countess of Ormond proprietrix of the said two colpes and a halfe in fee by descent from hir ancestors. The said George Hamilton held a lease from the Earle of Ormond at which tyme the said Sir George Hamilton paid six hundred and fifty pounds fine to the said Earl of Ormond. The said lands being the inheritance of the now lady of Ormond… The Countess of Ormond Sir George Hamilton… The mannor Castle towne and lands of Roscrea containing two colpes and halfe… There is in the said two colpes and a halfe on castle two turrets and one grinding mill as is above expressed. (Simmington, Vol. I, p. 29)*

Rathnaveogue Castle (Saint Mobheog's Ringfort)

O Meagher claims the name Rathnaveogue means the "Rath of Saint Mobheog." This would imply that Saint Mobheog was the local saint from whom the area got its name. Ratnaveogue Castle was built by an Ó Meachair chieftain upon a hillock on the lower western slopes of the Devil's Bit Mountain overlooking the village of Dunkerrin. The remains of this castle are fairly well preserved and rather impressive. The main tower block stands in a lonely field quite a distance from the Dunkerrin-Roscrea Road. It is a square castle with a small square tower that is circular on the inside.

Rathnaveoge on the engraved map of the Down Survey is written Rathmoveog, which means the Rath of Saint Mobheog. The old runs (of the church) are nearly disintegrated. The castle stands on a rising ground about three quarters of a mile north of the church. It has four floors, all of wood, and was lighted by eleven rectangular windows. It had three ornamented chimney pieces of limestone and was owned in 1641 by John O'Meagher of Clonakenny, who also owned the castle of Balymoneen nearby. (O'Meagher, p. 120)

Figure 13-20 Rathnaveogue Castle, Roscrea

> *The castle is located on a natural rise of limestone bedrock affording a limited view of the surrounding countryside. It is square in plan rising to four storeys containing a spiral stairs attached to the northeast corner ... There are musket holepositioned strategically inside the turret... There are the remains of three ornamental fireplaces present in the three upper storeys. (Stout, pp. 135–136)*
>
> *John O Magher of Clonekeany Esqr. Irish Papist, Rathmoveage and Cappaghnorane three quarters of a colpe ... The said John O Magher proprietor of the said lands in fee by descent from his ancestors as wee are informed. Upon ye said lands there is a stumpe of a castle, which was never finished, and many cabins. (Simmington, Vol. I, p. 16)*

Rathnaveogue Church (Saint Mobheog's Church)

Figure 13-21 Rathnaveogue Church and Graveyard

Just across the field from Rathnaveogue Castle there appears to be a small graveyard, which continues to be used. Within the walls of this graveyard are the ruins of a small chapel called Rathnaveogue Chapel. This little chapel is situated on a huge circular mound in direct view of the castle. The remnants of three original walls are crumbling earthward. In keeping with the established tradition of the O Meaghers, it is highly probable that Rathnaveogue Chapel belonged to the O Meagher Castle.

Tullowmacjames Castle (Mac James' Hillock)

Figure 13-22 Tullowmacjames Castle, Templetuohy, View 1

This massive structure is found in the townland of Tullow. It sits impressively upon a hill with extensive views of the surrounding lands and the village of Templetuohy. "In the townland of Tullowmacjames near Templetuohy there is a square castle of considerable dimensions and in good preservation. This was one of the oldest residences of Clan–Meagher, and it furnished many distinguished representatives at home and abroad. In 1641 Richard Butler of Carrickcarrig was in possession." (O'Meagher, p. 122)

> *Tullow castle is built of split stone, randomly coursed masonry. The building is four storeys high and rectangular in plan with a circular angle turret projecting at the northeast corner... There are fragmentary remains of a chimney breast set against the north wall... a spiral staircase gives access to the second floor... The fireplace in the north wall is a tall, wide, well preserved example... the cross-slit loops in the turret may be of an earlier medieval date. This would suggest that the turret, at least, may be Norman in origin. (Stout, p. 136)*

Figure 13-23 Tullowmacjames Castle, Templetuohy, View 2

> *There is in this parish one castle in Repayre in the town of Tullow with an old Bawne destroyed also the ruines of a grinding mill in Listineen… Piers Lord Viscount Ikerine Irish Papist… Tulloe one fouerth part of a colpe… The said Lord Viscount Ikerine proprietor of the said lands by way of inheritance upon this land stands the castle of Tulloe and a bawne much decayed and some good cabins. (Simmington, Vol. 1, p. 27).*

A considerable portion of this mighty castle still stands. J. C. O'Meagher claims this castle for the O Meaghers, although many claim that it was Anglo-Norman built. In 1641 it belonged to Richard Butler. In 1654 it belonged to the Viscount of Ikerrin, who was of the Butler of Ormond family. In 1667 Edmond Meagher had two hearths in Tullowmacjames, Templetuohy. It can be assumed that he occupied the tower house in fee from his ancestors. In the early eighteenth century, a John Maher (RIP 1761) of Tullowmacjames married Catherine Lanigan of Kilkenny. She died, and he married Mary Gore of Goreyhiggen. They had three sons and one daughter: Nicholas of Turtulla (RIP 1810), who was father of Valentine Maher (1781–1844) a member of parliament (MP) for County Tipperary; Mathias Maher (RIP 1824) of Ballymullen and Ballinkeel, who was father of Mathias Aiden Maher (1846–1893) a MP for County Wexford; Gilbert Maher of Loughmore, father of John and Nicholas (Nicholas was murdered on June 6, 1810 in Loughmore, County Tipperary); and Margaret Maher who married Dr. Martin Maher of Cashel and was mother of Nicholas Valentine Maher (RIP 1871), who succeeded his cousin Valentine of Turtulla as MP for County Tipperary. The pedigree of this Maher family is well documented.

According to O Meagher, at the outbreak of the war in 1641, there were twenty-seven castles in the Barony of Ikerrin, of which twenty belonged to Ó Meachairs. Twenty of these castles have been outlined here, and Joseph C. O Meagher claims all for the O Meaghers. However, some historians claim that Tullowmacjames, Crannagh, and Kiltillane were built by and belonged to the Butlers, while Sir Hervé De Montmorenci built Castleiney Castle for his O Meagher wife.

Joseph C. O Meagher also claims the following castles: Derrylahan, Lisnahalosky, Killawardy, and Ballina. "Lisnahalosky Castle, near Templemore, was owned by Thaddeus O'Meagher in 1624." (O'Meagher, p. 119) "The old castle of Ballina is situated on a cnocan or hillock not unlike a moat." (O'Meagher, p. 122) "The castle of Derrylahan was owned by John O'Meagher in 1641." (O'Meagher, p. 119) Further information on these three castles could not be found.

Chapter 14: The Flight of the Earls

During the reign of Edward VI, son of Henry VIII, the English continued their policy of subduing the Irish. Conditions became so intolerable that Hugh O Neill felt compelled to write a letter of complaint to Pope John XXII, informing him of the abuses of power by the English monarchs in Ireland and the terrible persecutions that were being inflicted upon the Catholic clergy. The following quotes found in the *Scotic Chronicle of John of Fordun*. Vol 3, 908-et seq, provide some details from O Neill's letter:

> *To our Most Holy Father, John, by the grace of God, sovereign pontiff, we his faithful children in Jesus Christ, Donald O'Neill, King of Ulster, and lawful heir to the throne of Ireland, the nobles and great men, with all the people of the kingdom recommend and humbly cast ourselves at his feet... in this letter a faithful description, and a true and precise idea of the real state at present of our monarchy... a kingdom that has groaned so long beneath the tyranny of the kings of England, and that of their ministers and barons... has stripped us, by the most flagrant injustice, of the rights of our crown, and left us a prey to men, or rather to monsters who are unparalleled in cruelty. More cunning than foxes and more ravenous than wolves, they surprise and devour us; and if sometimes we escape their fury, it is only to drag on, in the most disgraceful slavery, the wretched remains of life more intolerable to us than death itself... They have given us instead a code of their own making, Great God! Such laws! If inhumanity and injustice were leagued together, none could have been devised more deadly and fatal to the Irish... The following are the fundamental rules of English jurisdiction established in this kingdom...*
>
> *1st. Every man who is not Irish, may for any kind of crime go to*

> law with any Irish man, while neither layman nor ecclesiastic, who is Irish, (prelates excepted) can under any cause or provocation, resort to any legal measures against his English opponent.
>
> 2nd. If an Englishman kills an Irishman perfidiously and falsely ... of whatsoever rank, the Irishman may be noble or plebeian, innocent or guilty, clergyman or layman, secular or regular, were he even a bishop, the crime is not punishable before our English tribunal . . .
>
> 3rd. If an Irishwoman... marry an Englishman; on the death of her husband, she becomes deprived, from her being Irish, of one third of the property and possessions, which he owned.
>
> 4th. If an Irishman fallen beneath the blows of an Englishman, the latter can prevent the vanquished from making any testamentary deposition, and may likewise take possession of all his wealth.
>
> 5th. The law prohibits all religious communities, in that part of Ireland of which the English are in peaceful possession, to admit any into them but a native of England... (Mc Geoghegan and Mitchel, p. 328)

In response, the Pope addressed a letter to the boy king, Edward VI (1547–1553), reprimanding him for the purported injustices inflicted upon the Irish and requesting that he investigate the situation. Little changed during the six-year rule of Edward. Following Edward came Mary (1553–1558), who continued the policy of oppression in Ireland. She also requested that Pope Paul IV grant her permission to include Ireland as part of her kingdom. In 1555 the Pope agreed to her request. Mary confiscated the lands of the O Moores and the O Conners of Laois and Offaly and renamed these counties Queen's County and King's County respectively. Fortunately the O Moores and the O Conners rebelled at least eighteen times and ensured the plantation would be a failure.

Elizabeth I in Ireland

When Elizabeth took the crown of England (1558–1603), many European countries were grappling for power and wealth through the accumulation of foreign colonies. England needed to be sure of its position in Ireland before it could expand worldwide. It was also concerned that France or Spain, its Catholic enemies, would plot an invasion of England using Ireland as a stepping-stone. In 1560 the Act of Supremacy installed Elizabeth as Queen of Ireland and the head of the Church in Ireland. In the same year she introduced the Act of Uniformity requiring all Irish people to attend the State Church on Sunday. They were also to use the Book of Common Prayer. By 1570 she had made it clear that she planned to conquer Ireland in its entirety. Fines and imprisonment laws were introduced for failure to cooperate and conform. Ireland was divided into counties, and sheriffs were appointed to enforce English law and outlaw the traditional Brehon law. A president of Munster and Connaught were also appointed. Elizabeth also planned to rid Ireland of the rebellious chieftains who blocked her way to absolute control.

According to English law, land and property belonged to the chieftain and his heredity heirs in a grant from the Crown. When a chieftain was accused of treason, his lands and title were forfeited. He was imprisoned or executed, while the clanspeople escaped to the forests and hills or were killed. Elizabeth used this tactic abundantly in Ireland. She sent mapmakers to make exact maps of the territorial boundaries and to chart the value of the land. Confiscated properties were divided among her favorite nobles, who brought lesser English settlers with them to secure the property and work the land. When the Queen began to colonize Munster in 1586, the territory of O Meagher was not included. Their lands were considered to be the property of the Earl of Ormond, who was a loyal subject and a relative of Queen Elizabeth.

With the widespread confiscation of property, the remaining clans of Ireland feared for their lives and their lands. They knew it was only a matter of time before Elizabeth put them under close scrutiny with the intention of dispossessing them. Laws became more and more anti-Catholic and anti-Irish. This disturbed the Old Irish and Anglo-Irish alike. The latter were usually of Norman stock, but ardently

Catholic. The Crown was infringing upon their rights, forcing them to become English Protestants. They were, until now, content to be English, but they refused to be swayed in their religious convictions. It was for this reason the Old Irish and the Anglo-Irish were eventually able to unite and fight alongside each other against the English.

During this century County Tipperary earned the reputation of being a troublesome county. In 1576 Sir Henry Sydney reported that the Queen's law was of no value in Tipperary. Also, in 1579, James Fitzmaurice returned from Lisbon with one hundred men. His plan was to fight for Irish freedom. Many of the Irish were tired of war and refused to support him. Fitzmaurice headed for Tipperary knowing that "the fuel of rebellion was always most ready to kindle there," (O'Meagher, p. 21).

At this time O Meagher territory became a hotbed of activity. There was constant strife between the O Meaghers and their immediate overlords, the Butlers of Ormond. The O Meaghers were also harried by the English administration. In 1549 Captain Walter ap Poyll reported from Nenagh that there was dissent between O Meagher and the Lord Marshall. Nine years later Sir Henry Ratcliffe, Knight, Lieutenant of King's and Queen's Counties, had to punish O Meagher, O Dunnes, and O Carrolls with fire and sword. In 1562 Elizabeth's advisor, the Earl of Sussex, suggested that she should gain control of the Irish inhabitants of Upper Munster and that a tax should be levied upon O Carroll and O Meagher. In 1560 the tax levied on O Meagher was 160 pounds. This money was used to support English soldiers who were quartered with Irish families outside the Pale. Only two years later this tax was increased to 360 pounds. Later that year Sussex reported, "O Meagher and the other Irish lords lived in obedience." (Brewer and Bullen, Vol. I, p. 346)

Sir Henry Sydney was sent to Ireland in 1567 to survey the situation between the Anglo-Normans and the Irish. When he returned to England he reported that, while the Earl of Ormond was on business in England, Pierce and Edward, his younger brothers, led an attack into Ikerrin and plundered everything in sight. The younger Ormonds had taken it upon themselves to carry out revenge on the O Meaghers, whom they deemed had lost sight of their allegiance to the Butlers. On January 11, 1571, Gillenowe O Meagher was pardoned. This same year, thirty pardons were given to O Meagher foot soldiers.

This constant plundering and pillaging of O'Meagher land forced the chieftain, Tadhg O Meagher, to agree to terms with the Earl of Ormond. In 1572 it was decided that O Meagher would be given full possession of his lands if he paid one knight's fee to the Earl.

> *The Earl of Ormond entered a deed with Teigue O'Meagher granting him all the manors, lordships, lands, rents, etc. in the whole cantred or country of Ikerrin, reserving all deer and all bucks of all kinds, all pheasants, partridges, rabbits and the nests of young falcons called in English the eyries of great hawks; to have and to hold for the life of the said Teigue by the service of one knight's fee, when scutage runs, doing suit at the court of the Earl's manor of Corkatenny (Templemore) and at the court of the liberty of Tipperary, paying also yearly 4p for every cow in the cantred, and for every town or village a summer sheep; also Teigue shall render all other services as do the other free tenants of Ormond, Ileigh, and Eliogarty. (Curtis, Vol. VI, p. 218)*

O Meagher reasoned that it would serve his people better to keep the peace and their territorial lands rather than suffer constant ravishing by the enemy. Ten years later, in 1582, the Earl of Ormond plundered Ikerrin once again.

This act of aggression was in violation of the treaty of 1572 between the Earl and Tadhg O Meagher. In 1582, pardons were given to Conor Mac Keadagh O Meagher of Clonmore and John Mac Prior O Meagher of Roscrea on the condition that they were not of the O Meaghers septs that were deemed rebels. Should this be found to be the case, their pardons would be reversed.

The Ulster Chieftains

Elizabeth's policies were relatively successful in the south of Ireland, but things changed when she set her sights on the province of Ulster. Ulster had a strong history of powerful leaders who traced their origins back to the first Celt, Eremon. These proud and powerful Ulster men resented the English occupation of Ireland and bitterly regretted submitting to the English Crown. While Con Bacach O Neill (the O Neill) lay on his deathbed, he cursed all those who had anything to do with the English.

After seventeen years as an English earl, Con lay on his dying bed, a broken, dispirited man, despised by his subjects. He called his people to him and pronounced malediction on all his descendants who should trust in English faith or give credence to English promises. He cursed those who would speak the English tongue, "for language bred confusion;" who built houses after the English fashion, "to be beaten out by the hawk;" who grew corn in the open, unfortified country, "to nourish the ravishers and destroyers." (MacManus, p. 364)

Shane O Neill, son of Con Bacach, heeded his father's lament and spent his life fighting against the English. He renounced his title of earl and used the Irish title of the O Neill. In a message to Queen Elizabeth, he made his sentiments quite clear,

> *If Elizabeth your mistress be queen of England, I am O Neill, king of Ulster. I never made peace with her without having been previously solicited to it by her. I am not ambitious of the abject title of earl, both my family and birth raise me above it; I will not yield precedence to anyone; my ancestors have been kings of Ulster; I have gained that kingdom by my sword, and by my sword I will preserve it. (Cox, p. 221)*

The Reply of Shane the Proud

-Ethne
I scorn your Lady's honours; I scorn her titles vain,

A Prince am I of high degree, and of a fair domain;
Peace have I never craved of her, but ever she from me;
I am a king in kingly right, and hold my kingdom free.

Heremon's blood is in my veins—I feel it swelling high-
And Eoghain's of the iron arm and of the flashing eye;
Their forms are melted into dust—their spirit is not gone;
I owe no fealty to your Queen, and I will yield her none.

She boasts her ancient Norman line, but tell me can she trace
A pedigree as long and proud as of my royal race?
And can she dream that I would stand among her modern peers,
Whose sires were princes in the land for twice a thousand years?

Go, tell her, tho' Mac Carthy Mor has bent him like a churl,
And risen from beneath her hand a belted English earl,
That Shane the Proud is prouder far, and not for England's crown
Would he exchange the name O Neill, or lay its honours down.

Say that ye found him all prepared for peace, or for the fray,
Standing upon his native hill, as stern, as free as they;
And that, were all the rest her slaves, there would he stand alone,
Defying from their rocky crests the foemen of Tyrone.
(Reading Time, pp. 88, 89)

The Nine Years War (1594-1603)

In 1594 Shane O Neill's nephew, Hugh O Neill, joined forces with Red Hugh O Donnell, uniting the two most powerful Ulster clans to fight against the English. United against a common enemy, these two clans began what would later be known as the Nine Years War. (1594–1603).

> *This war began with the battle of Enniskillen, where the Irish attacked an English garrison at the castle. The English retreated, leaving their ammunition and supplies to the delighted Irish. In 1595 O Neill routed*

three thousand English soldiers under the leadership of Sir John Norris. In 1596, when the Lord Justice and the Council of Ireland saw the bravery and power of the Irish against them, and that all those who had previously been obedient to themselves were now joining the aforesaid Irish against them, they came to the resolution of sendingambassadors to O Neill and O Donnell, to request peace and tranquility from them. The persons selected for negotiating between them were Thomas Butler, Earl of Ormond, and Mulmurry Magrath, Archbishop of Cashel. The Earl of Ormond repaired to Traigh-Bhaile (Dundalk) and there halted; and he sent his messengers to O Neill, to inform him of the purport of his coming; upon which O Neill sent the same intelligence to O Donnell; O Donnell came to the place where O Neill was with a body of cavalry, both set out for Faughart-Muirtheimne. Here the Earl and the Archbishop came to meet them. They stated to the chiefs the object of their embassy, namely, a request for peace; and they stated the rewards promised by the Lord Justice, namely, the appropriation to them of the province of Conchobhar (Ulster) except the tract of country extending from Dundalk to the river Boyne, in which the English had dwelt long before that time... They also promised that the English should not encroach upon them beyond the boundary, excepting those who were in Carrickfergus, Carlingford, and Newry, who were at all times permitted to deal and traffic; that no stewards or collectors of rents or tributes should be sent among them, but that the rents which had been some time before upon their ancestors should be forwarded by them to Dublin; that beyond this no hostage or pledges would be required; and that the Irish in the province of Connaught, who had risen up in alliance with O Donnell, should have privileges similar to these. O Neill and O Donnell and all the chiefs of the province who were along with them, went into council upon those conditions... having reflected for a long time upon the many that had been ruined by the English, since their arrival in Ireland, by specious

> *promises, which they had not performed, and the numbers of the Irish high-born princes, gentlemen, and chieftains, who came to premature deaths without any reason at all, except to rob them of their patrimonies, they feared very much that what was promised would not be fulfilled to them; so they finally resolved upon rejecting the peace... The Lord Justice and Council sent messengers to England and to the Queen, to tell her the news; so that she then sent a great number of men to Ireland, with the necessary arms. Their number was no less that twenty thousand; and they were composed of mercenaries and native soldiers. (O'Donovan, Vol. 6, pp. 1997–1999)*

In 1597 the rebel Irish forces took control of most of Connaught and forced Sir Conyers Clifford, governor of Connaught, to retreat to Boyle, County Roscommon. At the time of this battle, Walter Tyrrell wiped out an English army sent to help Clifford. This battle was subsequently known as the Battle of Tyrrell's Pass. In 1597 the English were again routed at Drom Fliuch Hill near Benburb, County Tyrone.

In 1598 the Irish attacked an English fort at Portmore on the Blackwater. Marshal Bagenal left Dublin with a huge army and set out to help defend Portmore. The Irish ambushed Bagenal at the Yellow Ford in County Armagh, killing Bagnel and two thousand of his men.

Under the intelligent leadership of the Northern chieftains, the Irish forces experienced great success. Their armies were strong and gathered confidence supplies, arms, and forces as they marched toward Connaught, Leinster, and Munster. King Philip of Spain had agreed to send a fleet of ships and soldiers to aid the Irish. This fleet was to arrive in Ulster where the Ulster chieftains could fight against the English on their own land. Unfortunately the Spanish army of four thousand men under Don Juan D'Aguila arrived in Kinsale. O Neill and O Donnell had to march the entire length of the country to meet the fleet. When they reached Tipperary, they found that the O Meaghers were ready to take up arms alongside them.

In 1599 Keadagh O Meagher of Boolbawn Castle was the captain of his nation. He amassed an army of three hundred men from his fellow clansmen, relatives, and friends. These included such names as the Graces and Thomas Butler, third son of Viscount Mountgarrett. Keadagh also had sixthy foot soldiers and thirty horse soldiers under his command. Sir George Carew, the president of Munster, offered a reward for the capture of Keadagh O Meagher and other rebels.

There was another encounter between the Earl of Ormond and the O Meaghers in January 1601. Sir Walter Butler made a surprise attack on O Meagher, O Kennedy, and others along the River Nore. Sixteen of O Meagher's men were drowned. Sir George Carew reported, in 1602, that Captain Flower had burned all O Meagher's corn and had killed some armed men. Lord Mountjoy laid waste to most of the land in north Tipperary with his army of twenty thousand men. Supplies were sparse and help unavailable. As a result of this constant harassment, it is no surprise that the O Meaghers threw in their lot with the Ulster men. O Neill and O Donnell were welcomed by Keadagh O Meagher and enjoyed the full extent of O Meagher hospitality for twenty days. O Neill camped with O Meagher at Druim Saileach, Roscrea, and in Templetuohy. Sir George Carew had blocked off the marching route through north Tipperary, forcing Hugh O Donnell to march his army across the Slieve Bloom Mountains into the territory of Ikerrin.

At Kinsale the Irish army surrounded Mountjoy's troops. Their plan was to starve the British into surrender. O Donnell was eager for a surprise attack. O'Neill was more cautious but agreed with O'Donnell. A spy within the Irish camp leaked the information to the English. It was Mountjoy who surprised the Irish. He won the day, and the Irish were devastated. Their supplies were depleted, their arms reduced, and their morale shattered.

The demoralized Irish leaders retreated to their various homes and territories. They knew that they could not defeat Mountjoy. O Neill advised O Donnell to go to Spain and seek further aid from King Philip. King Philip promised O Donnell military aid and issued orders for the amassing of these forces. While O Donnell waited for his troops, he was poisoned. It is believed that an English agent was responsible for his early death at the young age of twenty-nine.

Mountjoy began a campaign of terror in Ireland. His area of concentration was Ulster. He intended to eradicate the powerful families who reigned there. He went so far as to smash the ancient coronation stone of the O Neill's at Tullahogue Rath in northeast County Tyrone. In 1603 O Neill agreed to make terms with Mountjoy. He and the O Donnell clan were unaware that Queen Elizabeth had just died. The treaty they agreed on was more stringent than it could have been. They could have negotiated a treaty more favorable to the Irish had they known the throne was temporarily vacant.

According to the Treaty of Mellifont, the chieftains of Ulster could keep their land, but only under English law. They also had to accept to be governed by the local county sheriff and the acting president of the province. They were no longer Gaelic chieftains, but English landlords. Despite the treaty, several attempts were made upon their lives. Eventually the O Neill and O Donnell families decided to leave Ireland. To stay meant eventual capture, imprisonment, and possible execution. Hugh O Neill went to France, then Spain, and, finally, to Rome, where he died in 1616. In the years that followed, many Irish chieftains and their families fled Ireland. They hoped for a chance of survival on the continent of Europe. Some hoped to return with armies of their own and continue the struggle for freedom. The mass movement of Irish families and Irish patriots to the continent in the early 1600s is known as "the Flight of the Earls."

During 1603 and 1604 there was a period of treaty signing and pardons. Over three hundred O Meaghers were pardoned for their "crimes" during the war. They came from every walk of life: soldiers of every rank, gentlemen, tradesmen, and tenant farmers. In 1604, *The Patent Rolls of James I* tells how Keadagh O Meagher was given a general pardon on October 14. This was one year after the Treaty of Mellifont. Elizabeth was dead, and James VI of Scotland was now the Stuart king of England. Since he was Scottish, Catholic, and Celtic, the Irish assumed he would favor their cause and exercise a certain leniency toward them.

Though the battle of Kinsale was lost, the O Meagher's spirit of rebellion remained strong. Being a lesser clan, the O Meaghers were not subjected to close scrutiny by the Crown and faired much better than those who were.

Chapter 15: The Demise of Celtic Ireland

After centuries of conflict, the leading Irish families were finally subdued. Henry VIII crushed the powerful Fitzgeralds of Kildare. This Norman family had integrated with the Irish and was very popular among the Irish chieftains. The rebellion and execution of Silken Thomas brought an end to their power. The O Neills and the O Donnells, the most powerful Gaelic chieftains, were crushed during the reign of Queen Elizabeth. Ireland was now leaderless. There was no family strong enough to unite the Irish against the enemy, leaving the door for conquest wide open. England took full advantage of this situation, and from 1603 to 1641, the English campaign to anglicize Ireland was in full swing.

The Dirge of Rory O'More (AD 1642)

Aubrey De Vere (1814–1902)

Up the sea-saddened valley at evening's decline,
A heifer walks lowing—the Silk of the Kine;
From the deep to the mountains she roams, and again
From the mountain's green urn to the purple-rimmed main.

What seek'st thou, sad mother? Thine own is not thine;
He dropped from the headland; he sank in the brine!
'Twas a dream! But in dreams at thy foot did he follow
Through the meadow-sweet on by the marsh and mallow!

Was he thine? Have they slain him? Thou seek'st him, not knowing
Thyself too art theirs, thy sweet breath and sad lowing!
Thy gold horn is theirs; thy dark eyes and thy silk!
And that which torments thee, thy milk is their milk!

'Twas no dream, Motherland! 'Tis no dream, Innisfail!
Hope dreams, but grief dreams not—the grief of the Gael!
From Leix and Ikerrin to Donegal's shore

Rolls the dirge of thy last and thy bravest—O'More!
(*The Student Treasury of English Verse III*, p. 50)

Finding the Ulster lands leaderless, James I of England quickly took advantage. He reneged on the pardon that had been issued at Mellifont in 1603. His court declared the earls guilty of treason and their lands forfeit to the Crown. This misuse of justice made it clear to the Irish that the king had no scruples. There was no protection against his whims. England went on to claim the six counties of Tyrone, Donegal, Derry, Armagh, Cavan, and Fermanagh.

> *Pitiable, indeed, was the state of the Gaels of Ireland after the death of O'Donnell: for their characteristics and dispositions were changed; for they exchanged their bravery for cowardice, their magnanimity for weakness, there pride for servility; their success, valor, prowess, heroism, exultation and military glory, vanished after his death. They despaired of relief, so that most of them were obliged to seek aid and refuge from the enemies and strangers, while others were scattered and dispersed, not only throughout Ireland, but throughout foreign countries, as poor, indigent, helpless paupers, and others were offering themselves for hire as soldiers to foreigners; so that countless numbers of freeborn nobles of Ireland were slain in distant foreign countries, and were buried in strange places and unhereditary churches… In a word it would be tedious and impossible to enumerate or describe the great evils which sprang and took permanent root at that time in Ireland from the death of Huge Roe O'Donnell. (O'Donovan, Vol. 6, p. 2229)*

In 1605, Lord Deputy Sir Arthur Chichester arrived in Ireland demanding full cooperation with Crown law. Penal measures against Catholics continued. The Ulster Irish were dispossessed and their territories planted by English and Scottish settlers.

> *The publication, in 1633, of Spencer's Tractate on Ireland, under the patronage of the Lord Deputy, accompanied by a suggestion that the remedies proposed in the work for "reformation of the natives" were "for the most part excellent," excited serious apprehensions among the Irish. Lord Stafford, during his reign of office, hanged every person found traveling through the country who could not give a good account of himself, his excuse being that martial law had been executed at all times in Ireland and never so sparingly as by him, so that for many years previous to 1641, causes of grave discontent underlay an apparently tranquil surface in Ireland, and conduced to prepare the way for that revolt against the existing system of government as soon as favorable circumstances should present themselves, as might be expected in the face of those acts of cruelty and oppression. (O'Meagher, Appendix J, p. 39)*

The Anglo-Irish were disturbed by the anti-Catholic sentiments of the Crown. They believed they should be allowed to remain Catholic and still be accepted as loyal English subjects. When this right was denied them, they decided to join the Irish insurrection. In October 1642 a Confederation was organized in Kilkenny. When the war broke out, the O Meaghers joined this Confederation.

The Confederation of Kilkenny

The Confederation of Kilkenny was a council of twenty-five people, the majority of whom were Old English. Their goal was to carry out most of the duties of government.

> *The main object of the Confederation was to defend themselves against attacks of the Puritans, to maintain the Prerogative of the Crown as well as the privileges of the Irish Parliament, to reinstate the Roman Catholic Church as it stood in the reign of Henry VII, and to annul all penal laws against its members. Declaring by public oath their allegiance to the King, but resenting the authority of the English Parliament, the Confederates, through their supreme council, organized forces, nominated commanders and officials, collected the public revenue, levied taxes, minted coins, treated with foreign powers, and governed a considerable part of the land.*
>
> *(O'Meagher, Appendix J, pp. 39–40)*

The Confederation proved to be a failure for many reasons. Its home base was in Kilkenny, which was the seat of the earl of Ormond, who was also the lord deputy. The Old English had a different outlook and agenda than the Irish, who were represented by a minority on this council. The Old English were Catholic, but ardent loyalists. The Irish were Catholics who refused to be dominated by a Protestant monarchy. Owen Roe O Neill was one of the many Irishmen who had returned to Ireland with plans to lead the people in rebellion. The Irish wanted Owen Roe O Neill to lead their army, but the Earl of Ormond refused. He was jealous of the popularity awarded this young man, who happened to be a nephew of the great Hugh O Neill. Another major split occurred when the King ran into difficulties with his parliament. The Old English wanted to raise an army and send it to England to aid the King. The Irish wanted to use their forces to rid Ireland of the Crown's army for good. The Irish decided to go ahead with their rebellion regardless of the loyalists. It was in Ulster, as to be expected, that the first sparks of rebellion were ignited.

The dispossessed Irish rebelled against the planters. English settlers were killed in the fracas. Rumors went back to England describing how the Irish had butchered thousands of English settlers. The English described the rebellion as a massacre of loyal Englishmen by the disloyal, unruly Irish. These exaggerated accounts had a huge impact on Oliver Cromwell, who later in 1649 conquered Ireland in the name of those dead English settlers.

In Laois and Offaly, the counties known as Queen's and King's counties, the O Moores rebelled and drove many of the English planters back to the safety of the Pale. Factions in Tipperary also took up arms.

In 1641, Teige Óg O Meagher, the son of John O Meagher of Clonakenny, raised a foot regiment and joined Colonel Philip O Dwyer of Dundrum, Theobald Purcell Baron of Loughmore, Thomas Purcell of Annfield, Theobald Purcell of Killoskehane, Richard Butler of Drom, Walter Burke of Ardmayle, Philip Ryan of Upperchurch, Thomas Ryan of Clonoulty, and Philip McGrath of Blean, Toomevara, to fight with the Confederation of Irish forces in Kilkenny. Teige Óg O Meagher held the rank of colonel.

Figure 15-1 Purcell Castle, Loughmore

> *It was a series of outrages by the Lord President of Munster, William St. Leger that lit the flames of the rebellion in Tipperary. As a reprisal against these outrages of St. Leger, local farmers from the Cashel area drove off some cattle and damaged property belonging to St. Leger's brother-in-law, Kingsmill, who lived at Ballysheehan, Cashel. Kingsmill duly reported this to St. Leger, who ordered two troops of horse cavalry to Cashel. These soldiers created such depredation at Ballymoreen, Galbertstown, Ardmayle and Clonoulty that women and children were left dead in their trail. This campaign of terror led to a deputation from the Catholics being sent to protest to St.Leger at Clomnel. The Lord President gave the deputation a very cold reception. "I consider it most prudent to hang you all"... The deputation withdrew brooding revenge in their hearts over the insult. This rebuke by St. Leger had the effect of sending all the Catholic gentry to join the Catholic Confederacy. Baron Purcell of Loughmore, Lord Dunboyne of Kiltinan Castle, Philip O Dwyer of Dundrum, and Richard Butler of Bansha were the members of the deputation who were insulted by St. Leger. These were the principal leaders of the new Catholic army formed in Tipperary, with the avowed object of getting revenge on the Lord President and relieving the Catholics from persecution. (Ryan, Seán, pp. 16–17)*

The above group, along with O'Meagher and his men, led an attack on the ancient town of Cashel. This attack was a reprisal for the atrocities committed by St. Leger's army as outlined earlier.
Protestants in the area had gathered for safety within the town walls. On December 31, 1641, Purcell demanded the surrender of the town. The clergy agreed to terms of surrender on the condition that the inhabitants of the town would be left unharmed. Purcell agreed to these

terms. Philip O Dwyer was put in charge of the surrendered town. Some of O Dwyer's men were from Clonoulty, where St. Leger's men had done many outrages. These men set about exacting personal revenge, and fifteen Protestants were killed.

O Dwyer, O Meagher, and their followers fought another battle against the parliamentary force on March 23, 1652. They lost this battle, and O Dwyer surrendered to Shankey, the commander of the parliamentary forces. O Dwyer and the commissioned officers were allowed to leave Ireland and join any foreign army they wished. O Dwyer left Ireland with thirty-five hundred men to serve under Conte in the Low Countries. His brother, Lieutenant-Colonel Donough O Dwyer; Colonel Teige Óg O Meagher; Theobald Butler of Killoskehane; Ulick Burke; and some others were refused passage or pardon. They were accused of murder. In a Clonmel court on November 8, 1652, Ellice Jeanes gave testimony leading to the conviction of the above officers.

> *Ellice Jeanes came before the Commissioners on the 23rd of August 1642, and deposed that she was the wife of Thomas Jeanes, of Captain Perry's troop, In Lieutenant General Cromwell's regiment, that she was formerly married to Peter Porlfry of Cashel, that she did nurse a child for Richard Brown of Cashel, in the year 1641; she then deposed to the murders of Beane, his brewer and tapster, of Carrean, a "schloemaster" of Carleton, commonly called Thomas Saddler, of Land, and his two daughters; of Lyndsay, of Mr. Bannister, of one who was a "taylor," and his wife, of a glazier's sonne, of one Murdo's child, of Anderson and six men, whose names she could not remember, "and that the Confederates took many prisoners," and she continued, "and after opening of ye gate they (the prisoners) were sent out in froste and snow to Moydrom, two miles from Cashel, where they were entertained by James Sall of Moydrom, that all of them after were sent away by convoy towards Clonmell,*

> which was commanded by Patrick and Peter Boyton of Cashel that three of ye Protestants were, by said convoy, killed, and Edward Boakes wounded. (O'Meagher, pp. 40–41)

In the whole of this deposition given on August 23, 1642, Ellice Jeanes never mentioned Teige Óg O Meagher. Yet, ten years later at a court in Clonmel on November 8, 1652, Teige Óg O Meagher was sentenced to be hanged. The above deposition and the unreliable word of questionably secured witnesses were the only testimony used against him. The other witnesses gave testimony saying that they were robbed of goods at the hands of Theobald Butler, Teige Óg O Meagher, Donough O Dwyer, Theobald Purcell, and other Irish commanders. At no point was O'Meagher accused of murder in this court. It must then be assumed that he was sentenced to hang by the neck until dead, not because he committed a murder, but because he was guilty of the ambiguous crime of "traitorous or disloyal words or speeches." Teige Óg O Meagher was a proud Irish patriot until his last breath. Tradition holds that he rode with utmost dignity to the scaffolding on the day of his execution. After the execution, his black horse made its way back to Clonakenny and roamed freely until its death.

In 1645 Lord Castlehaven, a commander in the Irish Confederation, was marching from Limerick to Ikerrin. As he approached the O Meagher castle at Clonakenny, he was notified that the enemy had taken the castle. "I sent to the adjacent villages and got together crows of iron, pick axes, and whatever else could be found, and fell a-storming the castle, and three or four hours took it. In this place I left one hundred men, and being over pretty safe I lodged that night at ease."

In the summer of 1652, the Confederates surrendered to the crown. The leaders and forty thousand men were expelled to the continent. Here they joined foreign armies and became famous for their skill at arms and leadership qualities. Many of O Meagher stock were expelled at this time. The abundance of O Meagher names listed in the military rolls of Europe after 1652 gives testimony to this fact.

Some of the names were slightly changed to fit the linguistics of individual countries. Those O Meaghers who remained in Ireland did not return to their homes. They were put on trial, imprisoned, executed, or set free to take up positions as tenants on land newly possessed by English Planters. The Irishman was a tenant, where once he was a clansman or even a lord. Ireland's social order was changing.

Chapter 16: Cromwell

Civil war was raging in England. Oliver Cromwell, the leader of the Roundheads, led the Parliamentary revolt against Charles I. Cromwell was a popular military leader known for his decisiveness and strict discipline. He defeated the king in 1649 and was appointed chairman of the council of state. He promptly made Ireland a priority, planning to conquer the island in a hurry, because he was much needed back in England. With twelve thousand well-trained men he set sail for Ireland, arriving in Dublin on August 16, 1649, and was joined by the Anglo-Irish who had remained loyal to England. As a result his army grew to twenty thousand men. A campaign of terror began almost immediately. He marched along the eastern coast quickly, gaining control of the major cities and trade routes. A legendary battle was fought at Drogheda, where thirty-five hundred people were killed. Because many of the dead were civilians, women, and children, this attack upon Drogheda was referred to as a massacre. Youghal, Cork, Cashel, and Cappaquin all surrendered thereafter. Wexford held out, but later a massacre similar to Drogheda occurred there. Kilkenny surrendered in 1650 and the Confederation disbanded. Those members of the Confederation who held out were counted among the many sent to "Hell or to Connaught."

Cromwellian forces conquered northwest Tipperary in 1650. They captured Roscrea Castle and used it as a base to quell further rebellion. Roscrea was the principal town in the Barony of Ikerrin and the nucleus of staunch O Meagher territory. The local chieftains were evicted from their properties, and their lands were confiscated. This was a tremendous defeat for the proud landowning O Meaghers, who had successfully retained their lands throughout the preceding centuries. Yet they had no choice but to surrender to the occupying forces whose motto was "surrender or slaughter."

On May 26, 1650, Cromwell rushed back to England, leaving his son-in-law, Ireton, in charge. Ireton continued the conquest of Ireland in the manner his father-in-law had begun. He showed little mercy to the native Irish.

Immediately after the Cromwellian invasion, England needed to decide what to do with the thirty thousand soldiers who had fought against Cromwell. Many were allowed to go into exile on condition that they only join foreign armies that were allies of England. Irish landowners were accused of treason or treasonous acts and punished for their treachery by total loss of property, partial loss of property, relocation to a lesser property in the west, exile, deportation to slavery in the West Indies and the American colonies, or by death. Their land was needed to pay the soldiers and adventurers who had helped fight and fund the war. The landless clansmen and laborers were pardoned because they were valued at less than ten pounds and were seen as a valuable skilled labor force needed to tenant the huge properties divided out among the English.

The Act of Settlement defined explicitly how Ireland was to be treated after the rebellion. All those who had rebelled against the Crown the first year of the rebellion (1641–1642) should lose their lives and their property to England. Those who fought after 1642, or any other time during the rebellion should lose their lands and be banished to Connaught, where they would be granted one third the value of their original property. All those who had not fought for the Irish cause, but who had supported it, should forfeit their lands and get two thirds of the value of these lands in Connaught. All those who were Irish and Catholic, except those with laboring skills and other skills needed for the upkeep of English estates, should under penalty of death evacuate to Connaught before the first of May 1654. The healthy-looking youths, who had been left orphaned and homeless as a result of the war or the transmigration, were rounded up and taken to the coast of Galway. Here they were forcibly put on ships for the West Indies. Anyone found wandering aimlessly on the roads and hills of Ireland suffered the same fate.

In 1653 the Act of Satisfaction arranged for the distribution of the confiscated lands. These lands were divided among English soldiers in payment for their service, to adventurers who had loaned money to Parliament and the war effort, and to friends and relatives of Cromwell. The coastal strip of Connaught and Clare was to be planted with English settlers to prevent the Irish from getting further aid from abroad. The dispossessed Irish and those promised partial properties in Connaught and Clare were ordered under pain of death to evacuate across the Shannon immediately.

Between the years 1654 and 1655, forty-five thousand Irish citizens trudged westward; "To Hell or to Connaught" was the cry of the oppressor at their backs.

When a family or group was ordered to move west, a certificate was issued to the head of the household describing the immediate family, friends, and other company traveling to Connaught together. It also described the property they were allowed to take with them. The Transplanter's certificate belonging to Anne O Meagher of Cloyne Castle lists as follows: "1653, January 6 . . . Clonmell . . . Anne Ó Machar of Clonyne, widow, in the Countie of Tipperary, hath on the seaven and twentieth December 1652, seaventy-five persons, 2 acres of summer corne, 4 cows and 4 garonns (horses) . . . Dated the one and thirtieth day of January 1653."

Tipperary was divided into land grants of various sizes. Huge land grants were made to people of consequence, while smaller plots were allocated to adventurers and soldiers. O Meagher land was confiscated and divided among prestigious Englishmen and adventurers. The following is an account of how some of the larger clan lands were divided. John O Meagher of Clonakenny was the documented owner of almost three thousand acres of land spanning from Templemore to Roscrea. Most of this land was granted to the Duke of Ormond. John O Meagher also lost his lands and castles at Rathnaveogue to Sir Martin Noele and Knockballymeagher to the Duke of Ormond. Thomas Meagher of Bawnmadrum was evicted from Bawnmadrum Castle and lands. His property was allotted to Sir Martin Noele and the Duke of Ormond. Roger O Meagher of Clonan or Cloneen lost his castle and estate of seventeen hundred acres to the Earl of Roscommon. Thomas O Meagher of Boulabane lost his castle and estate to Sir Martin Noele. Conor O'Meagher of Cloncrackin in Corbally, Roscrea, lost his 333 acres to Sir Martin Noele. William Buckley got O Meagher land, Morris lands, and Butler land in Barnane, County Tipperary. Acre by acre the ancient homeland of the O Meaghers was divided out among the English. The Duke of York, the Duke of Ormond, and Sir Martin Noele received the largest shares of Ikerrin.

The inhabitants of Ikerrin and Clonlisk were to be sent to the Baronies of Tulla, Bunratty, Island, Corcomroe, Clonderlau, Moyasty, and Ibrican in County Clare, and the Barony of Bellamo in County Galway. Many O Meaghers couldn't bring themselves to leave the old clan ground. It was their ancestral territory. They had no identity elsewhere. Rather than leave their homeland, they succumbed to being laborers or tenants on their own property. They worked the fields as they watched the new landowners erect stone mansions on their old clan grounds. They labored to provide the new English owners with a life of affluence and luxury.

Soon the Barony of Ikerrin was littered with the ruins of the old chieftain tower houses. They were replaced by the newly erected English-style country homes. Often they stood side by side. Sometimes the English lord built his mansion onto the old O Meagher tower house. Even more poignantly painful, were the landlords who used the stones from the O Meagher tower houses to build their own great residences. Needless to say, throughout the following years tensions between the new planters and the Old Irish grew to explosive levels.

In many counties rebellious groups hid in desolate places such as the forests, bogs, and hills. They fought against the landlords in their own local area. Thomas O Meagher of Ballinamoe organized such a band of rebels who were noted for attacking individuals, burning crops and houses, cattle raiding, and many other atrocities. Such outlaw gangs were known as the rapparees. Another famous rapparee, Captain John Meagher, was captured and hanged in 1690. This John Meagher and a band of eleven men launched an attack on a group of patrolling English soldiers about four miles from Thurles. When the raparees fled on foot into the bog, the soldiers went in pursuit and captured Meagher and his men. They were taken to Maryborogh Prison, where they were hanged. It would appear from William Wolseley's letters to the king in 1690 that John Meagher was tortured before his death and forced to divulge information referred to as his "confession." Documents were also found on his person and sent to the king for evaluation. The sincere opinion of William Wolseley was that, "An Irishman is to be taught his duty only by the rod."

The Irish Raparees
Charles Gavan Duffy (1816–1903)

Righ Shemus, he has gone to France and left his crown behind
I'll luck be theirs both day and night put running in his mind!
Lord Lucan followed after with his Slashers brave and true,
And now the doleful keen is raised,
What will poor Ireland do?
What must poor Ireland do?
Our luck, they say, has gone to France, what can poor Ireland do?
Oh, never fear for Ireland, for she has soldiers still,
For Rory's boys are in the wood, and Remy's son on the hill;
And never had poor Ireland more loyal hearts than these—
May God be kind and good to them!
The faithful Rapparees!
The fearless Rapparees!
The jewel were you, Rory, with your Irish Rapparees!
Oh, black's your heart, Clan Oliver, and colder than the clay!
Oh, high's your hand, Clan Sassanach, since Sarsfield's gone away!
It's little love you bear to us for the sake of long ago
But hold your hand, for Ireland still,
Can strike a deadly blow,
Can strike a mortal blow,
Oh! By my word! 'Tis she that still could strike the deadly blow!
The master's bawn, the master's seat, a surly bodach fills;
The master's son, an outlawed man, is riding on the hills,
But God be praised that round him throng, as thick as summer bees,
The swords that guarded Limerick wall,
His loyal Rapparees!
His loving Rapparees!
Who dares say, No, to Rory Óg with all his Rapparees?
Now, Sassanach and Cromweller, take heed of what I say—
Keep down your black and angry looks that scorn us night and day:
For there's a just and wrathful Judge who every action sees,
And he'll make strong, to right our wrong,
The faithful Rapparees!
The fearless Rapparees!
The men that rode at Sarsfield's side, the roving Rapparees!
(Colum, P., pp. 279–280)

As a result of local Irish hostility, some English landowners decided to sell their properties and return to England. Irish Catholics were allowed to purchase such properties. However, this was only feasible until the introduction of the Penal Laws, which forbade Irish Catholics from buying property of any kind.

The pre-Cromwellian Civil Survey of 1654 shows that more than fifth percent of the land in the Barony of Ikerrin belonged to the O Meagher Clan. It also shows that for the most part, they still practiced the old Gaelic system of commonage. The post-Cromwellian Census of 1658 shows that the population density of O Meaghers in the barony still remained high. There were in fact 193 O Meagher families living in the barony as tenants on the large English estates. The surveys of this era seem to confirm that a substantial number of O Meaghers did not move west.

During the years 1664 to 1668, the English devised a new taxation system known as the Hearth Tax. This involved an extensive survey of the country. Counties were divided into parishes and town lands. Families who lived in homes with hearths or fireplaces were noted, and a tax of two pence per annum per hearth was levied on the head of each household. According to this survey there were 283 Meaghers listed as the heads of households in sixty-five parishes spanning County Tipperary and neighboring counties. The greatest concentration was in County Tipperary. Again this record gives further testimony to the fact that many Meaghers stayed behind and lived in extremely poor circumstances following Cromwell's invasion.

Prendergast's description of Ireland in the post Cromwellian period shows the frightful state of the nation:

> *Ireland, in the language of scripture, lay void as a wildness. Five-sixth of her people had perished. Women and children were found daily perishing in ditches, starved. Wolves preyed upon the bodies of many wandering orphans, whose fathers had been*

> *killed or exiled, and whose mothers had died of famine. In the years 1652 and 1653 the plague, following the desolation wars, had swept away whole counties, so that one might travel twenty or thirty miles and not see a living creature. Man, beast and bird were all dead, or had quit those desolate places.*

As a result of Cromwell's plantation in Ireland, land ownership changed dramatically. By 1700, Irish natives held one eighth of the land in freehold, while two thirds of the land belonged to the English. Thus ended the ancient Gaelic order. The old days of clan commonage were gone. Never again would the Ó Meachair ride on horseback through the barony declaring himself, "Captain of the Nation."

Chapter 17: The Wild Geese

Cromwell died in 1658. Charles II (1660–1685), son of the executed Charles I, was invited back to England as the new king. Charles II relied upon bribery to maintain his power and to extract favors from the court. He restored lands to some of the more powerful and influential Irish families who promised allegiance to him. Many old Irish families returned from their places of exile with hopes of regaining their property. The majority of them were disappointed.

When Charles died, his Catholic brother, James II (1685-1688) ascended to the throne. Having failed to secure their property under Charles, the Irish were not hopeful of any changes under James. Much to their surprise James relaxed the stringent laws that discriminated against Catholics. They were now allowed to practice their religion freely, to join the English army, to hold public office, and to participate in government. During this period there was a resurgence of power, confidence, and fellowship between the old Irish and the Catholic Anglo-Irish. Parliament and the English Protestants resented James's obvious favoritism toward Catholics. Tensions grew and, fearing for his life, James fled to France. While in exile, his vacated throne was offered jointly to William of Orange and his wife, Mary. Mary, the daughter of James II, was married to William of the Royal House of Orange in Holland. William was a staunch supporter of Protestantism and willingly accepted the English throne.

The Irish rallied an army of five thousand to support James's efforts to reclaim his throne. This Jacobite army consisted of disorganized, untrained men who were short on finances, arms, and supplies. The stage was set for what was later to be called the Williamite War. In April 1689, the Jacobite forces lay siege to Derry City. This siege lasted 105 days. Derry held fast even though those within were starving and dying of disease. Reinforcements and food eventually arrived from England. Similarly, at Enniskillen the Protestant forces held fast. The Jacobite siege was abandoned, leaving William in control of Northern Ireland.

Figure 17:1 The Harp, Ireland's National Symbol. Stained-glass window, Library of Saint Patrick's, Thurles

The Harp That Once

Thomas Moore (1799–1852)

The harp that once through Tara's halls
The sound of music shed
Now hangs as mute on Tara's walls
As if that soul were fled.
So sleeps the pride of former days
So glory's thrill is o'er
And hearts that once beat high for praise
Now feel that pulse no more.
No more to chiefs and ladies bright
The harp of Tara swells;
The chord alone that breaks at night,
Its tale of ruin tells,
Thus freedom now so seldom wakes,

The only throb she gives,
Is when some heart indignant breaks,
To show that still she lives.
(Soodlums, 1982, p. 72)

The Battle of the Boyne

In l690 James's army of twenty-five thousand men marched north while William's army of thirty-six thousand marched south to meet him. On July 1, 1690, their forces met on the banks of the River Boyne near Drogheda. Initially the battle seemed to go well for the Irish, who killed many Williamites as they crossed the river. However, the Irish were forced to retreat because of the sheer weight of the numbers coming against them. When James realized the seriousness of the situation, he fled the battlefield, and, with his leading officers, he returned to France, leaving Patrick Sarsfield in command of the army. The Irish lost the day, making William of Orange the undisputed king of England and the continually disputed king of Ireland.

Patrick Sarsfield, a Dubliner of Norman stock, trained as a soldier in France before joining the English army under James II. He eventually became one of James's most valuable bodyguards. After the Battle of the Boyne, Sarsfield and the Jacobite army retreated to Limerick City. The Williamite army followed closely, sealing the Irish army within the city walls. William delayed attacking the city because he was waiting for ammunition and supplies to arrive from Waterford via Cashel. When Sarsfield got word of William's plan, he and his horsemen secretly left the city to intercept the arms train at Ballyneety. They attacked the Williamite camp and destroyed their provisions. This secret ride was later known as "Sarsfield's Ride." The sixty-mile trip took twenty-nine hours. Sixteen of the rear guard were killed in the fray. Galloping Hogan, the famous Tipperary Rapparee, acted as Sarsfield's guide on this expedition.

William waited for further supplies to arrive and eventually launched an attack on Limerick, but the Irish held the city. Subsequently he returned to England, leaving General Ginkell in charge. Ginkell was determined to gain full control of Ireland before the winter set in. By the end of 1690, he controlled most of the land east of the Shannon River. He marched west toward Athlone with plans to cross the River Shannon and take to the west. The Jacobite forces battled hard to prevent him from crossing the river. They even dislodged the bridge across the Shannon at Athlone. Here is a poem that describes the bravery of the Irish men under Sergeant Custume, who managed to dislodge the bridge in shifts. The felling of the Bridge of Athlone slowed the westward progress of Ginkell and his army, but they managed to ford the river further south.

The Bridge of Athlone

Aubrey De Vere (1814–1902)

Does any man that a Gael can fear?
Of a thousand deeds let him learn but one!
The Shannon swept onward, broad and clear,
Between the leaguers and broad Athlone.
"Break down that bridge." Six warriors rushed
Through the storm of shot and the storm of shell.
With late but certain victory flushed,
The grim Dutch gunners eyed them well.
They fell in death, their work half done:
They wrenched at the planks "mid a hail of fire"
The bridge stood fast; and nigh and nigher
The foe swarmed darkly, densely on.
Oh, who for Erin will strike a stroke?
Who hurl yon planks where the waters roar?
Six warriors forth from their commanders broke,
And flung them upon that bridge once more.
Again at the rocking planks they dashed
And four dropped dead; and two remained.
The huge beams groaned and the arch down crashed.
Two stalwart swimmers the margin gained.
(Flowers from Many Gardens, p. 56)

Louis XIV of France sent an army under the command of General St. Ruth to help the Irish in their fight against the Williamites. The combined forces of both the French and the Irish faced the Williamites at Aughrim. When it looked like the Irish would win the day, misfortune struck: A cannon ball decapitated St. Ruth, leaving the French army leaderless. They retreated in disarray, allowing Ginkell to win the battle.

Ginkell continued on his westward march, conquering Galway and Sligo. He then led the army south to Limerick City, where the Irish forces had regrouped under Sarsfield. Sarsfield was hopeful that more supplies and arms would soon arrive from France. For six weeks the Irish held Limerick City, yet no further help came from France. Sarsfield knew it was only a matter of time before they would have to surrender. Ginkell, on the other hand, was growing tired of the battle and anxious to be back in England before the winter. Both sides agreed to terms. After ten days of deliberations, on October 3, 1691, the Treaty of Limerick was drawn up. Ginkell outlined both the Military Articles and the Civil Articles of the treaty as follows.

The Treaty of Limerick Military Articles

All members of the garrison had the following choices:

- Go to France and join the foreign army there.
- Return home without punishment for the rebellion.
- Join William's army!

The Treaty of Limerick Civil Articles

Citizens of the rebellion were to be pardoned and not punished for their part in the rebellion.

- Catholics would be allowed religious freedom.
- Catholics could carry arms to defend themselves and for gaming.
- Catholics would not be deprived of their lands if they took the Oath of Loyalty to William and Mary.

In summary, all fighting men and their families would not be evicted or dispossessed. Catholicism would no longer be suppressed. An Oath of Allegiance would replace the Oath of Supremacy. Those who wished to go into exile would be allowed to leave the country without harassment. Shortly after this treaty was signed, three thousand French soldiers sailed into the Shannon Estuary ready to support Sarsfield in battle. Sarsfield refused to renege on his terms with the British. The French fleet was sent back to France, carrying with it several hundred Irishmen who chose to go into exile. When the treaty was presented to King William, he agreed to the terms on both sides. However, in the years that followed, the Protestant Parliamentary resistance pressured William into reneging upon the treaty of Limerick.

Abbe Mc Geoghegan, chaplain to the Irish Brigade and author of *The National History of Ireland,* stated that according to records in the office of the French War Department, 450,000 Irish men died in

Figure 17-2 Treaty Stone, Limerick City

the service of France between 1691 and 1749. This number does not include the Irish men who chose to go to Spain and other European countries. With the Wild Geese gone, Ireland was again leaderless, her most powerful men abroad soldiering for other countries.

Many O Meaghers are listed among the various divisions of King James's army. John Meagher was an officer in Sarsfield's Horse. Daniel O Meagher was an officer in Butler's Foot; John, Edmund, and Thomas O Meagher in Bagenal's Foot; Philip O Meagher in Oxburg's Foot; and John and Thomas O Meagher in Mountcashel's Foot. Cornelius, Brian, and Edmund O Meagher were officers in Purcell's Yellow Horse Brigade. Many of these men and their kinsmen were part of the mass exodus to the continent after the Treaty of Limerick.

> *We find O'Meaghers serving in the French regiments of Bulkeley, Clare, Galmoy, and Lee; in the Spanish regiments of Hibernia, Irlanda, Wauchop, and Waterford; in the Prussian army in Von Derfinger's Dragoons, and in the garrison of Custrin; and in the Polish Saxon Army, Thadee de Meagher became a Lieutenant-General and Colonel Proprietor of the Swiss Guard, and Chamberlain to the King: he was commissioned by his sovereign to negotiate with Frederick the Great a treaty of neutrality on the breaking out of the Seven Years War. (O'Meagher, p. 24)*
>
> *A list of members of the Irish brigade in France 1706-1774 include the names of five O Meaghers: three Captains, a Lieutenant, and a Major... In the French Army... one Captain Patrick O'Meagher... served in the "Regiment Irlandois de Bulkeley" for over thirty years. In 1745 he was created first Lieutenant, and in 1774 a Major. He participated in sixteen major European battles and sieges including the French taking of Corsica in 1761. In the Spanish Army the names of seven O'Meaghers appear serving in four different Regiments including the Waterford Regiment and the Regimento de Infanteria de Irlanda. (Hewson, p. 16)*

This Wild Geese exodus was the first time that O Meaghers left their homeland enmasse. Even Connaught did not see this number of O Meaghers during the Cromwellian banishment. Meaghers who went with the Wild Geese retained the O Meagher spelling. Those who went into exile between 1700 and 1800 generally kept Meagher, while many at home became Maher.

After the Williamite War and the breaking of the Treaty of Limerick, the Penal Laws were extended and became more stringent. These laws reduced Ireland to a land of uneducated tenants subject to the Protestant landlord ascendancy. It was the beginning of another new era for Ireland.

Chapter 18: The Penal Laws

The Wearing of the Green

O Paddy dear, and did ye hear the news that's goin' round?
The Shamrock is by law forbid to grow in Irish ground!
No more Saint Patrick's day we'll keep, his color can't be seen,
For there's a cruel law ag'in the wearin' o' the Green.
I met with Napper Tandy, and he took me by the hand,
And he said, "How's poor ould Ireland, and how does she stand?"
She's the most distressful country that ever yet was seen,
For they're hanging men and women there for the wearin'o the Green.

So, if the color we must wear be England's cruel red
Let it remind us of the blood that Irishmen have shed:
And pull the shamrock from your hat, and throw it on the sod,
But never fear, 'twill take root there, though underfoot 'tis trod.
When laws can stop the blades of grass from growin' as they grow,
And when the leaves in summer time their color dare not show,
Then I will change the color too, and wear in my caipín
But till that day, please God; I'll stick to the wearin' o' the Green.

But if at last the color should be torn from Ireland's heart,
Her sons with shame and sorrow, from the dear ould isle will part.
I've heard the whisper of a land, that lies beyond the sea,
Where rich and poor stand equal, in the light of freedom's day.
Ah! Erin must we leave you, driven by a tyrant's hand,
Must we seek a mother's blessing from a strange and distant land,
Where the cruel cross of England shall never more be seen,
And where please God, we'll live and die, still wearin' o' the Green.

After the Williamite War the English overlords, otherwise known as the Ascendancy, set about reducing the Irish to servile, uneducated peasants. They implemented a series of laws known as the Penal Laws to ensure that the Irish would have neither the wealth, the arms, the education, nor the impetus to organize another rebellion. The English ruling class would be left in comfort with the property of the dispossessed Irish, which they had been granted from their English monarchs. The prominent historian and essayist W. E. H. Lecky (1838–1903) said of the penal days in Ireland, "One of the blackest pages in the history of persecution . . . It was intended to make the Irish poor to keep them poor, to crush in them every germ of enterprise, and degrade them into a servile race who could never hope to rise to the level of their oppressor." Edmund Burke (1729–1797), political writer and parliamentarian, described the penal laws in Ireland, "As well fitted for the oppression and degradation of a people, and the debasement in them of human nature itself, as ever proceeded from the perverted ingenuity of man."

Repressive measures were introduced during the reign of Elizabeth I and continued for almost another century. The Penal Laws were strictly enforced between the years 1715 and 1745. These laws affected the practice of Catholicism, education, land ownership, public life, and occupations. Failure to obey or live within the law was severely dealt with. However, the astute Irish found ways to avoid conforming to the laws and observed only those necessary for survival.

Penal Laws Relating to Religion

It was a common thought among the Protestant Ascendancy that Catholics were lazy and that their numerous holy days encouraged this laziness. In 1695 legislation was introduced obliging all laborers to work holy days not recognized by the Established Church (Anglican Church). Failure to comply with this law resulted in a two-shilling fine. Failure to pay the fine resulted in a whipping. There was a twenty-pound fine for doing pilgrimages to holy wells. Ireland has numerous holy wells dedicated to the memory of various local saints. Pilgrimages to these wells, called patterns or patron days, were annual events. Throughout the centuries patron days became local fairs with vendors, peddlers, and farmers, each selling and buying wares both religious and secular. These gatherings aroused the suspicion of the ruling classes, who suspected that the Irish were using them to plot a rebellion. As a result of the prohibitive Penal Laws, patron days were abandoned. Catholics were also required by law to pay tithes to the Established Church. This tithe system became a contentious issue that lasted until 1883.

> *The Banishment Act of 1695 ordered all archbishops, bishops, monks, friars, deans, Jesuits, and other popish clergy to leave the country before May 1, 1698. All found after this date would be transported. Those who returned to Ireland were liable to be convicted of treason and executed. A reward of five pounds was offered for the capture of a priest and ten pounds for the capture of a bishop. Without bishops there would be no one to confer holy orders. "In 1654 five pounds was paid to Thomas Thompson and William Symons for apprehending Donogh Meagher, a popish priest; he was lodged in Clonmel jail. (Skehan, p. M38)*

In 1703 the Popish Clergy Registration Act required that parish priests register for a specific parish. Each parish was allowed one priest who could only minister within the confines of that parish. Curates were not allowed. In some cases curates circumvented the law by registering for parishes that had become defunct or had previously been amalgamated. Priests without parishes, or who were affiliated with various religious orders, had to go into exile or hiding. Mass was celebrated whenever and wherever it was feasible to do so. Secret pathways or Mass Paths led to the places of worship. Local houses, huts, ruins, or tabletop mountain rocks were used to celebrate Mass. The Catholic Irish were fiercely loyal to their clergy. They sheltered, hid, disguised, and smuggled them in and out of the country during the penal days.

During these penal days a very curious event caused quite a stir in the Moyne-Templetouhy Parish community. The parish priest, Dr. Andrew Meagher, publicly renounced his Catholic faith and embraced the Protestant faith. While it was not unheard of to find secular landowners converting from Catholicism to Protestantism in order to maintain ownership of their property, it was most peculiar for a clergyman to change faiths. Andrew Meagher was born in Cooleeney, Moyne, County Tipperary. Because of the Penal Laws against the Catholic faith, many aspiring priests were sent abroad to study for the priesthood. Meagher went to Paris for his ecclesiastically studies and was ordained to the priesthood in 1742. He remained in Paris to pursue further studies, earning a licentiate in theology at the Sorbonne in 1753. Dr. Andrew Meagher was appointed parish priest to his native place of Moyne-Templetuohy in 1758. On July 6, 1766 the bishop suspended him from his pastoral duties. Three stories abound as to the cause of his suspension.

He was expounding Protestant views from the pulpit. He got into a heated argument with a local family over a church pew and refused to apologize. He got into a heated argument with a parishioner for stepping on the hem of his sister's dress in church and refused to apologize. The suspension, for whatever reason, edged Meagher toward his decision to recant his Catholic faith and become Protestant. It seems that Meagher was an interesting intellectual who preached heretical ideas and had a volatile and stubborn temperament, which rankled both the Catholic hierarchy and his parishioners, causing him to come under the scrutiny of the entire community. Knowledgeable historians, such as William Hayes, suggest that Meagher's conversion was indeed sincere and that he appeared to have had issues with Catholic doctrine from the outset, particularly the "Popish Mass." From 1771 Meagher served as Protestant curate at Thurles. He died in 1781 while living at Church Lane, Thurles. He is buried in St. Mary's Graveyard, Thurles. His famous work is entitled, The Popish Mass Celebrated by Heathen Priest for the Living and the Dead, for several ages before Birth of Christ, printed by T. Walsh, 1771.

It was also said that some O Meaghers attended both Catholic Mass and Anglican services in order to retain their leases. "They stood at the back of the Protestant church hats in hand just to be seen to have been in attendence." (Enda Maher, Knocka)

Penal Laws Pertaining to Land

The Gavelkind Act of 1703 obliged Irish landholders to bequeath their land to all their sons. This subdivided large Catholic estates, leading to the break up of the estates over several generations. Catholics could not own, buy, inherit, or receive property as a gift. If the oldest son of a Catholic converted to Protestantism, he was entitled to the entire property of his Catholic father. A Catholic could not lease land for longer than thirty-one years. These inheritance and land laws were strictly enforced.

In 1760 a further blow was dealt to the Catholic landholder and tenant; the landlords who already led extravagant lifestyles began demanding increasingly high rents. In the same year, they closed the common lands, which was considered an outrage. Since ancient Celtic times, common land had been set aside to allow the poor to graze their animals for free. This ancient Brehon law helped prevent poverty. Never in the history of Ireland had anyone questioned the rights to this land.

The Irish Mother in Penal Days

John Banim (1798–1844)

Now welcome, welcome, baby-boy unto a mother's fears,
The pleasure of her sufferings, the rainbow of her tears,
The object of your father's hope, in all he hopes to do,
A future man of his own land to live him o'er anew.

How fondly on thy little brow a mother's eye would trace.
And in thy little limbs, and in each feature of thy face,
His beauty, worth, and manliness, and everything that's his,
Except, my boy, the answering mark of where the fetter is!

Oh! many a weary hundred years his sires the fetter wore,
And he has worn it since the day that him his mother bore;
And now, my son, it waits on you, the moment you were born:
The old hereditary badge of suffering and scorn!

Alas, my boy, so beautiful! Alas, my love so brave!
And must your gallant Irish limbs still drag it to the grave?
And you, my son, yet have a son, foredoomed a slave to be,
Whose mother still must weep o'er him the tears I weep o'er thee!
(Colum, P., p. 284)

Penal Laws Pertaining to Public Life and Occupations

By 1695, Catholics had no civil rights and no political representation. From 1691 all members of the Irish Parliament were required to take the Oath of Allegiance to the Crown, which included a declaration against the Catholic Mass and Transubstantiation. They were also required to take the Abjuration Act, which included an oath denying the spiritual supremacy of the pope. Since a Catholic in good conscience couldn't agree to terms that were regarded as sacrilegious, there was little Catholic representation in Parliament. In 1697 any Protestant who married a Catholic was forbidden to sit or vote in either house of Parliament. In 1727 no Catholic was allowed to vote for a member of Parliament, magistrate, or a civil office of any city or town. All Crown officials had to take a test of loyalty by taking communion in the Established Church. This was called the Test Act.

In 1703, Catholics were forbidden to carry arms either to protect themselves or for fowling and hunting. All arms had to be turned in by an appointed day to the justices of the peace or to local civil officers. Failure to do so resulted in fines, prison, the pillory, or whippings. Catholics could not hold the position of gunsmith or any position relating to the manufacture of guns, arms, knives, or swords. Catholics were banned from careers in teaching, law, and the government. They could not build houses within the confines of certain towns or urban areas. This excluded them from any rights or say in the governing of the urban area. Catholics could only own a horse if it was worth less than five pounds. The British hoped to restrict their ability to organize an army, because, without horses, farming, transportation, and communication were more difficult.

Penal Laws Pertaining to Education

In order to maintain their position of privilege and power, the Protestant Ascendancy needed to keep the Irish poor, subservient, and illiterate. In 1695 an act was introduced to prohibit the education of Catholics at home or abroad. It was a tradition among wealthy Catholics to send their children abroad to study at the numerous Irish monasteries and colleges throughout Europe. The new law forbade this practice. It also outlawed schoolmasters, teachers, and tutors. A five-pound reward was offered for the capture of any educator. Catholics who studied at Trinity College could not earn a degree unless they took the Oath of Supremacy. Failure to obey the law could result in the loss of one's estate.

During the reigns of Henry VIII and Elizabeth I, schools were established in many dioceses with the intention of teaching Irish children the English language and alienating them from their native tongue and culture. Later in the eighteenth century, charter schools provided another option for education. These charter schools were similar to boarding schools. The ordinary Catholic people could not afford the education offered, nor were they willing to have their children indoctrinated with Protestantism. Only two choices remained: illiteracy or the "hedge school." Since money was not available for education, illiteracy grew to almost 50 percent in some parishes.

Those who could pay limited fees sent their children to the hedge schools. These schools were migrant schools, depending on the availability of teachers. Local or wandering teachers set up classrooms in cabins, barns, ditches, hedges, and old ruins. The children who came to them got a rudimentary education as well as an introduction to some literature, classics, and even Latin and Greek. The teacher was paid for his instruction through fees. An example of such fees is as follows: spelling, one shilling and eight pence a quarter; reading, two shillings a quarter; writing, three shillings a quarter; arithmetic, three shillings a quarter; and Latin, eleven shillings a quarter. During school sessions the students took turns standing watch for soldiers or spies. Hedge schools remained popular for almost a century and a half. A William Meagher in the Washbin, Castleiney, near Templemore, ran the most famous hedge school in the Templemore area. He was so popular that students came from other counties to attend his classes. They boarded in local houses.

> *In William Meagher's school there were between 80 and 90 scholars, one third at least coming from Kilkenny and Cork and Waterford. The student came for classics. The scholars were lodged in the houses of the neighboring farmers. Bedding was free, butter was three and halfpence per pound, eggs were four pence a dozen, potatoes one and a half pence per stone. Some of the scholars were over twenty years of age and helped with the seasonal work of the farm. Turf cutting they did not like. The Ulster men were smart. All, especially the Connaught men, spoke Irish. Wealth was forgotten and class distinction was unknown. Candidates for the Church or Medicine or other vocations vied with each other in acquisition of knowledge. William Meagher was a tall, raw-boned, harsh featured, serious, and low spoken man. He dressed carelessly in the dress of the time. He had a scolding tongue. He had an approved manner of imparting knowledge. His custom was to pace up and down the school, repeating long verses of Homer, the speeches of Cicero, and lectured learnedly on the various phases of war as described in the Fourth Book of Quintus Curtius and Caesar's Commentaries. He was humorous on Lucian's Dialogues of the Dead and witty when he came to dissect Anacrem, but his glory was the Mantuan Bard, particularly the descent of Aeneas into the Lower Regions and his dissertations on the Georgics on which he became rapturous. He laughed to show the nervous energy of Juvenal and as he constantly kept the scholars to their books he taught them more in short time than did Roger Ascham to Queen Elizabeth. The schoolhouse was small. In fine*

> *weather he examined the scholars in their shelters on the ditch and under trees. The usual books were Erasmus, Corderius Justin, Caesar, Horace, Livy, Tacitus, Homer, and Lucian. No Mathematics were taught but the mathematics students attended Templemore Mathematical School. Fees were eight shillings one and a half pence per quarter . . . Rev. Fr. Mullally P.P. frequently visited and examined the pupils. William Meagher removed to Tipperary and was succeeded by his pupil Martin Kennedy. (Limerick Reporter, February 23, 1877)*

As a result of the Penal Laws, the gap in affluence, land ownership, and education between the Protestant planter and the Catholic Irish grew. What remained of the Irish aristocracy was practically destroyed. Very little land was left in Irish possession. Education standards declined. The Irish began to resent the authorities and their oppressive laws. Social structures broke down. Some Irish men took to crime; many drank heavily to drown their misery, while still others emigrated. It was during the eighteenth century that emigration among Catholic tenants began. At first it was a slow trickle overseas. By the mid-nineteenth century, this trickle had grown to a flood.

Around 1760 a resistance movement called the Whiteboys formed among the tenants. They wore white garments, sheets, and cockades. The Whiteboys retaliated violently to the miserable existence forced upon their fellow people. They committed many outrages and punished the perpetrators of perceived injustice wherever and whenever they could. They were considered rebels and when arrested were brutally punished or hanged. In 1822 a John Maher of Templetuohy took tenancy of a thirty-two-acre farm from his landlord, John Lloyd of Lisheen. The previous tenant had been evicted. It is not clear if he was evicted for lack of rent payment or if Maher went behind his back and offered to pay a higher rent for the property. The latter is unlikely because of the violent consequences of such an action at that time. As was expected, the local Whiteboys led an attack on Maher.

Maher rented the thirty-two-acre property in May. In July twelve men arrived at his home armed with guns, pikes, and clubs. They broke the windows, forced entry, and attacked Maher and his son. They forced Maher to his knees at gunpoint and demanded that he agree to quit the tenancy within six days. Maher reported the incident to the authorities, and a trial ensued. No charges were made, but Maher's testimony suggests that the ringleader of the attack was in fact the previous tenant of the property. Five years later, in 1827, the Tithe Applotment Book lists John Maher as tenant of a thirty-two-acre property in Lisheen.

Figure 18-1 A solitary couple stands in their cottage doorway.

The Suppression of Irish Industry

Few Irish Catholics were directly involved in business, trading, or industry. It was the Anglo-Irish Protestant entrepreneurs who developed Irish industries. Their reputation for fine goods resulted in very lucrative markets abroad. Huge amounts of corn, wool, cattle, glass, linen, and crystal were exported to Europe and the colonies. When English industries suffered from competition with Irish industries, it was decided that Ireland's resources should be exploited to increase the economic prosperity of England. Strict trading laws were introduced. Industries that were not in direct competition with England were encouraged, while those similar to English industries were taxed. Restrictions on the quantity of goods produced were also imposed. To make matters even worse, the English authorities decided to restrict Irish trade with other countries by mandating that all trading go through England first.

The English also feared that the Cromwellian descendants and subsequent Protestant settlers in Ireland had too much control over the Irish Parliament, so they revived Poyning's Law. Henry VII (1485–1509) had introduced Poyning's Law in 1494 with the expressed purpose of limiting the power of the Irish Parliament. According to this law the Irish Parliament could not convene without English approval or pass laws without ratification by the English Parliament. Over the subsequent centuries this law had been relaxed, but now the English authorities decided to revive it. In 1719 a further law allowed the English authorities to independently make laws for Ireland, which meant bypassing the Irish Parliament. Without Irish representation in the English Parliament, there was no one to petition for Ireland's cause. The Anglo-Irish Protestants were furious. They considered themselves English and expected to enjoy all the rights and privileges of the English who resided in England.

In late 1775 the American colonies rebelled against England. They shared many of the same grievances as the Irish Protestants, such as taxation, trade restrictions, governmental grievances, unjust laws, and insufficient representation. France came to the colonies' aid in their struggle against England. The British government realized that France might respond similarly to Ireland and use it as a landing ground to attack England. The tenant population of Ireland would gladly support the French who were Catholic and anti-British.

The Irish Volunteers

The Anglo-Irish ruling class was anxious to protect its interests, lands, industry, and lifestyle from the threat of war from either England or France. They decided to form a volunteer army that would defend Ireland in case of attack or invasion. Members of the Volunteers were mostly Protestant and, by 1779, had become a powerful military presence. The British government grew concerned that Ireland would follow the United States' lead and demand independence. In 1780 it agreed to solve the trade grievances. Using the Volunteers as a pressure group, the Anglo-Irish presented other grievances to Parliament for ratification. By 1782 Poyning's Law was repealed. Henry Grattan, the leader of a movement for freedom of both Catholics and Protestants in Ireland, pushed hard for the right of Catholics to participate in Parliament. The members of Parliament, however, were afraid to grant voting rights or government positions to the Catholic majority, because they feared that the Catholics would become too powerful and demand the return of their land and property through acts of Parliament. Catholics did, however, enjoy a certain reprieve from persecution at this time, because the Anglo-Irish Ascendancy was busy using the Volunteers as leverage to alleviate their own grievances.

Repeal of the Penal Laws

Having been successful with its own demands, it was not long before the Ascendancy began to cast a sympathetic eye upon the plight of the tenants. In 1778 Gardiner's Relief Bill allowed Catholics to lease land on longer leases (sixty-one years as opposed to thirty-one) on condition they take the Oath of Allegiance. The Gavelkind Act was repealed, and Catholics were no longer expected to divide their land equally among all their sons. In 1780 the Test Act, which demanded that in order to hold a government post one had to receive communion in an Established Church, was repealed. In 1782 Gardiner's Relief Act II allowed Catholics who had taken the Oath of Allegiance in 1778 to purchase, hold, and bequeath free holdings. Clergy and schoolmasters were reinstated and allowed to carry on with their professions. By 1782 most of the Penal Laws were repealed, and a more independent Irish parliament was recognized. It was known as Grattan's Parliament in honor of Henry Grattan, who had worked tirelessly to establish it. Grattan declared, "Ireland is now a Nation. In that character I hail her . . ." In 1789 a law was introduced that allowed the owner of land reclaimed from the bog to be exempt from tithes for seven years. Many Mahers who lived on bog lands availed of this tax exemption. Again Grattan proclaimed, "As Irishmen, Christians, and Protestants, we rejoice in the relaxation of the Penal Laws against our Roman Catholic fellow subjects." In 1792 a Catholic Relief bill allowed Catholics the freedom to become lawyers and the right to send their children abroad to be educated. In 1793 Hobart's Relief Bill allowed forty-shilling freeholders to vote. Forty-shilling freeholders owned their land or had lifetime leases. Their property was worth forty shillings annually after rent, taxes, and tithes were paid. With the Hobart's Relief Act, Catholics could now bear arms, join corporations, act as grand jurors, take degrees at Dublin University, and hold military commissions. The Hearth Tax of 1665, a tax of two shillings per fireplace in each home, was abolished by 1793.

The repeal of these oppressive laws led to a period of economic progress. Mills were built, mansions erected, towns developed, and trading and business flourished. Catholic traders and large leaseholders prospered. Between the years 1706 and 1799, the population of Ireland increased from 1.5 million to 4.5 million.

> The Church of Ireland ascendancy, which possessed all the jobs and owned five-sixths of the land, but formed only one-tenth of the population, had indeed done much for Ireland in civilization, wealth, architecture, a free parliament, and even religious toleration. But gratitude for all this could hardly be expected from an Irish speaking tenantry steeped in the past and subjected to a harsh landlord system. All the dramatic events and "nation-making" of the last thirty years has scarcely touched them, and almost nothing had been done to win their loyalty or even manly consent to the established order." (Curtis, p. 333)

Even though Catholics enjoyed some reprieve from the Penal Laws, they still could not hold state positions and had no representation in Parliament. Members of Parliament were still required to obey the Test Act and the Anti-Roman Oath of 1692. If further reprieves were to be gained, Catholics needed to demand the right to Parliamentary representation.

The United Irishmen

Theobald Wolfe Tone, a Protestant farmer's son and barrister at law, abhorred the injustices of the day. He entered politics believing that further reforms could be achieved peacefully. In 1791 he, along with Samuel Neilson and Thomas Russell, founded an organization called the Society of United Irishmen. At first, most of its members were well educated Ulster Protestants. The goals of this society as stated by Wolfe Tone were "To subvert the tyranny of our execrable government, to break the connection with England, the never-failing source of all our political evils, and to assert the independence of my country—these are my objects. To unite the whole people of Ireland, to abolish the memory of all past dissentions, and to substitute the common name of Irishman in place of the denominations of Protestants, Catholics, and dissenters."

The year 1793 was a momentous one. France was declared a republic and waged war on England. King Louis XVI was executed. The United Irishmen organization was outlawed, because England feared that the French would help them organize a rebellion. United Irishmen members discovered by the authorities were declared traitors and executed. The organization went underground and quickly abandoned their nonmilitary stance. By 1795 their membership was estimated at four hundred thousand. In 1796 Theobald Wolfe Tone was sent to France to petition for military aid. He was granted a fleet of forty-three ships and fifteen thousand troops under the control of General Lazare Hoche. The fleet left Brest, France for Ireland but was delayed by huge storms at sea, dense fog, and coastal rocks. Only sixteen ships eventually made it into Bantry Bay, but they failed to dock because of the high seas and raging storms. They returned to France. As a result of this abortive attempt to import French soldiers, the British suspicion of an Irish insurrection was confirmed. On March

30, Ireland was declared to be in a state of rebellion. The 1796 Insurrection Act forbade insurrection and allowed the authorities to put any area under martial law. Leaders of illegal organizations were captured and imprisoned. Arms and ammunition were to be turned in to the local authorities, and those found guilty of administering unlawful oaths faced the death penalty, while those taking the unlawful oath were deported. The authorities also became more vigilant in their observation of local gatherings.

The Rebellion of 1798

In the summer of 1798, thirteen counties staged rebellions. Fifty battles were fought. Some of these were brutal and bloody massacres, others nothing more than crossroad skirmishes. The most famous battles of 1798 were fought in Wicklow and Wexford. Though these counties were normally peaceful, in 1798 they joined the insurrection. The British sent troops fresh from England to quell the rebellion in the southeast. The last battle of this rebellion was fought at Vinegar Hill on June 21. Among the leaders of the Wexford rebels were Father John Murphy and Father Mogue Kearnes. Father John Murphy from Boolavogue led his men in a successful battle at Camolin. The following day the British destroyed the chapel and homes of the people of Boolavogue. On June 21, 1798, Father Murphy and his men suffered a defeat at Vinegar Hill, County Wexford. The leaders of the rebellion were either shot, hanged, or transported.

A traditional ballad tells the story of Vinegar Hill:

Boolavogue

Patrick Joseph McCall (1861–1919)

At Boolavogue as the sun was setting
O'er the bright May meadows of Shelmalier,
A rebel hand set the heather blazing
And brought the neighbors from far and near.
Then Father Murphy, from old Kilcormack,

Spurred up the rocks with a warning cry,
"Arm, Arm!" he cried, "for I've come to lead you,
For Ireland's freedom we'll fight or die."
He led us on 'gainst the coming soldiers,
And the cowardly Yeomen we put to flight;
'Twas at the Harrow the boys of Wexford
Showed Bookey's regiment how men could fight.
"Look out for hirelings, King George of England,
Search every kingdom where breathes a slave.
For Father Murphy from the County Wexford
Sweeps o'er the land like a mighty wave."
We took Camolin and Enniscorthy
And Wexford storming drove out our foes.
'Twas at Slieve Coilte our pikes were reeking
With the crimson blood of the beaten Yeos.
At Tubberneery and Bally ellis
Full many a Hessian lay in his gore
Ah! Father Murphy had aid come over
The Green Flag floated from shore to shore!
At Vinegar Hill, o'er the pleasant Slaney,
Our heroes vainly stood back to back,
And the Yeos at Tullow took Father Murphy
And burned his body upon the rack.
God grant you glory, brave Father Murphy,
And open heaven to all your men;
For the cause that called you may call to-morrow
In another fight for the Green again!
(Soodlums, p. 49)

    On August 22, 1798, when it was thought that all was lost for the United Irishmen, French troops arrived in Killala Bay on the west coast of Ireland. They had minor successes initially but were eventually crushed by the superior British forces. Two months later, Wolfe Tone arrived at Lough Swilly with another French fleet. The

British were waiting and captured Tone. He was sentenced to death but died before his execution.

County Tipperary does not figure among the thirteen counties that rebelled in 1798. It had already been disarmed and subdued before the national rising. In March 1798 martial law was declared for the Barony of Ikerrin, the O Meagher homeland. In April it was declared for the whole of County Tipperary. Tipperary was subjected to severe cruelty at this time. The High Sheriff and chief magistrate for the county was Thomas Judkin Fitzgerald, nicknamed the "Flogger Fitzgerald." Fitzgerald implemented martial law with brutal force. Prisoners were flogged, tortured, deported, or executed. Fitzgerald used individual cases, as examples to the general population of what would befall them should they refuse to cooperate with him. As a result threats of punishment and death were taken seriously and led to the surrender of information and ammunition. Fitzgerald was proud of his achievements in subduing Tipperary and requested the title of baron in recognition of his success. He was granted this reward and became Sir Thomas Judkin Fitzgerald.

In spite of the Flogger Fitzgerald's threats, a number of Tipperary men were still willing to pull out their pikes and fight. In Slievenamon Captain John Meagher of Ninemilehouse led an attempted uprising. Spies informed the British of the plan, and a trap was set to capture the rebels in action. Days before the appointed uprising, a false signal was ignited on a nearby hill. John and his United Irishmen were tricked into an early insurrection. They were captured and subjected to the usual brutalities of the Flogger Fitzgerald. In the wake of the rebellion, many O Meaghers figured among those who were transported for life to Australia, Tasmania, and New Zealand.

The Memory of the Dead

John Kells Ingram (1823–1907)

Who fears to speak of Ninety-Eight?
Who blushes at the name?
When cowards mock the patriot's fate
Who hangs his head for shame?

He's all a knave or half a slave
Who slight his country thus:
But a true man, like you, man,
Will fill your glass with us.

We drink the memory of the brave,
The faithful and the few—
Some lie far off beyond the wave,
Some sleep in Ireland, too;
All, all are gone-but still lives on
The fame of those who died;
And true men, like you, men
Remember them with pride.

Some on the shores of distant lands
Their weary hearts have lain,
And by the stranger's heedless hands
Their lonely graves were made;
But though their clay be far away
Beyond the Atlantic foam,
In true men, like you, men
Their spirit's still at home.

The dust of some is Irish earth,
Among their own they rest;
And the same land that gave them birth
Has caught them to her breast;
And we will pray that from their clay
Full many a race may start
Of true men, like you, men,
To act as brave a part.

They rose in dark and evil days
To right their native land,
They kindled here a living blaze
That nothing shall withstand.
Alas! That Might can vanquish Right—
They fell, and passed away;
But true men, like you, men,
Are plenty here today.

Then here's their memory—may it be
For us a guiding light,
To cheer our strife for liberty,
And teach us to unite!
Through good and ill, be Ireland's still,
Though sad as theirs, your fate;
And true men, like you, men,
Like those of Ninety-Eight.
(Mc Mahon, S., p.54–55)

The Act of Union

As a result of the 1798 rebellion, the British decided that they needed to abolish the Irish Parliament and rule Ireland directly from Westminster. They felt it was imperative to implement this promptly, because they were tired of the constant insurrection and threat of foreign aid. They resented having to heavily bribe members of the Irish Parliament to favor their position. They also feared that the United Irish mentality would spread through Parliament, and sympathy would grow toward emancipation and total separation from England. War with European nations posed a constant threat, and enemies might use Ireland as a base to invade England. Finally, it was agreed that if Catholics were to be given emancipation, it would be better to implement it from the greater Parliament in England.

According to John Caismir O' Meagher, the leading families of the O Meaghers strongly and adamantly opposed the Union. His list runs as follows:

> *This measure was vehemently opposed by a majority of the leading men of Cineal Meagher, a few only, who were allied by family or other ties to the nobility and gentry, favoring the Union . . . the Meaghers of Clonburre; Dr. Pierce Meagher of Cashel; Gilbert Meagher of Loughmoe; Edmund Meagher of Clonmel; William Meagher and Nicholas Meagher of Thurles; Daniel, James, Thomas, and Dr. Richard Meagher of Waterford;' Francis Meagher, Samuel, William and Thaddeus O Meagher of Dublin; John O Meagher of Fethard; John Meagher of Tullamaine Castle; Patrick Meagher of Slanestown Castle; James Meagher of Coolquill Castle; The Meaghers of Cloneen and Kilbury; John and Nicholas Meagher of Ballymorris; William O Meagher of Tourine; Denis O Meagher of Kilmoyer; Edward O Meagher of Marhill; Francis O Meagher of Bansha; Dr. Thomas O Meagher of Tipperary; The Meaghers of Snugboro; The O Meaghers of Cloyne and Clonakenny; of Roscrea and Templemore; of Templetuohy and Barnane; Brian O Meagher of Drangan; The O Meaghers of Kilkenny and Callan; the Mahers of Carlow and Meath. (O Meagher, p. 156)*

On June 7, 1800, the final reading of the Union Bill was held in the House of Commons. On January 1, 1801, the United Kingdom of Ireland and England was formed. Ireland lost her Parliament. She was now represented in England as a minority. Three months after the forming of the Union, the proposal for Catholic emancipation was abandoned.

The Union brought many changes for Ireland. The Anglican Church was formally declared the established religion of the Union. Free trade was agreed upon. Ireland was expected to pay two seventeenths of the imperial expense to the United Kingdom. Compatible taxation systems were introduced. Ireland was now considered part of the United Kingdom.

A Local Look

The oral history of three Meagher families in the Templemore area provides an example of how the general Irish person and local Meagher lived after Cromwell's dispersion. In an effort to be consistent from this point forward, the variant forms of the name Maher and Meagher are used when attached to specific families; otherwise it is standardized to the Maher form. The Penal Laws helped secure the new landlords in their estates and establish them as the ruling class of Irish society. There was little resistance from the dispossessed Catholics. These landlords became, as the name suggests, lords of the land. Here ended 513 years of Anglo-Norman rule and here began 224 years of English landlord rule.

It had not been fifty years since most of the Mahers had lived within the security of the clan system with their chieftain, John Meagher of Clonakenny. Some hoped the English landlords would be a new style of chieftain concerned about their welfare and their lives. Others secured tenant plots, confident that in a few years they would be able to rally enough support to oust the landlords and send them back to England. However, those Mahers who were spared exile were glad to secure a plot of land from any landlord anywhere.

The Maher Goss of Killanavogue, Clonmore, County Tipperary

The nickname "Goss" means "long and lean." All the members of this Maher family were tall and slender, thus their nickname, Goss. The Goss Maher family claims a relationship with John Meagher of Clonakenny, the O Meagher chieftain in Cromwellian times. The Goss Mahers lived in and around Clonakenny when Cromwell's forces stormed the village and surrounding area. When the inhabitants were ordered to evacuate, the Mahers Goss left their ancient homeland and fled to a place called Killinavogue, Clonmore, County Tipperary. This was also staunch Maher territory. Here they settled among their relatives and remained tenants on their ancient clan land until they finally bought their family farms from the landlords in the late nineteenth and early twentieth century. The Goss Mahers were known for their intellectual ability. Many became priests and nuns, while others emigrated to the United States, Australia, and England.

The Killea Mahers

The Killea Mahers have a colorful and exciting history, which is more typical of the average Irish tenant's experience. In 1640 there were twenty-six people living on the eighty-six acres in the town land of Gortroane, Killea, County Tipperary. This was a total of 2.6 people per acre!! Obviously a large number of people were living on common clan land owned by a few select people. The Civil Survey drafted from information collected between 1640 and 1656 shows the land of the Barony divided as follows. Select Mahers owned huge tracts jointly in fee from their ancestors. Landholders of the Maher name in the Barony were probably of the *derbfine* (direct bloodline) of various chieftains and, therefore, entrusted with the guardianship and government of the ancient clan lands. When the surveys were drawn up, these men were listed as the owners of their various town lands. Most were listed as joint owners with no clear boundaries. Such evidence strongly suggests that the Mahers were still practicing the ancient clan system of commonage up to the Cromwellian invasion. This was most unusual, since many of the major clans had been dispersed after the Treaty of Limerick or the flight of the Wild Geese. It would appear that the Maher Clan was among one of the last Irish clans, if not the last clan, to be dispersed.

Cromwell

When Cromwell came to Ireland in 1649, he began the systematic destruction of the native Gaelic way of life. He evicted Irish landholders and redistributed their lands to adventurers, soldiers, and friends, who had helped fight or fund his invasion. Strangely enough the Mahers of Killea did not remove to Connaught as ordered, but remained living on their clan land as before. It was not until the arrival of Joseph Lloyd that they were eventually forced to leave their ancient homelands.

Lloyd

The adventurers, who were granted the Maher townlands of Barnaballylegane and Gortroane, Killea, allowed the Mahers to remain undisturbed on this property until Joseph Lloyd acquired it. Joseph Lloyd, a Welsh man, came to Ireland in 1630. He eventually settled in north Tipperary. Joseph Lloyd married Mary Heather (c. 1670), the daughter of William Heather, a wealthy Cromwellian adventurer who had been granted land in Crannagh, Castleiney, County Tipperary. His son, Joseph Lloyd Jnr, married Mary Elizabeth Otway and took up the estate at Barnaballylegane and Gortroane. They built the first Lloyd house in the town land of Barnaballylegane. Gortroane became estate grounds. Lloyd promptly changed the name of his new estate to Lloydsborough. The old town land names of Barnaballylegane and Gortroane were soon forgotten.

Figure 18-2 Lloydsboro House, renamed Ikerrin Hall by Patrick Maher (1870–1961)

Their son, John, wed Elizabeth Blunden and lived at Lloydsboro. John and Elizabeth had three sons. Their oldest, John, wed Deboriah Clutterbuck in 1746 and went to live at Crannagh (another castle connected with the Mahers). John and Deborah lived in the tower house at Crannagh until the completion of the attached Georgian house in 1768. Their son, John, married Amy Brazier in 1777. This John inherited Lloydsboro and went to live there. John and Amy renovated the original home and rebuilt it as the English manor it is today. The final renovations were completed at the outbreak of the French Civil War in 1789. The Lloyds subsequently purchased many other properties in the county.

When the first Joseph Lloyd's offspring took ownership of the townlands of Gortroane and Barnaballylegane, life changed dramatically for the local inhabitants, many of whom were Mahers. The land was cleared of tenants to make room for the new landowner's private demesne. According to oral tradition, the great ancestors of the Killea Mahers were a Thomas and/or Daniel Meagher, who lived at Barnaballylegane and Gortroane. The Civil Survey of 1654 to 1656 lists a Thomas Meagher and a Daniel Meagher owning land in this area. In fact Daniel, along with various partners, is associated with the townland of Barnaballylegane and Gortruane; Thomas, along with his partners, is associated with Gortroane. The Book of Distribution (1659–1666) shows Thomas Meagher and partners as holding sixty-one acres in Gortroane. These Meaghers were evicted when the Welsh landlord built his mansion on their lands, calling the estate Lloydsborough in honor of his family. John Maher (1913–1991) of Ikerrin Hall (formerly Lloydsborough House) claimed that Lloyd admitted to his father, Patrick Maher (1870–1961) that the estate land formerly belonged to his Maher ancestors. John Maher also claimed that when his father, Patrick Maher (1870–1961), a direct descendant of the Killea Meaghers, bought Lloydsboro from John Lloyd in 1947, Lloyd gave Patrick an oil painting of a gentleman called Dolphy Maher. He said that the man in the picture was the original owner of the property when the Lloyds came.

The name Dolphy Maher is not on any survey for this time frame. Could Dolphy have been the above Daniel? Could the name have been distorted over the centuries (especially in the English tongue by English people)? Or could Dolphy have been a nickname for Domhnaill, which is the Irish for Daniel? One should also note that the man in the portrait bears a remarkable resemblance to the current generation of this line.

Figure 18-3 Dolphy Maher Photo of the original oil painting taken by George Willoughby, Thurles. (Courtesy of Mary Maher, Ikerrin Hall)

When Lloyd evicted the Killea Mahers to build his manor, they had nowhere to go. The descendants of Daniel and Thomas took refuge in the common lands of the Killea and Barnane area. It was in the commonage that many of Ireland's poor and dispossessed managed to scrape out a living for themselves and their families. The Killea Meaghers lived on the commons until 1760. However, in 1760 the landlords throughout Ireland decided to expand their acreage by closing the commons. Yet again the inhabitants were evicted to make room for the landowners and their livestock. John Meagher (c. 1730), a descendant of Daniel, and his compatriots were forced to relocate. This time there was no commonage to provide relief for the poor. In fact there was no place left for the dispossessed tenant to go, except for the vast wastelands, marshes, and bogs that spread about the foot of the Devil's Bit Mountain. One cannot but notice the density of inhabitants in these desolate places during the 1700s and 1800s. John Meagher found a place for his family on a plot of bog outside the town of Templemore.

The bog plot of Gortbrack was a tiny town land situated between two larger town lands called Jockey Hall and Forest near the town of Templemore. In the early 1800s Gortbrack was absorbed into the town land of Forest. The name Gortbrack was almost forgotten; it was only kept alive in the oral tradition of the Maher family and in some parish records. When John Maher (c. 1730) moved to Gortbrack, he cut a hole in the bog and built a sod house for himself and his family. His children and some of his grandchildren were born and reared on this same bog.

While Lloyd and his descendants were evicting tenants and acquiring land in the Barony of Ikerrin, another English family was also acquiring huge tracts that spanned both the Barony of Ikerrin and the Barony of Eliogarty. This new landlord was also to play an important role in the lives of all Mahers at the foot of the Devil's Bit Mountain and in Barnane, Killawardy, Templemore, Drom, and Loughmore.

John Carden was not a Cromwellian adventurer. He bought his land from the planters and other dissatisfied landholders of the time. In 1698 John Carden (c. 1623–1728) came to Templemore from Lincolnshire, England. He leased three thousand acres from Charles, Earl of Arran (Butler of Ormond). In 1701 he bought the Barnane estate from Sir John Morres. In 1704 he bought the three thousand–acre estate of Templemore from the Duke of Ormond. The latter was in need of cash and sold this tiny fragment of his huge estate to Carden.

When the Carden family arrived in the Templemore area, they resided at the Black Castle in the town park. (The Mahers claim that this was one of their castles taken from them by the Butlers of Ormond.) This castle was accidentally burned down in 1740. The Carden family was forced to draw up plans for a new home. The site of the new residence, the Priory, was chosen. Locals claim that the Priory site was, in fact, the site of an ancient abbey. There is no archeological evidence to prove this.

John Carden came from a landed family and was a skilled farmer. Unlike Cromwell's adventurers, he settled into his new estate with relative ease and began procuring suitable tenants for his property. A Meagher family from Barnane and their neighbors, the Healys, were transplanted from Barnane to Borrisbeg, Templemore. The Meagher and Healy family each had four sons. These sons were given tenancy as they came of age. John Carden made the conditions of their tenancy quite clear: "One fault, all out." If any one of the four families faulted, the entire group would be evicted. To this day descendants of the Meaghers and Healys still live in and around Borrisbeg. This branch of Meaghers is known as the Borrisbeg Meaghers. Obviously John Carden made a very successful choice of tenants for this area. He was not as fortunate elsewhere. Many Maher families were Rapparees, Whiteboys, and land agitators. John Carden and his descendants were not spared the disdain of these Mahers in any generation.

Figure 18-4 "The Day after the Ejectment" (Makeshift Home), *The Illustrated London News,* 1848

The first John Carden died in 1728. His family boasts that he lived to the ripe old age of 105 years. His body is interred in a plot atthe back of the old church in Templemore Town Park. He was the first of his family to be buried there. The plot remained in the family for all those Cardens who lived and died in Templemore.

Figure 18-5 The Priory, Templemore (courtesy of the National Library of Ireland)

John Carden II (c. 1675–1747) succeeded his father in 1728. By this time many landlords lived in fear of a tenant revolt. Fortunately for them, the Penal Laws were still stringently enforced, and infractions of the law were severely punished. A strong dislike for the landlords developed among Carden's tenants. In 1743 John Carden II had the opportunity to purchase more land that bordered his estate. He bought 403 acres from Sir John Morres of Knocka. Several Maher families were tenants on this property. Some remain there to this day. They are known as the Mahers of Knocka and are descendants of the original Thomas and Daniel of Killea. John Carden II died in 1747. His son, John Carden III, succeeded him.

By the mid-1700s, landlords had the confidence of several generations of established English order in Ireland. When John Carden III (1720–1774) inherited his father's estate in 1745, the Penal Laws were still being enforced. The severity of their enforcement was largely dependent upon the attitude of individual landlords and their agents. Throughout Ireland different standards of the law were enforced. John Carden also joined with his fellow landlords and closed the commons on his large estate. In retaliation for this unprecedented action, the local Whiteboys destroyed his Deer Park walls.

John Carden's stance on Catholics was demonstrated by his treatment of the clergy and their flock. In 1754, when other parishes were building more substantial churches with land grants from their landlords, Carden's town of Templemore had little more than a hut for a church. It sat at the foot of the Devil's Bit Mountain in the College Hill area. A local tale tells how Carden even went so far as to destroy this church in a vengeful rage. There are two different versions of this story.

> *The man whom Fr. Ryan stood up for was a young man from Drom who when making his way home from Roscrea went cross-country through some of the Carden estate, only to be accosted by Carden, called a 'rebelly papist' and threated with horsewhipping. The young man, taking to his heels out ran the mounted landlord, and sought refuge in a house where Fr. Ryan was administering to a dying man. The parish priest presented himself at the door as Carden rode up demanding that the young fugitive be presented to him, and declared that Carden would have to horse whip himself first. In a fury Carden rode away, vowing vengeance on the priest.' Hence, he stampeded his cattle down the hill and toppled the little hut church where Fr. Patrick Ryan was parish priest. (Hayes, Moyne-Templetuohy Appendix 2, p. 66)*

> *In 1752 Archbishop Butler visited College Hill, Templemore, where Fr. Patrick Ryan ministered in a straw covered church. Appointed in 1740 he lived in Knockinroe and Aughall. The latter church was dedicated to St. Michael. This was the church destroyed by a Carden. He was pursuing a Whiteboy with soldiers. The Whiteboy took refuge in a house where Fr. Ryan was baptizing a child in Gortruah. Fr. Ryan defended the Whiteboy, hot words followed and Carden left determined on revenge. He drove a herd of cattle down a hill where the level of the church was on a slope. The church was wrecked… Fr. Ryan changed to Moycarkey in 1755. In the same year Fr. William Maher, a native of Killea, was appointed Parish Priest. He built a church in Killea in 1758, and dedicated it to Saint James. The present building was erected by Father Fant in 1832 when he also built one at Clonmore. ("Bearnán Éile," Hasset, John J., The Guardian, 1952)*

From the time of his eviction by Lloyd in the early 1700s, John Maher worked hard to rear his family on the tiny bog plot at Gortbrack. John Carden III was friendly with this particular Maher family and came to the rescue. He allowed John Maher to farm a twelve-acre plot of land adjacent to Gortbrack. This was the same twelve acres that was leased to the British Army Barracks in 1800. It seems bizarre that in these troubled times John Carden III would show such benevolence to John Maher of Gortbrack. This was a curious arrangement. When questioned about this arrangement, the immediate descendants replied that the Carden and this particular Maher family were always on good terms. They claim that their families were often invited to parties and balls at the Abbey! Sr. Áine Ní Chearbhaill, Convent of Mercy, (RIP), Templemore, added that, "When the Carden came to Templemore he was very much aware that he was in possession of the ancient land of the Ó Meachairs. He seems to have made a point of staying on friendly terms with them."

Thankful for the benevolence of the Carden, John Maher farmed the twelve-acre plot of land in Templemore until he had accumulated enough money to procure a seven-acre tenancy opposite the old graveyard in Drom Village. John took up the tenancy at Drom and left Gortbrack to his oldest son, John, who married a lady from Killea named Mary Kate O Brien.

John and Mary Kate had ten children. When the oldest son, John, came of age, he was sent to his grandfather in Drom to secure the farm there. John and Mary Kate remained at Gortbrack. They had six more sons to settle. Unfortunately, at this time the law stated that Irish Catholics, upon their death, must divide their property equally among all their sons. It is not surprising then that the Maher boys remained on the bog at Gortbrack and were married adults with families before they managed to find better opportunities elsewhere.

Figure 18-6 Templemore Barracks, County Tipperary (courtesy of the National Library of Ireland)

In 1774 John Carden III died. His son, John Craven Carden (c. 1757–1820), inherited the estate. This John was honored with the title of baronet of Ireland in 1787. Hence he became known as Sir John Craven Carden, or simply, Sir John. He lived in the time of Grattan's Parliament and the United Irishmen. Sir John became involved in local politics and was colonel of a unit of Volunteers in 1776. In 1798 he thought it prudent to disband the unit because he discovered that some of the members were UnitedIrishmen. He did not want to be associated with an illegal underground organization.

With growing tensions and talks of an uprising, Sir John worried that his tenants would join in the revolt. He wrote to the government, demanding that troops be sent into his area. He was refused. John took matters into his own hands, and, with the use of paid spies, he was kept informed of local and United Irishmen activities. He also invited High Sheriff Thomas Judkin Fitzgerald (the Flogger Fitzgerald) to come visit his estate with the express purpose of intimidating his tenants into submission. The Carden's tenants were ordered to appear before the Flogger Fitzgerald and were subjected to a three-hour lecture in both Irish and English. When the meeting was over, suspected traitors were called forward to kneel before the high sheriff and pray for the king of England. The conscientious efforts of the Carden and the very realistic threats of the Flogger Fitzgerald had the desired effect of cowing the tenants into submission. It was no surprise then that Tipperary was poorly represented in the 1798 rebellion.

As a direct result of the rebellion and the lack of adequate government support, Sir John Craven Carden decided that he needed military fortifications in his territory. When he heard that the British were looking to build another barracks in County Tipperary, he immediately put forward plans to lease the British a suitable plot of his land. Sir John offered to lease the land for 155 pounds, 8 shillings, and no pence, annually, plus a further 100 pounds for the training ground. His offer was accepted, and, in 1800, the ground was broken for the building of a British military barracks in Templemore. This barracks took ten years to build and was completed in 1810. Sir John felt morecomfortable knowing that the British Army was now camped on his doorstep.

Believing the promises of the English authorities, he voted for the Act of Union in 1800. Comfortable in the knowledge that his estates were secure, Sir John devoted his time and energies to developing his new town, Templemore. He died in 1820.

Chapter 19: Catholic Emancipation

After the Act of Union in 1801, many landlords returned to England and left their estates in the hands of bailiffs or land agents. They took their money and businesses with them. This loss of industry led to an economic drain on the entire country, which seriously affected the standard of living for the average tenant, who already paid high rents, rates, and tithes to the Anglican Church.

Daniel O Connell and the Repeal Association

Daniel O Connell from County Kerry came to the fore at this time. He had studied in France and England, where he qualified as a barrister. Upon returning to Ireland, having spent years abroad, he was shocked by the intolerable misery of his fellow Catholic Irish. O Connell was totally opposed to bloodshed and violence as a means of reform. He had lived in France at the time of the bloody revolution and left that country the day King Louis XVI was beheaded. O Connell and Richard Shiel founded an organization that had, as its goal, Catholic emancipation by peaceful, political, and legal means. This Catholic Association was established in 1823.

To maintain the organization, a membership fee of one penny a month was collected from each family. This fee, known as the Catholic Rent, was inexpensive enough to include the poorest of tenants. It was collected at the church gates or by house-to-house canvassing. O Connell held meetings the length and breadth of Ireland. He chose sites of particular historical significance for these meetings. Because of the huge tenant turnout, these meetings were called "Monster Meetings."

In 1826 O Connell's Catholic Association put forward Villiers Stuart as the Waterford candidate for Parliament. He ran against the landlord's choice, Lord George Beresford. Even though it was open ballot, Villiers Stuart won the seat. The Catholics were jubilant. As a result of this success, Daniel O Connell decided he would contest the next Parliamentary seat. In 1828 a vacancy arose in County Clare. The opposition was Vesey Fitzgerald. O Connell was elected but could not take his seat, because he refused to take the Oath of Supremacy, which acknowledged the king, not the Catholic pope, as the supreme head of the Church. The elections were held again. O Connell was triumphant the second time. When the second election reaffirmed O Connell's Parliamentary seat, the prime minister recognized that the time had come to grant Catholic emancipation. In 1829 the Roman Catholic Relief Bill allowed Catholics to enter Parliament.

     Having achieved Catholic emancipation, O Connell continued to bring to light the many other injustices suffered by the Catholic tenants, the Cess taxes, rates, and tithes. The Cess Tax helped pay for the upkeep of Protestant church buildings. In 1832 the Cess Tax was abolished, but tithes and rates were not. In 1838, tithes were reduced to one quarter of what they used to be. The landlord was responsible for paying the tithes. Some landlords paid the tithes themselves, while others added the fee to the tenants' rent. O Connell's next agenda was the repeal of the Act of Union.

     O Connell continued the tradition of holding Monster Meetings throughout Ireland in an effort to raise consciousness of the necessity to repeal the Act of Union. He decided to organize a huge meeting at Clontarf. The date was set for October 8, 1843. This was a poignant setting for such a meeting. The Battle of Clontarf in 1014 was one of the most famous battles ever fought in Ireland. It was here that Brian Boru defeated the Norse men, putting the Irish back in control of their land. The authorities became suspicious of the proposed Clontarf meeting and labeled it an illegal gathering. Troops were called in. Fearing bloodshed, O Connell canceled the meeting. He and his colleagues were arrested and charged with the crime of trying to overthrow the Irish government. Following imprisonment, a trial, and a hefty fine, they were set free. O Connell's health failed, and he decided to go on a pilgrimage to Rome. He died at Genoa, Italy in 1845. In keeping with his last wishes, his heart was taken to Rome, and his body was sent back to Ireland.

Education

In 1832 a national education system was founded to educate the poor. These public schools were open to everyone regardless of creed or culture. Classes were conducted through the medium of English. Religious instruction was allowed at an appointed time when the clergy of choice came to the school to teach. The following excerpt from Skehan's Cashel and Emily Heritage shows how some Catholic clergy reacted to the national schools.

> *Meagher, (Maher, O Maher) John, PP Murroe and Boher 1850-1859, born in Thurles town at the Suir Bridge end of the Square; nephew of Fr. William Bryne, PP Ballina (B133). Entered Rhetoric Class, Maynooth, 25th August 1826. Ordained at Maynooth towards the end of 1832. After fifteen months in Ballina as CC to his uncle, he was sent as CC to Murroe, 1834-1850. He lived for the spiritual and material welfare of his flock and during the Famine he shared all he had with them. So beloved was he that when the news of his appointment as the PP reached Murroe in July 1850 bonfires blazed through out the parish for two days; He was appointed Canon, 1857. As a result of a slight fall he became paralyzed and died November 11, 1859, aged 55. He was buried in Boher Church. His class fellows, Archbishop Leahy and Dr. Russell, President of Maynooth, attended his funeral. Dr. Leahy paid him the tribute of preaching at his funeral, something he had not done before. He spoke of the personal loss to himself and of a life long friend. Scenes of great sorrow were witnessed at his burial.*
>
> *Visitation 1852: 495 confirmed; 4 National and 3 private schools; Curates collection in October; no lease for Murroe church site but a lease dated 1838 for Boher. Visitation 1855: 764 confirmed; 4 National schools, 4 private schools, The NS at Barrington's Bridge, Kishiquirk and Murroewere double schools, the female school at Murroe being closed at the time.*

> *The closure of the latter arose as follows; J. Barrington, son of Sir Matthew Barrington, was patron of this school, built by Lord Cloncurry. A Protestant schoolmistress, Eliza Miller, was introduced. Fr. Meagher forbade his parishioners to attend it. Barrington ordered his employees to send their children there under pain of dismissal for refusal and many were dismissed; but the PP's unbending determination over came this effort at proselytism and the school had to be closed for lack of pupils. There were seven perverts in the parish during the famine, all but one (of whom emigrated) were received back into the Church. (Skehan, M52, p. 1993)*

The Poor Law

The Poor Law Act passed in 1838, divided Ireland into poor law districts. Taxes were collected to help the poor. Workhouses, which served several districts, were built to accommodate the destitute who came in search of food and shelter. Initially many Irish refused to go to the workhouses, because families were separated into men, women, and children's quarters. It was not until famine times that the workhouses became the final option for so many, particularly during the harsh winter months.

The Young Irelanders

The Young Irelanders, led by William Smith O Brien, became a splinter group of O Connell's Catholic Association. Unlike O Connell, who abhorred bloodshed and violent means, the Young Irelanders believed that the sword was the only way to gain Irish emancipation. They shared Wolf Tone's idea of a United Ireland, with Protestants and Catholics all living in harmony. The founders of this organization were Charles Gavan Duffy from Monaghan, John Blake Dillon from Mayo, and Thomas Davis, a Protestant from Cork. Duffy and Davis were poets, and Duffy was the founder of their newspaper, *The Nation*.

John Mitchel, an Ulster Protestant, joined them later. He was a notable writer and contributed many articles to their newspaper. Thomas Francis Meagher, a Waterford man, was their orator, and William Smith O Brien was their leader. Their newspaper included the popular opinions of the day, with many stirring articles and poems that encouraged rebellious ideas. The Young Irelanders seemed to imply that it would be far better to die in battle than to die of hunger in the ditches.

James Clarence Mangan, a renowned poet, contributed regularly to *The Nation*. His most famous contribution was probably "Dark Rosaleen." This poem uses the code name Rosaleen for Ireland. Its content is typical of the cryptic manner used by *The Nation* to incite the Irish Catholic to take up arms for Ireland.

Dark Rosaleen

James Clarence Mangan (1803–1849)

O! my Dark Rosaleen,
Do not sigh, do not weep!
The priests are on the ocean green,
They march along the Deep.
There's wine . . . from the royal Pope
Upon the ocean green;
And Spanish ale shall give you hope,
My Dark Rosaleen!
My own Rosaleen!
Shall glad your heart, shall give you hope,
Shall give you health, and help, and hope,
My Dark Rosaleen.

Over hills and through dales,
Have I roamed for your sake;
All yesterday I sailed with sails
On river and on lake.
The Erne . . . at its highest flood
I dashed across unseen,
For there was lightening in my blood,

My Dark Rosaleen!
My own Rosaleen!
Oh! there was lightening in my blood,
Red lightening lightened through my blood,
My Dark Rosaleen!

All day long in unrest
To and fro do I move,
The very soul within my breast
Is wasted for you, love!
The heart . . . in my bosom faints
To think of you my Queen,
My life of life, my saint of saints,
My Dark Rosaleen!

Woe and pain, pain and woe,
Are my lot night and noon,
To see your bright face clouded so,
Like to the mournful moon.
But yet . . . I will rear your throne
Again in golden sheen;
'Tis you shall reign, shall reign alone,
My Dark Rosaleen!
My own Rosaleen!
'Tis you shall have the golden throne,
'Tis you shall reign, and reign alone.
My Dark Rosaleen!

Over dews, over sands
Will I fly for your weal;
Your holy delicate white hands
Shall girdle me with steel.
At home . . . in your emerald bowers,
From morning's dawn till e'en,
You'll pray for me, my flower of flowers,
My Dark Rosaleen!
My fond Rosaleen!
You'll think of me through daylight hours,
My virgin flower, my flower of flowers,
My Dark Rosaleen!

I could scale the blue air,
I could plough the high hills,
Oh, I could kneel all night in prayer,
To heal your many ills!
And one . . . beamy smile from you
Would float like light between
My toils and me, my own, my true,
My Dark Rosaleen!
My fond Rosaleen!
Would give me life and soul anew,
A second life, a soul anew,
My Dark Rosaleen!

O! the Erne shall run red
With redundance of blood,
The earth shall rock beneath our tread,
And flames wrap hill and wood,
And gun-peal, and slogan cry,
Wake many a glen serene,
Ere you shall fade, ere you shall die,
My Dark Rosaleen!
My own Rosaleen!
The Judgement Hour must first be nigh,
Ere you can fade, ere you can die,
My Dark Rosaleen!
(Gibbons, D., p.21–25)

The Young Irelanders planned a rebellion for the fall of 1848. It was destined to fail for a variety of reasons. The year 1848 was the height of the famine. Tenant farmers were in a desperate state. Their potato crop was partially blighted again. Thousands were malnourished and facing destitution. The authorities were vigilant in their observation of the Young Irelander's movements. They read *The Nation* with the intention of finding treasonable offenses against the leaders. Thomas Davis, their beloved comrade and patriotic leader, died. William Smith O Brien, Thomas Francis Meagher, and John Mitchel were arrested. A packed jury found Mitchel guilty of treason, and he was sentenced to transportation for fourteen years. Meagher and Smith O Brien were acquitted, because the government had failed to pack the juries. But they were under constant surveillance. Eventually, warrants for their arrest were issued. Impulsively they decided to rush forward the rebellion and make a brave stand for Ireland before their capture. The rebellion was nothing more than a skirmish at the Commons, Ballingarry, County Tipperary. In a few other places it was sporadic and equally unsuccessful.

Shortly after the failed uprising, Thomas Francis Meagher, William Smith O Brien, and the other leaders were arrested, tried, convicted, and sentenced. William Smith O Brien was to be hanged, drawn, and quartered. "The sentence is that you, William Smith O Brien, be taken from hence to the place whence you came, and be thence drawn on a hurdle to the place of execution, and be there hanged by the neck until you are dead; and that afterwards your head shall be severed from your body, and your body divided in four quarters, to be disposed of as Her Majesty shall think fit. And may the Lord have mercy on your soul." (Lord Chief Justice) Later this sentence was commuted to transportation for life.

Thomas Francis Meagher was also sentenced to execution, but his sentence was commuted to transportation to Van Dieman's Land (Tasmania). Duffy was sentenced to prison and much later released generations. The seeds of discontent and rebellion that were sown by Wolfe Tone and the United Irishmen in 1798 had blossomed with the Young Irelanders in 1848 and would grow again when, in 1916, Padraig Pearse led another rebellion.

Figure 19-1 The affray at the Widow McCormack's house, on Boulagh Common, *Illustrated London News,* August 12, 1848

As a result of the failed rebellion, his transportation for life, his subsequent escape, and his rise to fame in the United States, Thomas Francis Meagher became the most popular Meagher of the nineteenth century. Though a failed and exiled revolutionary, he is credited with the design of the current Irish flag. In 1848 he was one of three Young Ireland delegates who traveled to France to congratulate the government of the new French Republic. The red, white, and blue flag of the new French Republic inspired Meagher to design a similar tricolor for Ireland. On April 15, 1848, he presented this flag to the nation. Below is an excerpt from his presentation speech.

Figure 19-2 The War House, Commons, Ballingarry, County Tipperary (2005)

Figure 19-3 Plaque at the War House Ireland

> *I present you with this flag . . . From Paris the gay and Gallant City of the tri-color and the barricade, this flag has been proudly borne. I present it to my native land, and I trust that the old country will not refuse this symbol of a new life from one of her youngest children.*
>
> *I need not explain its meaning. The quick and passionate intellect of the generation now stirring into arms will catch it at a glance. The white in the centersignifies a lasting truce between the "orange" and the "green,"mand I trust that beneath its folds the hands of the Irish Protestant and the Irish Catholic may be clasped in generous and heroic brotherhood. If this flag be destined to fan the flames of war, let England behold once more, upon that white center, the RED HAND that struck her down from the hills of Ulster, and I pray that heaven may bless the vengeance it is sure to kindle. (Cavanagh, 1892, p. 164)*

Though the flag was not immediately adopted as the flag of Ireland, it billowed from the top of the General Post Office during the rebellion of 1916 and was adopted by the Irish Free State as the nation's flag in 1937. This was almost a century after Meagher presented it to the Irish nation. As the official flag of the Republic of Ireland it was hung in reverse order, the green at the staff. Meagher went on to become a famous soldier in the American Civil War. He was promoted from captain to major, to colonel, to brigadier general and fought for the North leading the 96th Brigade. In 1865 he was appointed secretary and acting-governor of Montana. On July 1, 1867 Meagher fell overboard from a steamer on the Missouri River. He was forty-four years old.

Figure 19-4 Memorial to the Young Irelanders at the Commons, County Tipperary

A Local Look

It was Sir John Craven Carden's father who had begun the building of Templemore town. Unlike many Irish towns, Templemore is not an ancient town that grew from a monastic settlement, a Viking settlement, or a trading route. Sir John Craven Carden meticulously designed Templemore according to his own tastes and the needs of the growing community. He wanted a market town, so he planned the unusually wide town square to meet this need. It would be large enough to accommodate small and large animal pens, food stalls, ware stalls, traders, hawkers, and the huge crowds that were expected to attend. Three-story Georgian-style houses with slates were encouraged. Thatch was allowed until the slates were purchased. Local tradesmen constructed the public buildings using their own transport and labor. These buildings included the Market House, the Bridewell Prison, and the Courthouse.

Figure 19-5 Thomas Francis Meagher (courtesy of Elaine Ryan Sullivan, Australia)

Continuing the legacy of his father, John Craven Carden worked hard to develop the new town. He built thirty-seven houses at "New Row" to accommodate weavers he brought from Belfast in hopes of starting a cloth industry. These newcomers were Protestant. Not only did their religion cause tensions, but their celebration of July 12 (the anniversary of the Battle of the Boyne) also caused quite a stir in the predominantly Catholic town. Local tensions inhibited a happy compromise, and the weavers emigrated to Canada. The townsfolk moved into their cottages and occupied the houses until they were demolished in 1940. John Craven Carden even became a benefactor of the Catholic community, giving Fr. Jeremiah Morrissey, P.P., a site for a Catholic church. Morrissey's successor, Fr. Patrick Fant, built the new church on this property in 1815. Fant's church was the first church to be built in the actual town of Templemore.

The town of Templemore grew quickly during the time of John Craven Carden. He died in 1820 and was succeeded by his son, Sir Arthur Carden (c. 1777–1822). Arthur died after being landlord for only two years. During his short span as landlord, Ireland's revolutionary spirit began to rise again. O Connell and the Catholic Association were gaining popularity and fanning the flames of discontent among the tenant population. O Connell held a Monster Meeting on Carden's land at College Hill, Templemore, on the slopes of the Devil's Bit Mountain in O Meagher territory. Here O Connell addressed issues of support for Irish industry and production, the repeal of the union, temperance and peaceful ways, and an avoidance of violence and factionalism. Below is an account of this meeting, known as "The Burial of the Tithes."

> *In 1841 Daniel O Connell addressed a meeting of about 50,000 people on the slopes of the Devil's Bit. They met him there and to express their joy they carried out what came to be known as the "burial of the tithes." Described very fully by Samuel Lover. Bands from the local parishes played for the dancers, aplatform was built for them, while the musicians sat on large stones, as this historic event was commemorated down through the years. Local people took great pride*

in having the hay saved by that day and the people on the Rock surveyed down below them, all the trams of hay neatly dotted on the slopes. In later years the Stations of the Cross were erected for the day and prayers were said. (John J. Hasset, "Bearnán Éile" Guardian, 1952)

Sir Arthur Carden feared a rebellion among his tenants and fortified his home by walling up the ground floor windows. He had cannon fittings built on the Market House in the center of town in readiness for the cannons he planned to order.

Figure 19-6 Templemore Town, c. 1900 (from the Cardall Collection, Courtesy of the National Library of Ireland)

Sir Arthur died and was succeeded by Sir Henry Carden (c. 1789–1847), his half-brother. Sir Henry was an army officer and served under the Duke of Wellington in the Spanish Peninsular War. Many Templemore streets were named after the great battles and officers of that war; Richmond, Talevara, and Wellington Lodge are but some examples. Sir Henry took the reigns of the Carden estate during troubled times. He owned huge tracts of land and had many thousands of tenants. His town of Templemore was home to hundreds of laborers, traders, and businessmen. At this time Daniel O Connell and his Catholic Association had given the tenants the courage to defy their landlords and to stand up for their rights. Sir Henry wanted to avoid a rebellion at all costs, so he began to make concessions. He signed the petition for Catholic emancipation in 1829 and gave generously to the Catholic Church. He also organized employment schemes.

A year after Sir Henry's death, the Young Irelanders brought trouble to the town of Templemore. They rebelled in South Tipperary under the leadership of Thomas Francis Meagher and others. As a result the authorities raided the homes of Maher tenants in the Templemore area looking for evidence of collusion. It was no secret that Thomas Francis Meagher had many allies in Templemore. In fact it was a Father Patrick Meagher of Borrisbeg, Templemore, who aided his escape after the rebellion.

The Borrisbeg Mahers

This family was transplanted from Barnane to Borrisbeg, Templemore, by the original Carden. They subsequently became known as the Borrisbeg Mahers. This group managed to hold onto their land through troubled times. They recalled the "one fault all out" agreement with the first Carden. By 1848 the original family branch had grown into a huge tree, and many families depended on the adherence of all to this agreement. The following incident with Thomas Francis Meagher and "The Book of Names" in Ballingarry as recounted by Billy Maher (RIP) proves this premise.

The Mahers of Borrisbeg spelled their name *Meagher* for many generations. An incident occurred in 1848 that caused them to change their name to *Maher*. In 1848 a group of freedom fighters called the Young Irelanders staged a failed revolt at Ballingarry, County Tipperary. One of the leaders of this group was the famous Thomas Francis Meagher of Waterford. He managed to flee south in an effort to escape capture by the British Forces. While fleeing, he dropped his book of names in south Tipperary. A woman found the book and, realizing immediately the delicacy of the material within, promptly turned it in to her local priest, Fr. Patrick Meagher. Though a native of Borrisbeg, Templemore, he was at this time the curate of Ballingarry. Fr. Meagher thought it prudent to destroy the book. He burned it on his own hearth.

Figure 19-7 The Market House (Town Hall), Templemore (2000)

Figure 19-8 The Garda College, Templemore (2000)

The authorities got news of the incident and raided the presbytery. Having searched the entire house, they found nothing. They went immediately to Fr. Meagher's home in Borrisbeg. Here they ransacked his house and every other Meagher home in search of the missing book. In the meantime Thomas Francis Meagher was captured and tried for treason. It was the firm belief of the Borrisbeg Mahers, at that time, that Thomas Francis Meagher endangered the lives of his fellow freedom fighters in order to save his own skin. As a result of this event, the Borrisbeg Meaghers had the name Meagher removed from their carts and replaced by Maher. They wanted it made clear to all that they were not one and the same with the Meagher who was willing to sell his comrades for his own safety.

Little did the Borrisbeg Mahers realize that Thomas Francis Meagher would become a hero in three countries: Ireland, Australia, and America! Mahers throughout the world and through successive generations changed their names to Meagher in his honor. Some even called their sons Thomas Francis.

Chapter 20: The Famine

The Irish Emigrant

Lady Helen Dufferin (1807–1867)

I'm sitting on the stile, Mary
Where we sat, side by side,
That bright May morning long ago
When first you were my bride.
The corn was springing fresh and green,
The larks sang loud and high,
The red was on your lip, Mary
The love-light in your eye.

The place is little changed, Mary,
The day is bright as then,
The lark's loud song is in my ear,
The corn is green again;
But I miss the soft clasp of your hand,
Your breath warm on my cheek,
And I will keep list'ning for the words
You never more may speak.

'Tis but a step down yonder lane,
The little Church stands near,
The Church where we were wed, Mary,
I see the spire from here;
But the graveyard lies between, Mary,
My step might break you rest,
Where you, my darling, lie asleep
With your baby on you breast.

I'm very lonely now, Mary,
The poor make no new friends;

But, oh! they love the better still
The few our Father sends.
And you were all I had, Mary,
My blessing and my pride;
There's nothing left to care for now
Since my poor Mary died.

Yours was the brave good heart, Mary,
That still kept hoping on,
When trust in God had left my soul,
And half my strength was gone.
There was comfort ever on you lip,
And the kind look on your brow.
I bless, you Mary, for the same,
Though you can't hear me now.

I thank you for the patient smile
When you heart was fit to break;
When the hunger pain was gnawing there
You hid it for my sake.
I bless you for the pleasant word
When you heart was sad and sore.
Oh! I'm thankful you are gone, Mary,
Where grief can't reach you more!

I'm bidding you a long farewell,
My Mary—kind and true!
But I'll not forget you, darling.
In the land I'm going to.
They say there's bread and work for all,
And the sun shines always there;
But I'll not forget old Ireland,
Were if fifty times as fair.

And when amid those grand old woods
I sit and shut my eyes,
My heart will travel back again
To where my Mary lies;
I'll think I see the little stile
Where we sat side by side,

And the springtime corn and bright May morn,
When first you were my bride.
(McMahon, S., pp. 333–334)

    Of the many hardships endured by the Irish throughout centuries of invasion, oppression, suppression, insurrection, expulsion, and famine, it was the famine that had the most devastating effect on the land, its people, its culture, and its language. Ireland was brought to her knees during the famine years. The blight was a mysterious and silent enemy.

    By the mid-nineteenth century, the majority of Irish lived in one-room thatched cabins with earthen floors. Often the extended family lived in these huts and depended on the same plot of land for sustenance. Farmers were tenants-at-will, which meant they had no security of tenure and could be evicted at the whim of the landlord or his agent. Farms were often as small as five acres, and crops were grown to pay the rent. Laborers usually lived on one-acre plots and farmed this acre in potatoes to feed the family. Their salary for labor was used to pay the rent. In 1844 an estimated 182,000 farms were less than five acres and 135,000 farms were less than one acre. Only 7 percent of the farms in Ireland were above thirty acres.

    The Irish tenant farmer lived on the edge. Wheat, oats, barley, and other cash crops were harvested and shipped abroad. Animals such as cattle and pigs were sold at the fair for exportation. Money from the sale of crops and livestock was used to pay the rent. Potatoes fed the family. Most farms had free-range fowl, which provided eggs and meat. Meat, however, was a rarity, being a special treat on Easter and at Christmas.

Old Skibbereen

(Anonymous)

Oh, father dear, I often hear you speak of Erin's Isle,
Her lofty scenes and valley's green, her mountains rude and wild,
They say it is a lovely land wherein a prince might dwell,

Oh, why did you abandon it? The reason to me tell.

Oh, son! I loved my native land with energy and pride,
Till a blight came o'er my crops—my sheep, my cattle died;
My rent and taxes were too high, I could not them redeem,
And that's the cruel reason that I left old Skibbereen.

Oh, well do I remember the bleak December day,
The landlord and the sheriff came to drive us all away;
They set my roof on fire with their cursed English spleen,
And that's another reason that I left old Skibbereen.

Your mother, too, God rest her soul, fell on the snowy ground,
She fainted in her anguish, seeing the desolation round,
She never rose, but passed away from life to mortal dream,
And found a quiet grave, my boy, in dear old Skibbereen.

And you were only two years old and feeble was your frame,
I could not leave you with my friends you bore your father's name.
I wrapped you in my cotamore at the dead of night unseen,
I heaved a sigh and bade good-bye to dear old Skibbereen.

Oh, father dear, the day may come when in answer to the call,
Each Irishman, with feeling stern, will rally one and all;
I'll be the man to lead the van beneath the flag so green,
When loud and high we'll raise the cry, "Remember Skibbereen."
(McMahon, S., pp. 44-45)

Throughout the history of Ireland, there were many mini famines. They were usually local and small in scale. During these famines the loss of the potato crop was of great consequence, but not life-threatening. From 1845 to 1848, the potato crop was continuously blighted. The loss of the potato over this period of time meant the loss of the Irish tenant's staple diet. Landlords continued to demand the rent regardless of the desperate situation of the tenants. When necessary, agents and bailiffs were ordered to take the animals off the farms and gather the harvest for shipping abroad.

Figure 20-1 "Searching for potatoes in a stubble field," the *Illustrated London Times,* Dec. 22, 1849

When the great national tragedy commenced; and after many a hope and fear, it was seen that, without doubt, Famine and all its ghastly train of evils was far and wide upon the land . . . When the potato was the sole sustenance of the people, we can imagine what a horror, slowly creeping on their minds, finally seized them with utter panic, when, in the autumn of '47 and again in the autumn of '48 that strange odor filled the atmosphere and told of the deadly blight . . . What must have it been in these far days, when no other food was to be had; when the granaries of the great prairies were yet unlocked, and a whole people might perish before the hands of the charitable could reach them. And they did perish; perished by hundreds and by thousands, by tens of thousands, by hundreds of thousand; perished in the houses, in the fields, by the roadside, in the ditches; perished from hunger, from cold but most of all from the famine-fever. It is an appalling picture, that which springs up to memory. Gaunt specters move here and there, looking at one another out of hollow eyes of despair and gloom. Ghosts walk the land. Great giant figures, reduced to skeletons by hunger, shake in their clothes, which hang loose around their attenuated frames. Mothers try in vain to still their children's cries of hunger by bringing their cold, blue lips to milk-less breasts. Here and there by the wayside a corpse stares at the passers-by, as it lies against the hedge where it had sought shelter. The pallor of its face is darkened by lines of green around the mouth, the dry juice of grass and nettles. All day long the carts are moving to the graveyards with their ghastly, staring, uncoffined loads. In the towns it is even worse. The shops are shuttered. Great fires blaze at the corners of streets to purify the air.

> *From time to time the doctors send up into the polluted air paper kites with a piece of meat attached. The meat comes down putrid. At the government depots, here and there, starving creatures dip their hands into the boiling maize, or Indian meal, and swallow with avidity the burning food. A priest is called from his bed at every watch of the night. As he opens his hall door, two*

> or three corpses fall into his arms. Poor creatures! Here was their last refuge! Here and there along the streets, while the soft rain comes down to wash more corruption into the festering streets, a priest kneels in the mud over a prostrate figure. He is administering the last rights, while a courageous by stander holds an umbrella above his head to guard the Sacred Species. No graves, but pits, as after the carnage of a great battle, are dug in the cemeteries and the burial service is read over twenty corpses at a time. Those who have managed to escape the dread visitation are flying panic stricken to the seaports. They heed not the coffin-ship, nor the sea perils before them. Anywhere, anywhere, out of this pestiferous, famine stricken Gehenna! The ships are full. Those who are compelled to remain behind in the quays send up a wail of lamentation. The dread spirits of Fever and Famine haunt them. There is no exorcism so powerful as to dispel them. There is nothing but flight, flight! (Sheehan, pp. 199–201)

The *London Times* reported the following statement with regards to the plight of Ireland: "They are going! They are going! The Irish are going with a vengeance. Soon a Celt will be as rare in Ireland as a Red Indian on the shores of Manhattan."

Since the Act of Union, Ireland had no legal means of addressing her burdens and relied upon England to implement legislation to address them. In the early years England sent scientists to with orders to study the situation. This, of course, offered no immediate relief of suffering. Later, money was allocated for distribution among the poor. However, much of this money was used to pay the civil servants who organized the relief. Later again, other relief projects were set up. They included soup kitchens, building projects, distribution of Indian corn, and the upkeep and maintenance of the workhouses. The Society of Friends also ran soup kitchens. They provided a daily meal for the destitute. Building projects were organized according to the philosophy of "charity with dignity." Peasants could "earn their bread by the sweat of their brow."

At this time the English government stringently believed in the economic system of Laissez Faire. Their relief laws stipulated that the building projects were to be of no economic benefit to the country and, on no account, was the money to be used to buy seed potatoes. Sick and starving tenants were put to work on these building projects. Emaciated bodies yielded heavy sledgehammers, broke rocks, hauled the rocks to building sites, and used shovels to dig foundations. Whole families worked on these projects to earn enough to feed everyone. In 1847 the government sent agricultural advisors to Ireland to educate the tenants. Many of the starving tenants had no seed, no money, no home, and no land. The advisors related this message to England.

The Passing of the Gael

Ethna Carbery (1866–1902)

They are going, going, going from the valleys and the hills,
They are leaving far behind them heathery moor an mountain rills,
All the wealth of hawthorn hedges where the brown thrush sways and thrills.

They are going, shy-eyed colleens, and lads so straight and tall,
From the purple peaks of Kerry, from the crags of wild Imaal,
From the greening plains of Mayo, and the glens of Donegal.

They are leaving pleasant places, shores with snowy sands outspread;
Blue and lonely lakes a-stirring when the wind stirs overhead;
Tender living hearts that love them, and the graves of kindred dead.

They shall carry to the distant land a tear-drop in the eye,
And some shall go uncomforted- their days an endless sigh
For Kathleen Ní Houlihan's sad face, until they die.

Oh, Kathleen Ní Houlihan, your road's a thorny way,
And 'tis a faithful soul would walk the flints with you for aye,
Would walk the sharp and cruel flints until his locks grew grey.

So some must wander to the East, and some must wander West;
Some seek the white wastes of the North, and some the Southern nest;

Yet never shall they sleep so sweet as on your mother breast.

Within the city streets, hot, hurried, full of care,
A sudden dream shall bring them a whiff of Irish air—
A cool air, faintly scented, blown soft from otherwhere.

They may win a golden store—sure the whins were golden too;
And no foreign skies hold beauty like the rainy skies they knew;
Nor any night-wind cool the brow as did the foggy dew.

They are going, going, going, and we cannot bid them stay;
Their fields are now the strangers', where the strangers' cattle stray.
Oh! Kathleen Ní Houlihan, your way's a thorny way!
(The Christian Brothers, pp.171–172)

Indian corn (maize) was imported from America to feed the starving masses. This corn was paid for by donations from the English, Americans, Irish Americans, and other nations. The imported maize was used to feed the Irish, while their wheat was sold in England at high prices to feed the industrial workers. Lady Jane Francesca Wilde, who used the pen name "Speranza," laments this particular situation in the following poem:

The Famine Year

"Speranza" Lady Wilde (1824–1876)

Weary men, what reap ye? "Golden corn for the stranger."
What sow ye? "Human corpses that await for the Avenger."
Fainting forms, all hunger-stricken, what see you in the offing?
"Stately ships to bear our food away amid the stranger's scoffing."
There's a proud array of soldiers—what do they round your door?
"They guard our master's granaries from the thin hands of the poor."
Pale mothers, wherefore weeping? Would to God that we were dead—
Our children swoon before us and we cannot give them bread."
Little children, tears are strange upon your infant faces.
God meant you but to smile within your mother's soft embraces.
"Oh, we know not what is smiling, and we know not what is dying;
But we're hungry, very hungry, and we cannot stop our crying.

And some of us grow cold and white; we know not what it means;
But as they lie beside us we tremble in our dreams"
There's a gaunt crowd on the highway—are ye come to pray to man,
With hollow eyes that cannot weep, and for words your faces wan?
"No, the blood is dead within our veins, we care not now for life;
Let us die, hid in the ditched, far from children and from wife;
We cannot stay to listen to their raving famished cries—
Bread! Bread! Bread!—and none to still their agonies.
We left an infant playing with her dead mother's hand;
We left a maiden maddened by the fever's scorching brand."
Better, maiden, thou wert strangled in thy own dark—twisted tresses!
Better, infant, thou were smothered in thy mother's first caresses!
"We are fainting in our misery, but God will hear our groan.
Yes, if fellow men desert us, He will hearken from His throne!
Accursed are we in our own land, yet toil we still and toil,
But the stranger reaps our harvest; and the alien owns our soil.
Oh, Christ, how have we sinned, that on our native plains
We perish, houseless, naked, starved, with branded brows like Cain's."
Dying, dying wearily, with a torture sure and slow—
Dying as a dog would die, by the wayside as we go?
"One by one they're falling round us, pale faces to the sky.
We have no strength to dig them graves; there let them lie.
The wild bird when he's stricken is mourned by the others.
But we, we die in a Christian land—we die amid our brothers—
In the land which God has given—like a wild beast in this cave.
Without a tear, a prayer, a shroud, a coffin, or a grave."
Ha! But think ye the contortions on each dead face ye see
Shall not be read on Judgment Day by the eyes of Deity?
"We are wretches, famished, scorned, human tools to build your pride,
But God will yet take vengeance for the souls for whom Christ died.
Now is your hour of pleasure, bask ye in the worlds's caresses!
For our whitening bones against ye will rise as witnesses
From the cabins and the ditches in their charred uncoffined masses.
For the Angel of the Trumpet will know them as he passes.
A ghastly spectral army before great God we'll stand,
And arraign ye as our murderers, O spoilers of our land."
(*Ghosts of Kilmainham*, p. 20)

At this time there were over 130 workhouses in Ireland. They were all full. The daily death count determined the number of newly admitted. Conditions within the workhouses were abysmal. Most were breeding grounds for disease. Families were split up according to sex and age. Some never united again. For a nation with strong family bonds, this was the worst place one could possibly go. Destitute families, on discovering this reality, sneaked out at night and walked the roads toward home. They died in the ditches as they traveled homeward. Others, who had nowhere to go, wandered aimlessly till they dropped where they stood and were buried in unmarked graves.

Thomas Francis Meagher had the following to say about the famine in a speech delivered on Slievenamon, July 16, 1848:

> *A scourge came from God which ought to have stirred you up into greater action. The potato was smitten; but your fields waved with golden grain. It was not for you. To your lips it was forbidden fruit. The ships came and bore it away, and when the price rose it came back, but not for the victims whose lips grew pale, and quivered, and opened no more. Did I say that they opened no more? Yes, they opened in Heaven, to accuse your rulers. (Cavanagh, p. 239).*

Tipperary County had the highest rate of evictions during the famine. The main towns of North Tipperary, Nenagh, Thurles, and Roscrea were in a pitiful state. In a four-month period Nenagh ordered the making of 1,130 coffins. Its people were dying from starvation and cholera. At the peak of the famine, Roscrea's workhouse death toll went from 940 to 2,025 deaths. The Thurles and Rahealty Relief Committee sent a report to the British Association for the Relief of Extreme Distress in Ireland and Scotland in February 1847. From this report the following information was extracted.

The population of this area was fourteen thousand. They were in dire need of food and money for the distressed. Two thousand were employed in public works; these were paid ten pence a day. Nine hundred and forty were admitted into a poor house that was constructed to hold seven hundred. Many of the poorhouse residents died of malnutrition and disease. The weekly death toll had increased fivefold. A further report submitted by the Relief Committee of the Society of Friends for this area disclosed that there were six hundred people in dire need of food but incapable of labor. The report also gave an account of the landlord status at this time. There were sixteen absentee landlords and fifty nonresidents in this area.

Figure 20-2 Bridget O Donnell and children, *The Illustrated London Times,* Dec. 23, 1849

> *Landlords were impoverished by the famine either by great efforts to feed the needy or by the inability to collect rents. The Damer heir, Lord Portarlington had recourse to the Encumbered Estate Court to sell Roscrea town and Borrisoleigh, as had the Butler Matthew heirs Thurles, and Peter Holmes's widow in Nenagh. Templemore alone remained solidly in the 18th century hands of the Cardens. (Murphy, Donal A., p. 24)*

"Black '47," the year 1847, was one of the coldest winters in history. Following this bitter winter, the harvest was blighted again. Thousands died while thousands more emigrated. In less than a decade, the population of the island was cut in half. It went from eight million inhabitants to four million. Large towns set up emigration offices to accommodate those who attempted to emigrate.

The language and culture of Ireland were equally blighted. During the famine, families lived in isolation. They avoided each other for fear of transmitting famine fever and related diseases. They didn't have the heart for socializing, dancing, and song. This isolation led to the loss of community gatherings, crossroad dancing, visiting, and storytelling. The *tintean* (the hearth), where the old stories were passed

Population of North Tipperary, 1841–1891

Date	North Tipperary Population Decline
1841	201,000
1851	147,000
1861	109,000
1871	93,000
1881	86,000
1891	76,000

from one generation to the next, was now a hollow cave of cold stones. The silent mist that brought the famine stole an entire curriculum of Irish folklore.

The Irish language had begun to decline during and after the Penal Laws, when education was forbidden. After the famine, almost a century later, the English language took precedence over Irish. English was the "get ahead" language. Irish was the predominant language in the west of Ireland. The vast majority of people emigrating from there took the language with them. This loss of the Gaelic-speaking population was a crushing blow to the native tongue.

By the postfamine years, the population of Ireland was halved. Whole villages were emptied. One million people emigrated to various parts of the world, mostly to Glasgow, Liverpool, Canada, and the United States. Many sailed on cargo ships without passenger facilities. Others got on board the "Coffin Ships," vessels that cast as many of the dead overboard as arrived safely on foreign shores. Some were put on ships chartered by the landlord and sent to Canada only to die of cholera in the quarantine shelters on such coastal islands as Grosse Isle. These voyages to North America took three weeks to three months, depending on the ship and the weather. Those who survived set about making a new life on foreign shores. Embedded in their brain were the horrors they had left behind. They held the English authorities responsible. This anger was passed from generation to generation. Even into the late twentieth century, Irish Americans continued to send arms and money to Ireland in support of a rebellion. They hoped to see the land of their fathers free and independent.

Ireland's Population Decline after 1841

Census Years	Approximate Population of Ireland
1841	8,500,000
1851	6,500,000
1871	5,798,000
1891	4,705,000
1911	4,391,000

The Deserted Village

Oliver Goldsmith (1728–1774)

Sweet was the sound, when oft at evening's close
Up yonder hill the village murmur rose;
There, as I passed with careless steps and slow,
The mingling notes came soften'd from below:
The swain responsive as the milkmaid sung,
The sober herd that low'd to meet their young;
The noisy geese that gabbled o'er the pool,
The playful children just let loose from school;
The watchdog's voice that bay'd the whisp'ring wind,
And the loud laugh that spoke the vacant mind;
These all in sweet confusion sought the shade,
And fill'd each pause the nightingale had made
But now the sounds of population fail,
No cheerful murmurs fluctuate in the gale,
No busy steps the grass—grown footway tread,
For all the bloomy flush of life is fled.
All but yon widow'd, solitary thing,
That feebly bends beside the splashy spring;
She, wretched matron, forced in age, for bread,
To strip the brook with mantling cresses spread,
To strip her wintry faggot from the thorn,
To seek her nightly shed, and weep till morn;
She only left of all the harmless train,
The sad historian of the pensive plain.
(Gibbons, D., p. 108)

A Local Look

Sir John Craven Carden (c. 1818–1879) succeeded Sir Henry at the height of the famine in 1847. He employed many laborers in building projects on his estate. Miles of cut stonewall were built to enclose the estate. These laborers were given one good meal of Indian corn a day for their labor. From 1856, tradesmen were hired in the rebuilding of his manor house, the Priory, which was subsequently renamed the Abbey. It is estimated that the rebuilding cost thirty-six thousand pounds. Also at this time he ordered the building of six lodges on the perimeter of his estate. These building projects provided much-needed employment for the locals, and the estate itself provided employment for agents, gardeners, gamekeepers, gatekeepers, maids, cooks, footmen, and stable hands. His cousin, John R. Carden of Barnane, on whose estate numerous Mahers lived, also tried to create employment for his distressed tenants. He employed two to three hundred people in

Figure 20-3 "Village of Moveen," the *Illustrated London Times,* Dec. 22, 1849

wall-building projects, the erection of a tower house on the Devil's Bit, and renovations to his dwelling house. Though it seemed that Sir John was making an effort to alleviate suffering and to provide employment, there were those who scorned him and his way of life.

Figure 20-4 The Abbey, Templemore (courtesy of the National Library of Ireland)

Carden's Wild Demense

Rev. Fr. Timothy Corcoran, Curraduff, Killea (1857–1928)

Of all the places on this earth, no matter where I roam,
I love you dear old Erin's Isle, my own dear native home.
Where're I stray by night or day, fond memories throng my brain,
Of pleasant, happy hours I spent, on Carden's Wild Demesne.

Of all the places on this earth, 'tis there I'd like to roam,
Were the pheasant, grouse and partridge, all find a happy home,
The wild jack hare he rises there, and scampers o'er the plain,

To try the swiftness of our dogs, round Carden's Wild Demesne.

The turtle dove sits cooing there, upon the tall oak trees.
The thrush and blackbird warble out, their notes unto the breeze.
The cuckoo's voice is hears to sound, along the flowering plain,
And echo through the woods around, on Carden's Wild Demesne.

'Tis sweet to roam those lovely walks, those fine and flowery dales,
To ramble through those grand old woods, and tell some happy tales,
Of bygone years, when homes were seen, all free from grief and pain,
As nature decked the verdant fields, of Carden's Wild Demesne.

It grieves me sore to see such land, oppressed by tyrant laws.
To strike a blow for freedom now, would be a righteous cause,
And stop our sons and daughters brave a-crossing o'er the main,
And leaving Paradise behind, in Carden's Wild Demesne.

Behold ye friends your native glens, behind their grandeur too,
Remember well tradition tells, that there's the place for your.
From the landlords and their agents, our rights we can regain,
And plant our homesteads one again, round Carden's Wild Demesne.

So rise up me old Tipperary boys and hasten to the fray,
And join your gallant comrades from Drom and brave Killea,
We'll free the land St. Patrick blessed, and break the tyrant's chain,
We'll hunt and shoot and reap the fruit, on Carden's Wild Demesne.

A local who said that the above was incomplete added the following verses. It is unclear whether these two stanzas were part of the original poem or were added later making them more immediate to the locality or the temperament of the times.

Come rise you men around Barnane and hasten to the fray
And join that noble country man Mc Sweeney from Killea
Led on by this brave mountaineer our lands we will regain
We'll plant our homesteads once again on Carden's Wild Demesne.

Cap and feather trimmed with green we'll march in grand array
Three cheers we'll give for every man that comes from sweet Killea.

The cruel orange Saxon brood we'll chase across the plain.
Their scarlet flag we'll tear to rags on Carden's Wild Demesne.

Sir John had political aspirations and considered running for Parliament. He knew that Irish Catholics generally supported the candidate endorsed by their bishop. He began a campaign of favors to the town and townsfolk, most especially the Catholic clergy. In 1861 Sir John gave a site to Rev. Dr. T. O. Connor, Parish Priest of Templemore, to be used as a Catholic graveyard, rent free. Again, in 1864, he gave a site to the Catholic Church, rent free, for the building of a new church. This was to be the current Church of the Sacred Heart. In 1863 Sister Mary Joseph Walsh, Sister Mary Regis Crean, and Sister Mary Acquin Mc Donnell came from Cork to Templemore with the intention of setting up a convent and opening a school. In 1872 Sir John Craven Carden leased a site to these Sisters of Mercy for the founding of their convent.

It was no surprise when, in 1865, Carden decided to contest a seat in Parliament. He chose to run as a Liberal. In order to gain the people's support, he wrote to the archbishop asking him to endorse the decision. In the letter he told the bishop that he had full intentions of supporting the tenant Catholic cause. As proof of his sincerity, he reminded the bishop of the favors already paid to the Catholic Church and to the people of Templemore. The bishop had another man in mind. Disappointed, Sir John decided to give up his efforts and return to his family, who was in England at this time. When it came time for elections in 1869, he decided to run again, but the bishop still offered no support. Sir John abandoned his plans for a political career.

Killea/Drom Mahers

It is interesting to look at how the three Maher groups survived during the time from 1800 to 1845. The Killea Mahers fared the worst, as can be expected. Tradition states that John and Mary Kate Maher had ten children. None of these children emigrated. This is no surprise, since mass Catholic emigration from this area began during and after the famine. All of John's sons were born in the bog at Gortbrack, Templemore. They grew to manhood on this very tiny holding. William, James, and Michael married while still living at Gortbrack, and they reared their families there. John went to Drom to his grandfather's plot, while Patrick went to Borrisoleigh. Thomas (1798–1882) married from Gortbrack into a farm in Larha, Drom. There was possibly another son named Daniel, who went to Knocka, Drom, and rented from John Lloyd, Esq. Many of these men lost infant children during the famine years. When their surviving children grew to adulthood, they emigrated, cousins going to cousins, younger brother's following older ones, and sisters facing the great unknown together.

The Borrisbeg Mahers

The Borrisbeg Mahers survived the famine. John Maher (c. 1800) married Judith Doherty (c. 1800). They had ten children. Of the ten, four emigrated: Margaret (c. 1848) went to Australia with cousins; Michael (c. 1838–1862), William (c. 1846–1862), and Thomas (c. 1852) emigrated to the United States. The remaining six, Anne (1832), Mary (1833), Denis (1836), John (1840), Johanna (1842), and James (1844), married locally.

The Goss Mahers

Michael Maher (c. 1810), of the Goss Maher line, married Catherine Martin (c. 1810) in 1840. Michael and Catherine had a large family, all of whom seem to have done very well for themselves. Paddy (c. 1845) inherited the home place. The second son, Michael (c. 1858), joined the Christian Brothers. When Margaret Maher (c. 1850) married Jim

Maher of the Borrisbeg line, the Goss Mahers and the Borrisbeg Mahers were subquently related. The Goss Mahers of this direct line survived the famine. Their farm remained in the family for one more generation.

The Borrisbeg, Goss, and Killea Mahers had large families. In the prefamine era, none of their children emigrated. However, many lost children to the famine, and those who grew to adulthood joined their countrymen as they sailed away to other lands.

Chapter 21: The Land Wars

After the famine there was a period of great despair in Ireland. Thousands upon thousands emigrated. The peak year of emigration was 1851. Never before and never after did so many rush to the shores of Ireland and sail away in hope of a better future. Those who stayed behind were about to enter another turbulent period. They were about to fight two wars simultaneously: the land war and home rule.

The Encumbered Estate Act of 1849 benefited landlords who were forced to sell their estates during the famine years. Almost seventy-five hundred estates changed hands over the next eight years. The new landowners decided to move from tillage to pasture and dairy farming. Dairy herds require large tracts of land for grazing and fodder. The small tenant plots had to be cleared. Those tenants who managed to maintain their tenancy were subjected to the practice of rack renting. If a tenant improved his land or made his home more comfortable, the agent or landlord assumed he had money to spare and raised the rent. Many Irish tenants lived in squalid conditions to avoid this rack renting. Evictions were commonplace. In the county of Tipperary, the Maher homeland, over sixty-five hundred families were evicted between the years 1849 and 1853.

The Eviction

William Allingham (1824–1889)
from Laurence Bloomfield in Ireland

In early morning twilight, raw and chill,
Damp vapours brooding on the barren hill,
Through miles of mire in steady grave array
Three score well-arm'd police pursue their way;
Each tall and bearded man a rifle swings,
and under each great coat a bayonet clings;
The Sheriff on his sturdy cob astride
Talks with the chief, who marches by their side,
And, creeping on behind them, Paudeen Dhu
Pretends his needful duty much to rue.
Six big-boned laborers, clad in common frieze,

Walks in the midst, the Sheriff's staunch allies;
Six crowbar men, from distant county brought,
Orange, and glorying in their work, 'tis thought,
But wrongly, churls of Catholics are they,
And merely hired at half a crown a day.

The hamlet clustering on its hill is seen,
A score of petty homesteads, dark and mean;
Poor always, not despairing until now;
Long used, as well as poverty knows how,
With life's oppressive trifles to contend.
This day will bring its history to and end.
Moveless and grim against the cottage walls
Lean a few silent men: but someone calls
Far off; and then a child "without a stitch"
Runs out of doors, flies back with piercing screech,
and soon from house to house is heard the cry
Of female sorrow, swelling loud and high,
Which makes the men blaspheme between their teeth.
Mean while, o'er fence and watery field beneath,
The little army moves through drizzling rain;
A "Crowbar" leads the Sheriff's nag; the lane
Is enter'd, and their plashing tramp draws near;
One instant, our cry holds its breath to hear;
"Halt!"— at the doors they form in double line,
And ranks of polish'd rifles wetly shine.

The Sheriff's painful duty must be done;
He begs for quiet—and the work's begun.
The strong stand ready; now appear the rest,
Girl, matron, grandsire, baby on the breast,
And Rosy's thin face on a pallet borne;
A motley concourse, feeble and forlorn.
One old man, tears upon his wrinkled cheek,
Stands trembling on a threshold, tries to speak,
But, in defect of any words for this,
Mutely upon the doorpost prints a kiss,
Then he passes out forever. Through the crowd
The children run bewilder'd, wailing loud;
Where needed most, the men combine their aid;

And, last of all, is Oona forth convey'd,
Reclined in her accustom'd strawen chair,
Her aged eyelids closed, her thick white hair
Escaping from her cap; she feels the chill,
Looks round and murmurs, then again is still.

Now bring the remnants of each household fire;
On the wet ground the hissing coals expire;
And Paudeen Dhu, with meekly dismal face,
Receives the full possession of the place . . .
(Kinsella, T., pp. 306–307)

The Land League

Michael Davitt (1846–1906) founded an organization called the Land League. Davitt was born at the height of the famine in County Mayo. When he was four years old, his family was evicted because of failure to pay the rent. Having nowhere to go, they moved into the local poor house. Upon entering the workhouse, their family was separated into men, women, and children. Even young Michael was separated from his mother. The Davitts were determined to keep their family together, so they left the workhouse and emigrated to England. At the age of nine Michael was sent to work in a cotton mill. When he was eleven he lost his right arm in a machine accident. Years later he was accused of being a gun-running Fenian and spent seven years of a fifteen-year sentence in English jails. Eventually he returned to Ireland and took up the case of the Irish tenant. Charles Stuart Parnell became the president of the Land League, while Michael remained the secretary. The aims of this new organization were to prevent evictions, procure legal leases, reduce rents, lower land prices, and work toward land ownership through peaceful means.

The Land League tactics included holding the harvest, refusing to pay excessive rent, offering a fair price or not paying (the plan of campaign), insisting on fixed rents, and boycotting. The latter tactic proved to be its most successful strategy. In 1880 Captain Boycott, a landlord's agent in County Mayo, refused his tenants' rent offer. The entire neighborhood shunned him. He was refused service from local stores, labor from the laborers, mail, and so on. When the laborers refused to help him save the harvest, he was forced to send for fifty orange order laborers and a police guard to harvest his crops. As a result of this incident, the word *boycott* was introduced to the English dictionary.

Michael Davitt traveled throughout Ireland, urging Irish tenants to join the Land League. Charles Stuart Parnell's sister, Fanny Parnell, formed the Ladies Land League. She wrote fiery poetry not unlike the Young Irelanders of 1848, urging the tenants to stand up for their rights.

Hold the Harvest

Fanny Parnell (1848–1882)

Now, are ye men, or are ye kine,
    ye tillers of the soil?
Would ye be free, or even more
    the rich man's cattle toil?
The shadow on the dial hangs that
    points the fatal hour
Now, hold your own, or branded
    slaves for ever cringe and cower.

Oh, by the God who made us all—
    the seignior and the serf
Rise up and swear this day to hold
    your own green Irish turf
Rise up and plant your feet as men
    where now you crawl as slaves
And make you harvest fields your camp
    or make of them your graves.

> But God is on the tenant's side,
>   the God that loves the poor;
> His angels stand with flaming swords
>   on every mount and moor
> They guard the poor man's flocks and herds,
>   they guard him ripening grain;
> The robber sinks beneath their curse
>   beside his ill-got gain.

In 1879 Tenant Farmer Clubs formed throughout North Tipperary. Later these clubs merged into the National Land League. By 1880 Templemore had joined their ranks, and by 1881 most towns in Ireland had branches. The Land League was quite successful in highlighting the tenant's plight, gaining extensive following both in Ireland and abroad. Money from the United States was used to help evicted tenants re-lease their property, provide temporary housing for the evicted, and give food and clothing to those in dire need. With the confidence of such support, tenants grew bolder and began making demands upon the landlords and the government. In 1881, at the height of their success, Davitt, Parnell, and the other leaders were imprisoned.

The Land League urged the Irish tenants to refuse to pay their rent in protest against the unjust imprisonment of their leaders. Skirmishes throughout the country caused great anxiety to the English, and the prisoners were released. It is interesting to note that in Templemore many horse-drawn cars took food, fuel, and supplies to the homes of the jailed men. These supplies came from the people of Templemore, Drom, Loughmore, Templetuohy, and Killea. Such was the reaction of many Land League groups throughout Ireland.

The Kilburry Meaghers

Figure 21-1 The Ejectment, the *Illustrated London Times,* Dec. 16, 1848

A branch of O Meaghers settled in South Tipperary during the sixteenth century. The Meaghers of Kilburry and Kilmoyer descendents of this line made national news during the Land League days. Subsequently Kilburry was nicknamed "The Cradle of the Land League." The Meagher family, which tenanted land at Kilburry, Cloneen, was a well-respected family in the community. In 1879 their rack rent was too high to be paid and an eviction notice was issued. Henry Meagher informed the local Land League of his plight. A meeting was called at Cloneen. Almost twenty thousand farmers and laborers attended. It was decided that no one would be allowed to rent the farm over the head of the current tenant and that the landlord was to be boycotted until he agreed to a fair rent and reinstated the Meaghers.

Below is an account of the Irish National League meeting at Clonmel taken from *The Nationalist,* Saturday, September 6, 1890.

> *The usual fortnightly meeting of above was held in the Catholic National Club on Tuesday evening. There was a large attendance of members. The Hon. Sec. read the following resolutions from the Drangan suppressed branch.*
>
> *Resolved—that we condemn the action of E. N. Going, late Traverstown, Nenagh, Co Tipperary, presently of Ballymagarvey, Balrath, Navan, Co. Meath for grabbing the Kilburry evicted farm.*
>
> *Resolved—that we again condemn the brutal and unjust eviction of the Meaghers of Kilburry by Mr. Henry Beasley, Blackrock, Co. Dublin, and confidently appeal to the branches throughout the county for their moral support in the aiding of the Meaghers to regain possession of their evicted farm.*
>
> *The committee unanimously adopted the resolutions, and also pledged themselves to give all the moral support in their power in aiding the Meaghers to regain possession of their farm. The charges against certain persons named were gone into, but decision was deferred to the next meeting pending further information...*

Neighbors and Land Leaguers boarded up the Meagher house and barricaded the driveway in anticipation of the eviction. Twenty farmers were ordered to protect the house for ten days. On eviction day the police tried to talk the men into surrendering their positions, but they refused. The police gained access to the house through backfields and arrested the farmers. As these men were being transported in wagons to Clonmel Jail, the crowds cheered and hailed them as "The Men of Kilburry." A huge celebration was held in Cloneen upon their release.

In 1882 the Meaghers agreed on a settlement and were reinstated in their tenancy. A year later they were ordered out, even though their crops remained unharvested in the fields. The local Land Leaguers—Michael Cusack, Thomas Ryan, and C. J. Meagher—rallied the neighbors to harvest the crops. Men, women, and children set to work and successfully harvested all thirty-six acres of Meagher's corn.

> *A Famous Victory . . . A Land League organizer named Boyton who had come from Dublin addressed all those assembled from a rise of ground in the Fíodh Mór (big field or big wood), and a tremendous cheer greeted the closing words of his address.*
>
> *For those who sow shall reap,*
>
> *And Kilburry's shown all Ireland*
>
> *How we did the harvest keep!*

The crowd then formed in procession, and, preceded by the band, marched in triumph through the little village of Cloneen—bound for Kilburry, where refreshments were served to all. The musicians then proceeded to play for the dancing which followed, and the younger people present spread all over the level lawn before Kilburry House to enjoy themselves in a victory dance. There was a moving scene when Mrs. Meagher appeared at the hall-door of her home, holding a spray of laurel leaves, and thanked the neighbors who had loyally come to the midnight reaping. There was a great hush as she repeated the lines from Kickham's song of the *Maid of Anner:*

> *Ah, cold and well—nigh callous*
>
> *This weary heart has grown,*
>
> *For thy hapless fate, dear Ireland,*

> *And for sorrows of my own.*
>
> *(Maher, James, pp. 182–185)*

The Kilburry Meaghers were eventually evicted from their Kilburry property. Henry Meagher died from the stress of the land war. However, his wife, Margaret Sheehy Meagher, held firm. She never gave up. When her cattle were seized in lieu of the rent, she followed the bailiffs all the way to the fair and prevented their sale. Despite her efforts, the family was eventually forced to quit the property at Kilburry. They procured another tenancy near Cahir, County Tipperary. Such was the fate of many Mahers during these times.

The Irish Republican Brotherhood/The Fenians

In 1852 Isaac Butt, a Donegal man and brilliant barrister, ran for Parliament and succeeded on the Unionist ticket. While in office he founded the Home Rule League (1873). His goal was to establish a Parliament for Ireland where laws could be made independent of Britain. The Home Rulers eventually became a powerful political party. By 1874 there were sixty Home Rulers in Parliament. In 1875 Charles Stuart Parnell was elected as the Home Rule candidate for County Meath. Parnell was also famous for his support of the tenant's rights. When Isaac Butt died, Parnell became the leader of the Home Rule party and founded a new organization called the National League. Its aim was to gain Parliamentary seats for Irish candidates and to continue to work toward Home Rule.

In 1858 a militant group formed under the name of the Irish Republican Brotherhood (IRB). The founding members were James Stephens, John O Leary, Thomas Clarke Luby, James O Mahoney, and Michael Doheny. Most of these had escaped capture during the 1848 rebellion. They founded this new militant group in the footsteps of the United Irishmen and the Young Irelanders. Charles Kickham, John Devoy, and Jeremiah O Donovan Rossa joined the IRB. Each was given a specific assignment. John Devoy was to enlist the support of Irish patriots in the English military and in government and jailers in Irish prisons. James O Mahoney and Michael Doheny formed a sister group in the United States called the Fenians. Their goal was to supply men, arms, and money to support a revolution in Ireland.

Unfortunately, at this time America was recovering from the Civil War, and few were willing to turn around and fight another war in Ireland. In 1865 the government arrested the leaders of the IRB, O Leary, Kickham, Luby, Stephens, O Donovan Rossa, among others. Stephens escaped to the United States. The others were convicted of high treason and given long sentences or penal servitude. In 1867 the IRB rebelled, regardless of the fact that their leaders were in prison or in exile. Like the Young Irelanders before them, this revolt amounted to nothing more than skirmishes in blizzard weather.

Templemore town was famous for it strong affiliation to the Fenian organization. Even though the town had a large military barracks with many British soldiers, locals continued to join the Fenian ranks. It was not unusual for Irish men to join the British army and, at the same time, be sworn in as secret members of the Fenians. It fact when it was discovered that many members of the regiments inside Templemore barracks were Fenian supporters, their units were transferred, because it was deemed unsafe to have British soldiers sympathetic to the Fenian cause housed in one of the most volatile towns in Ireland.

> *During the late 1850's and early sixties when the Fenian movement was being organized, a large number of Irishmen, soldiers in the British Army all over Ireland, were being sworn in as members of the Fenian Brotherhood. This happened extensively in Templemore Barracks. In December 1865 the 11th Depot Battalion, which was stationed here for a long time, was transferred to Newry and Enniskillen and were replaced by the 59th Regiment from Glasgow. The reason assigned for the transfer of the 11th Battalion from Templemore is that it was strongly suspected that those troops are tainted with Fenianism. Templemore is the H.Q. of a depot battalion and the majority of those soldiers are recruits, drafted from several parts of Ireland, but Tipperary men predominate. (Walsh, 1991, p. 58)*

Walsh goes on to say that these soldiers got rowdy in the public houses and socialized with questionable persons. Two of these soldiers were arrested for singing Fenian songs. When they were charged, they retorted that the entire company should be arrested on similar charges.

It was the policy of the Fenians to assign each local area a Volunteer who had returned from fighting in the U.S. Civil War. These men were well trained and had extensive experience in battle. Joseph Gleeson of Borrisoleigh led the Templemore Fenians in the rebellion of 1867. Captain Gleeson had fought in the U.S. Civil War among the 63rd New York Volunteers. His mission was to recruit and train the Templemore Fenian Circle for rebellion. When the time came for the rebellion, his assignment was to take a small group of men to the Railway Bridge at Aughall and destroy it. This would prevent the Dublin–Cork train from bringing supplies and munitions to the English military barracks in the town. He was also to assemble the remaining troops on the Devil's Bit Mountain, with plans to march to Limerick Junction, where General Godfrey Massey waited with a large army of Fenians.

Gleeson's mission was a failure. His men were ill equipped, having insufficient ammunition. In fact Gleeson sent some of his men home, because they had only two guns and several pikes between them. His forces on the Devil's Bit Mountain were equally ill equipped and swiftly dispersed by the superior forces of the British Army. Their plan to destroy the Railway Bridge also failed, because the Volunteer with the lighter fluid never arrived. The Fenian rising became yet another unsuccessful bid for independence since 1641.

Though the Fenian rising of 1867 was a failure, it demonstrated the determination of the Irish to win freedom through violent means. Gladstone recognized this fact and declared that the Irish would continue to revolt if their issues were not resolved. He pressured Parliament to consider this and managed to gain some land concessions, but he failed to secure Home Rule. Though the Fenian rebellion failed as an act of war, the IRB, as an organization, actually continued to survive and grow well into the twentieth century. All the signers of the 1916 proclamation were IRB members except for James Connelly.

The relentless pressure from the Home Rulers, the Land League, and the Fenians forced the English government to relax the land laws in an effort to divert attention from the Home Rule issue. "Killing Home Rule by Kindness" became their new motto. It was hoped that tenant satisfaction would distract from Home Rule demands. As a result it took almost half a century (1850–1921) to implement the laws necessary to return the land to the Irish, who had been dispossessed some seven hundred years before.

The Church Act of 1869 disestablished the Church of Ireland as the state church of Ireland. Catholics no longer had to pay tithes to the Protestant Church.

The Land Act of 1870 changed the status of tenant rights. The law now favored the tenant. If the tenant was evicted for reasons other than not paying the rent, the landlord had to pay the tenant "compensation for disturbance." Another clause gave the tenant the right to sell his interest in a plot of land. The tenant could also purchase the plot with the aid of government grants.

During the years 1879 to 1903, grants at low interest rates were given to farmers to help pay rent or buy out farms. Tenants were entitled to compensation for their interest in the land if they chose to move elsewhere and leave their plot to someone else. As a result of these agrarian reforms, landlords slowly disposed of their estates.

The Ballot Act of 1872 allowed the Irish to vote by secret ballot. No longer could the landlord force his political views upon his tenants under threat of eviction.

The Land Act of 1881 set up land courts where a fair rent was fixed. The courts also established fixity of tenure and free sale of land. Many landlords knew that it was only a matter of time before they were forced to sell their land at fixed prices, so they began selling their land to the tenants at agreed prices.

The Ashbourn Land Act of 1885 gave five million pounds to Irish tenants at 4 percent interest to be paid back over forty-nine years to help buy out their land. In 1885 the land commission lent money to tenants to purchase their holdings from the landlords.

In 1886 Gladstone, the prime minister of England, put forward a Home Rule bill, but this bill was rejected.

The Land Purchase Act of 1891 gave an additional thirty million pounds to tenants for the purchase of holdings. This act also provided for the setting up of the "Congested District Boards." Their goal was to alleviate congestion on land in the west.

Again, in 1893, Gladstone put forward another Home Rule Bill. This too was rejected. It passed the House of Commons, but the House of Lords rejected it.

The Balfour Act of 1896 allocated fifty million pounds to tenants in order to buy out holdings.

The Local Government Act of 1898 transferred power from the Grand Juries, who were formerly appointed by the landlord class, to a council elected by the people. Local governments formed into County Councils. In Tipperary, under the old system, the High Sheriff chose twenty-three landowners. The new system selected twenty-one members by public ballot. In Templemore in 1899, Sir John Carden was the only landowner elected to the council.

The Wyndham Act of 1903 allocated one hundred million pounds for land purchase. It also gave twelve million pounds to landlords to encourage them to sell their land.

The Evicted Tenants Act of 1907 forced landlords to sell their land. The land was distributed among evicted and current tenants.

The Saorstát Éireann Land Act of 1923 hastened the transfer of ownership. A judicial commission fixed the price of land for estates.

A Local Look

By the end of the nineteenth century, many districts in Ireland had cast off their landlord's yolk and were now farming their own land. This was not the case for the huge population of Mahers who lived on the lands of Sir John Craven Carden of Templemore. In 1863 John Craven Carden inherited a part of the Purcell Estate in Loughmore and increased his acreage to 7,850 acres. His tenants were highly agitated, because he refused to sell his property like so many other landlords had done. Sir John stood firm and continued to pursue a career in politics. Little changed up to the time of his death in 1879.

His son, John (1854–1931), succeeded him. John was the last Baronet born in Templemore. He was educated in England and was a staunch Unionist. He continued the political aspirations of his father. First, he became a justice of the peace; then, in 1882, he was appointed High Sheriff of County Tipperary; and finally, in 1899, he ran for local government. This bid for local political power failed. It was the landed people who voted for him and not the thousands of tenants who sat at will upon his estate. He ran for a County Council seat on the Unionist ticket and was elected by default. Two Nationalists, James Ryan and James Fogarty, ran against him and split the vote.

In 1898 the Local Government Act changed the political arrangements for each county. County Councils and District Councils were set up throughout the land. Their members were elected by the people and no longer appointed by the authorities. The Urban District Council replaced the Templemore Town Commissioners. This council had fifteen seats. The Grand Jury became the County Council, and Templemore was allowed one seat on this council. Two poor laws guardians could sit in the Thurles Poor Law Union. Lady Sybil Carden got one of two Poor Law seats; husband and wife were now local politicians.

Sir John began to suffer huge financial losses due to Land League pressure, boycotts, the no-rent campaign, and the plan of campaign. There were mass evictions, arrests, and fighting. Some of his rents were the highest among landlords. Pressure was put upon him to sell to the tenants, but he refused. In 1902 he left the country for England, placing his Irish estate in the hands of agents and solicitors. A year later, in 1903, the Land Act gave the Land Commission the power to force landlords to sell to the tenants. Still, Sir John Carden refused. Six years later, in 1909, Sir John had thirty-six cases against his tenants for refusal to pay rent. Though other landlords continued to sell to their tenants, Sir John refused to break up his vast Templemore estate.

According to Paul Walsh, a local paper reported in 1908,

> *Sir John Carden has proved himself to be one of the worst landlords in Ireland, and he has up to the present repeatedly refused to sell to his tenants under the 1903 act or to reinstate the evicted tenants of his holding. But it is generally believed that the Commissioners will soon reinstate those evicted tenants whether Sir John likes it or not... It is a matter of common knowledge that Sir John is in straights for money recently, and bailiffs have been in possession of his mansion for the past month. It is known that all the beautiful furniture, pictures, and other contents of the mansion are to be sold, by order of the Court. Sir John could relieve the pressure on himself by selling to his tenants, and by*

> *selling his vast grazing ranch. But with his characteristic obstinacy he refused to do so... Sir John's tenants met in the Town Hall Templemore and Father William Purcell C. C. presided. Mr. L. J. Ryan, Solicitor, Thurles, said he wrote to Sir John requesting him to sell to his tenants. Sir John replied asking for an offer to guarantee his present income. The tenants offered 20 3/4 years purchase. Carden wanted 23 years purchase, to give him an income of 3 ½ % basis. (Walsh, p. 38)*

Eventually, the estate commissioners were able to reinstate evicted tenants and distribute land to others. Sir John Carden was left with his Priory Demesne and Templemore Demesne. In 1922, when Ireland became a free state, a committee of local men known as the Big Five bought this property. They disposed of as much estate as they could by selling it in lots to local people for eighty to one hundred pounds per acre. However, they found it difficult to dispose of all the property, because many tenants lacked sufficient funds to purchase the land. The balance of the estate was given to the Land Commission, and the Land Commission Court in Dublin arranged for the allocation of the property among the locals.

The year 1922 was a jubilant year for the Maher families who tenanted the vast Carden estate. This was the year they finally bought the rights to the land taken from them several hundred years before. It was also the year the British departed Southern Ireland and Ireland was declared a free state. These Mahers were unique among Irishmen; they secured their land and their national freedom in the same year.

Sir John Carden left for England in 1902. In 1908 he disposed of the contents of the Abbey. A year later British Auxiliaries occupied the Abbey for the duration of the Black and Tan War. In 1921 the farm equipment was sold and the Auxiliaries were evacuated. Upon their evacuation, local Volunteers were ordered by their commanding officers to burn the Abbey. The cut stone was sold to Mount Saint Joseph Abbey, Roscrea, and it was used to decorate the Cistercian Abbey Church. It was not until 1925 that the final sale of the Abbey ruins occurred, and the rubble from the clearing of the site was used to repair the Barrack Square in Templemore.

The Killea/Drom Mahers

Thomas Maher (1798–1882) had been evicted from his farm in Drom. He found another tenancy in Shanakil. This farm lease fell to his son John (1832–1907) and his wife, Catherine Healy (1849–1921). Seven of their eight children were born on this property. It seems that John inherited the family home place along with his father's fiery temperament and nationalistic sentiments. The Home Rule movement was at its height in 1874. This was also the year of the general elections. Fr. O Connor, the parish priest of Drom, endorsed a nationalist candidate for the general elections. John Maher rallied support for this man and campaigned on his behalf. In doing so, he was leading an opposition to his landlord's candidate, who was a Unionist. John blatantly told his landlord, Mr. Roe of Loren Park, that he had no intention of voting his way on Election Day. Eviction papers were served after the election, and the Maher family was evicted. They went to live with relatives before finally settling at Ivy Hall, Templemore.

Another famous man of this lineage is Thomas Maher (1836–1876) of Knocka, a cousin of the above-mentioned John. Thomas lived at Knocka, Drom. He was born before the famine and was an adult at the time of the land wars. The following tale is attached to this John. A meeting had been called at Barnane to debate the local land situation. Most of the farmers present had walked to the gathering place from their local farms. Thomas Maher, in arrogant Maher style, rode into the meeting mounted like a chieftain upon his steed. The police must have known about the meeting, because they arrived on the scene rather suddenly while Thomas was still mounted. Thomas surveyed the situation and spotted an opening between the police and the crowd. He deliberately reared up the horse and charged through the gap. The police chased Maher all the way home to Knocka, while his fellow farmers were able to flee to the safety of their homes.

The Maher families who lived in Barnane, Knocka, and Drom were serious about land and land ownership. Many were tenants of John "Woodcock" Carden (1811–1867), a cousin of the Templemore Cardens. These Mahers felt strongly about their rights to the ancient

Figure 21-2 John Maher (1832–1907), trice evicted in his lifetime

territory of Ikerrin, particularly the Devil's Bit Mountain, Barnane, and the surrounding townlands. In fact two Barnane Mahers were accused of murdering John Carden's wood ranger, Timothy Cleary. When John R. Carden took over the Barnane estate in 1832, he was a youth of twenty-one years and an inexperienced landlord. He complained that some of his lands were "let up almost to my hall door." He wanted the tenants removed from this property so that he could convert it into demesne land. He named the tenants as follows: Patrick Carroll, Widow Carroll, Loughlan Shanahan, Widow Maher, and Michael Maher. They were offered compensation of 150 pounds to move elsewhere or take permanent employment upon the estate. A violent reaction ensued with a failed attempt upon the life of his steward. John R. Carden backed down.

Several years later, in 1844, a similar incident occurred. "A farm of 40 or 50 acres of very bad land is occupied by ten families living in poverty and idleness, trespassing in my plantations, and neither doing good for themselves nor anyone else. I offered five pounds a family merely to provide houses with an engagement to give them work winter and summer at ten shillings a day." (Letter written by John Carden to the *Nenagh Guardian*, October 16, 1844)

Timothy Cleary, Carden's wood ranger, served the eviction notices upon these tenants. They reacted violently and threatened his life. However, one family agreed to terms. Encouraged by this response, Cleary arranged to meet with the other tenants at a cabin in the townland of Ballymaher to petition the landlord's case. He was brutally murdered within the cabin, and his body was disposed of in a nearby ditch. Martin Maher (Tierney), William Maher, and John Shanahan were indicted for the murder. It was alleged that William Maher threatened Cleary, but that it was Martin Maher who cleaved him with a hatchet from behind. Martin was convicted and sentenced to hanging. The others were set free. Later the sentence was overturned due to questionable witnesses and evidence. It is not certain what happened to Martin Maher. Some say he was transported to Australia.

Subsequent to this murder, threatening notices were posted throughout the estate warning tenants and laborers against helping Carden harvest his crops or his potatoes. Carden offered five shillings a day to get his potatoes harvested, but no one dare accept the position. The notice stated clearly that anyone seen to cooperate with Carden would be murdered. As a result of the Cleary murder, these notices were taken seriously.

This incident gives testimony to the fact that Mahers were leading land agitators and tenant-rights activists. They joined the Land League and were actively involved in their local branches. They had a special Land League house where they helped plan strategy, set up evicted tenants in farmsteads, buy small places, and divide them out among evicted tenants. They also marched publicly and fought injustice with word and sword. They demanded fair rent, fixed tenure, and freedom of sale.

Enda Maher (1924–1999) of Knocka, told the author that the Mahers who lived in Barnane and around the Templemore area "were a hot-blooded lot who went after land rights with the appetite of a starving wolf." He also added that Barna Cross, at the foot of the Devil's Bit Mountain, was a hot spot for tenant-right battles. People gathered there to hammer out differences. Oftentimes these resulted in faction fights over land.

Chapter 22: Éire Saor

Éire Saor

John F. Her (1959)

I long await the day our fathers longed to see.
They struggled while the planter played
And wept in silence as their children strayed.
For glory's sake so many lives were wronged.
The boot and bayonet ne'er here belonged.
But empires fat fall victim to their preyed,
Especially when prejudice has overstayed
And pious poison in the air's prolonged.
A peace of man is purchased painfully
Slow when the piece that grips red tighter clings
To pages past before present things. This
Matrix puzz. has solution unity.
Through misty air and thorn field there rings
The call to symphony—trial wedded bliss.
(Her, J. F., p. 19)

Though the land of Ireland finally belonged to the Irishman, his island country belonged to another. It was a paradox of property. The Irish sought *"A land that could take its place among the Nations of the Earth,"* Robert A. Emmet. They were unwilling to abandon the ideal of an independent Irish Ireland. This was Ireland's last great struggle.

Four groups with similar cultural goals formed independently of each other at this time. Twelve men, including Archbishop Dr. Thomas Croke of Cashel, lamented the fact that Gaelic games had gradually been replaced in favor of British sports. These men decided to revive the native sports by setting up an organization called the Gaelic Athletic Association (GAA). The GAA was founded on November 1, 1884, at Hayes's Hotel, Thurles, County Tipperary. Its goal was to foster the revival of the ancient Irish games of football and hurling. Charles Stuart Parnell and Michael Davitt became patrons of the GAA. A year after the formation of the GAA, there were one thousand clubs nationwide. In 1887 the Thurles Blues won the first-ever All Ireland Senior Hurling Championship against Galway at Birr, County Offaly. Though the GAA was founded as an organization to foster the revival of Irish games, it eventually became a Nationalist organization with members using hurleys as guns to train for an uprising.

In 1893 Dubhglas De hÍde founded another cultural organization called Conradh na Gaeilge (the Gaelic League). Its ultimate goal was to revive Irish as the country's national language and to preserve the nation's folklore, songs, and oral traditions. It encouraged the use of the Irish language as the daily vernacular and in written literature. It broadcast its views through the weekly newspaper, *An Claidheamh Soluis* (*The Sword of Light*). Their first Oireachtas was held in 1897. This became an annual cultural fair promoting Irish language arts. They also held feiseanna, céilithe, aeríochta, and scóraíochtaí, which celebrated Irish music, song, dance, and language. In 1899 the Gaelic League held an annual conference called the Árd Fheis. The function of the Árd Fheis was to elect a committee to organize and coordinate its events. The Gaelic League lobbied hard to include Irish as a second language on the school curriculum. It also secured grants for schools that taught through the medium of Irish. It instituted Irish teacher training colleges and had Irish made a compulsory matriculation subject.

Though it seems that the ultimate goal of the Gaelic League was to foster the revival of the Irish language, a spirit of nationalism crept into its ranks. It was only natural that those working so diligently for an Irish Ireland would want a free Irish Ireland. As a direct result of the organization, there was a blossoming of Irish literature both in Irish and in English. Almost all the writers of the time wrote with strong nationalistic feelings. Some of the more famous Irish language writers at this time were An tAthair Peadar Ó Laoghaire (1839–1920), Dubhglas De hÍde (1860–1949), An tAthair Pádraig Ó Duinnín (1860–1934), Padraic Ó Conaire (1882–1928), Padraic Ó Siochfradha (An Seabhach) (1883–1964), Padraic Mac Piarais (1879–1916), and Padraic Colum (1881–1972).

Anglo-Irish authors included the following: James Clarence Mangan (1803–1849), Samuel Ferguson (1810–1886), Thomas Davis (1814–1845), Lady Gregory (1852–1932), George Moore (1852–1933), T.W. Rolleston (1857–1920), Katharine Tynan Hinkson (1861–1931), Daniel Corkery (1978–1964), James Stephens (1880–1950), Thomas Mc Donagh (1887–1916), and Joseph Mary Plunkett (1887–1916). The following Anglo-Irish writers are known as some of the greatest writers that the world has ever known: W. B.Yeats (1865–1939), George Russel (AE) (1867–1935), and J. M. Synge (1871–1909).

It had long been the policy of Britain to suppress Irish industry in favor of its own. Just as the tenants demanded fair rent, free sale, and fixity of tenure, the industrial workers deemed it time to demand labor rights. In 1905 the Industrial Development Association (IDA) was founded in Cork. Its membership spread quickly to Dublin and then throughout Ireland. Its goals were to encourage the growth of existing Irish industry, to promote the trademark and sale of Irish goods, and to foster the growth of new industry in Ireland. Since most Irish industries were agriculturally based, in 1930 the IDA was renamed the National Agricultural and Industrial Development Association.

James Larkin was the most prominent leader of the labor movement in Ireland. His unions in Belfast managed to unite Protestant and Catholic alike. However, when the police opened fire upon dissatisfied workers on the Catholic Falls Road, the sectarian differences were once again highlighted. In the south of Ireland, James Connolly united the Dublin laborers. He believed that unless Ireland was a free country, it could never achieve full labor and industrial autonomy. He joined forces with Larkin in 1908 and formed the Irish Transport and General Workers Union (ITGWU). James Connolly also organized the Citizen Army to protect striking workers from the police.

The GAA, the Gaelic League, the ITGWU, and the Citizen Army were independent organizations with separate goals and ideals. However, many of these groups had members in common. Slowly over time they were all drawn toward the common goal of an independent Irish Ireland.

Arthur Griffith (1871–1922) founded a newspaper that recalled the nationalistic ideals of the 1798 United Irishmen. He called it *The United Irishman.* This newspaper was most successful in spreading nationalistic ideas and strategy. In 1906 it was renamed *Sinn Féin* after the 1905 foundation of the Sinn Féin organization. The goal of the Sinn Féin organization was to free Ireland by her own initiative "all by ourselves." Sinn Féin was in fact a loose uniting of all of the earlier nationalist organizations. Griffith believed in nonviolent means to achieve his Irish Ireland. He expounded that the English administration in Ireland would become dysfunctional if the whole of Ireland refused to recognize it. He recommended that the Irish set up their own Dáil (Parliament), their own courts, and their own army. With an army, courts, and an Irish Parliament, the Irish would be encouraged to ignore the existence of English law.

Meanwhile, in England, the battle for Home Rule continued. Unfortunately, the Home Rule Party once strong under the leadership of Charles Stuart Parnell now began to lose momentum. Parnell fell out of favor with the Irish people in 1890. The Home Rule Party split into two factions: those who supported Parnell and those who refused to support him. It was not until 1900 that the two opposing groups reunited under John Redmond and continued to operate as a united Home Rule Party.

In 1907 an Irish Council Bill was offered by Britain. This bill gave Ireland a council in Dublin that would control education and other minor matters, while England controlled all foreign policy and major political issues. The Home Rule Party rejected this council. They felt it did not give Ireland sufficient autonomy. In 1912 Lord Asquith put through another Home Rule bill. This bill was acceptable to the Home Rule Party but refused by the House of Lords in England. A third attempt at Home Rule was offered in 1914. Though this bill did not account for any settlement on the Ulster question, the Home Rulers agreed to it, hoping to take what they could get for now and work for other concessions later.

World War I interrupted the negotiating process. Many Irish Volunteers joined the British Army in hopes that the British would look favorably upon them in the aftermath of the war and be willing to grant Ireland concessions. Two hundred thousand Irish soldiers went to war and fought in the British Army. Sixty thousand never returned.

The Home Rule Party's popularity declined radically during this period, while Sinn Féin's popularity increased phenomenally. In the 1918 general election, Sinn Féin won seventy-three seats, while the Home Rule Party won six and the Unionists won twenty-six.

At home Volunteers were restless and decided that England's preoccupation with the war was Ireland's opportunity for a rebellion. The leader of this group was Padraic Mac Píarais. He and the Irish Republican Brotherhood (IRB) planned a full-scale revolt for Easter Saturday 1916. A shipload of ammunition organized by Roger Casement was to come from Germany. This ship, *Aud,* was captured. Casement was convicted of treason and was hanged a year later. As a result of this loss of arms, the date for the uprising was moved to Easter Monday. This gave the IRB time to regroup. Eoin Mac Neill, who was the commander-in-chief of the Sinn Féin Volunteers, decided against the rising and sent word to his men that the rising was postponed. Padraic Mac Píarais and James Connolly, with his Citizen Army, decided to go ahead with the uprising as a statement of protest. The Volunteers chose the General Post Office (GPO) as their headquarters. They hung the tricolor flag from the GPO and stood outside to read their proclamation, Poblacht na hÉireann.

There was considerable loss of life among civilians during the 1916 Dublin City rebellion. In order to prevent further bloodshed among civilians, the Volunteers agreed to surrender. While there were minor skirmishes throughout the rest of Ireland, they were of little consequence, and the failed rising followed the path of Ireland's previous insurrections—Wolfe Tone and the United Irishmen in 1798, Robert Emmet in 1803, the Young Irelanders in 1848, and the Fenians in 1867. The leaders of the rebellion were arrested and imprisoned in Kilmainham Jail. Within a month, fifteen of them were executed. James Connolly, who was badly wounded during the rising, was unable to stand erect to face the firing squad. He was tied to a chair, blindfolded, and shot. In death these men became heroes. Padraic Mac Piarais predicted this when he claimed at the grave of O Donovan Rossa, "But the fools, the fools, the fools, they have left us our Fenian dead, and while Ireland holds these graves, Ireland unfree shall never be at peace."

I Am Ireland

Patrick Pearse (1879–1916)

I am Ireland:
I am older than the Old Woman of Beare.
Great my glory:
I that bore Cuchulainn the valiant.
Great is my shame:
My own children that sold their mother.
I am Ireland:
I am lonelier than the Old Woman of Beare.
(McMahon, S., p.107)

The spirit of nationalism grew to feverish levels after the execution of the leaders. Thousands of Irish soldiers were captured and shipped to English prisons, where they reorganized themselves as Volunteers choosing Eamonn de Valera as their leader. On returning to Ireland, de Valera was also elected leader of Sinn Féin. Sinn Féin joined the Irish Volunteers and formed the Volunteers or the Irish Republican Army (IRA). The old Fenian members and their followers formed a separate army called the Irish Republican Brotherhood (IRB). Together these groups provided a formidable guerilla army for Ireland. The Sinn Féin members of Parliament refused to sit in an English parliament. They set up their own Dáil in Dublin and immediately declared Ireland a republic independent of England. The Volunteers policed the country, encouraging all to ignore English law.

The IRA became synonymous with the Volunteers. Their tactics throughout Ireland were fiercesome. They shot anyone suspected of spying or leaking information to the British. They threatened the lives of those found speaking negatively of them and the new government. They attacked the British police force and British soldiers in guerilla-like attacks in units known as the Flying Columns. The British sent reinforcements to deal with the unrest. These troops were called the Auxiliaries and the Black and Tans (after their uniform

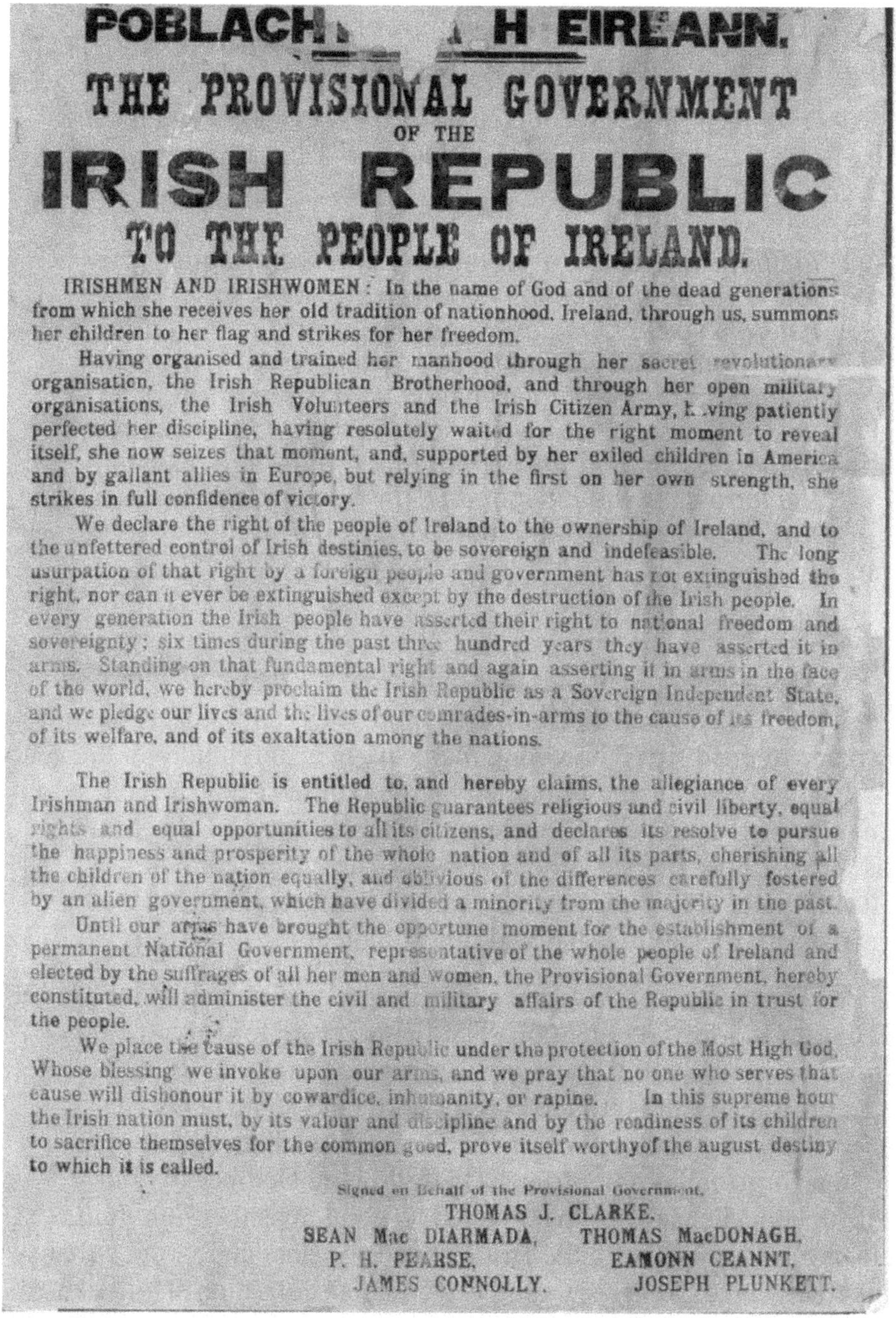

POBLACHT NA H EIREANN.

THE PROVISIONAL GOVERNMENT

OF THE

IRISH REPUBLIC

TO THE PEOPLE OF IRELAND.

IRISHMEN AND IRISHWOMEN: In the name of God and of the dead generations from which she receives her old tradition of nationhood, Ireland, through us, summons her children to her flag and strikes for her freedom.

Having organised and trained her manhood through her secret revolutionary organisation, the Irish Republican Brotherhood, and through her open military organisations, the Irish Volunteers and the Irish Citizen Army, having patiently perfected her discipline, having resolutely waited for the right moment to reveal itself, she now seizes that moment, and, supported by her exiled children in America and by gallant allies in Europe, but relying in the first on her own strength, she strikes in full confidence of victory.

We declare the right of the people of Ireland to the ownership of Ireland, and to the unfettered control of Irish destinies, to be sovereign and indefeasible. The long usurpation of that right by a foreign people and government has not extinguished the right, nor can it ever be extinguished except by the destruction of the Irish people. In every generation the Irish people have asserted their right to national freedom and sovereignty; six times during the past three hundred years they have asserted it in arms. Standing on that fundamental right and again asserting it in arms in the face of the world, we hereby proclaim the Irish Republic as a Sovereign Independent State, and we pledge our lives and the lives of our comrades-in-arms to the cause of its freedom, of its welfare, and of its exaltation among the nations.

The Irish Republic is entitled to, and hereby claims, the allegiance of every Irishman and Irishwoman. The Republic guarantees religious and civil liberty, equal rights and equal opportunities to all its citizens, and declares its resolve to pursue the happiness and prosperity of the whole nation and of all its parts, cherishing all the children of the nation equally, and oblivious of the differences carefully fostered by an alien government, which have divided a minority from the majority in the past.

Until our arms have brought the opportune moment for the establishment of a permanent National Government, representative of the whole people of Ireland and elected by the suffrages of all her men and women, the Provisional Government, hereby constituted, will administer the civil and military affairs of the Republic in trust for the people.

We place the cause of the Irish Republic under the protection of the Most High God, Whose blessing we invoke upon our arms, and we pray that no one who serves that cause will dishonour it by cowardice, inhumanity, or rapine. In this supreme hour the Irish nation must, by its valour and discipline and by the readiness of its children to sacrifice themselves for the common good, prove itself worthy of the august destiny to which it is called.

Signed on Behalf of the Provisional Government,

THOMAS J. CLARKE.

SEAN Mac DIARMADA, THOMAS MacDONAGH,

P. H. PEARSE, EAMONN CEANNT,

JAMES CONNOLLY. JOSEPH PLUNKETT.

Figure 22-1 Poblacht na hÉireann (courtesy of Sr. Gabriel Mary Gleeson) colors). The latter were a ruthless group who committed many outrages upon the innocent folk of Ireland.

Kathleen Maher recounted a story of her father and his men lying in the fields to hide from the Black and Tans. She explained,

> *In those days there were very few vehicles on the roads and the countryside was silent except for nature's voice. One could hear the rumble of the lorries from Thurles or Templemore. When the locals heard the trucks they went into hiding. It was not unusual for the soldiers to open fire on field hands or social gatherings among the farmers. My father lay between the furrows of the ploughed field when the lorries drove by. The women all ran indoors.*

She also talked of a Maher man from Loughmore who was lounging by a doorway in Thurles on market day. Soldiers sped into town and opened fire. The young man caught a stray bullet in the head. It lodged in his skull and remained there all of his life. The Black and Tans also set fire to several houses in Templemore. A Maher house was among those burned. The Black and Tans justified their indiscriminate acts of violence by calling them reprisals for the terrorist activities of the IRB and the Volunteers.

The amount of violence occurring in Ireland immediately after 1916 drew worldwide attention. The British were forced to respond. Prime Minister Lloyd George devised a plan for Home Rule. He partitioned the island into the current north and south. This was unacceptable to the Sinn Féiners and the Nationalists. In July 1921, Lloyd George called for a truce. The following October, Arthur Griffith and Michael Collins traveled to London as the Sinn Féin delegates. They met with the British heads of state and wrote a treaty. This treaty gave twenty-six southern counties dominion status like Canada or Australia. They were free to set up their own parliament in Dublin. Members would have to swear loyalty to the king of England. Military bases would be kept at the three ports of Cork, Berehaven, and Lough Swilly. Ulster was to choose its own destiny. It chose to be part of England with a parliament at Stormont. Griffith and Collins agreed to the treaty. They thought it prudent to accept what was being offered, with the intention of fighting for the rest when Ireland was in a position to do so.

When the delegates returned to Ireland, they presented the treaty to the Dáil. On January 7, 1922, Dáil Éireann accepted the treaty by sixty-four votes to fifty-seven. A provisional government was set up and Michael Collins was appointed leader of the transition from British to Irish rule. The Sinn Féin Party was split on the treaty issue. The Treatyites accepted the Saor Stát Treaty and were led by Michael Collins and Arthur Griffith. Those against the treaty became known as the Republicans and were led by Eamonn de Valera. The latter refused to accept Dominion status, the Ulster division, and the vote of fidelity to the king. A civil war broke out in 1922, and the Republicans fought against the Treatyites. During this vicious time, Griffith died suddenly, and Collins was assassinated. The entire country was torn apart physically, economically, and spiritually. In order to prevent further loss of life and economic destruction, Eamonn de Valera and his Republicans decided to surrender. A new government was formed, and Ireland was proclaimed Saor Stát na hÉireann (the Free State of Ireland). In the years that followed, the government of Ireland worked incessantly to rebuild the nation and develop the economy. Many Mahers joined in this effort on the national, county, and urban level.

The most renowned Maher of the twentieth century was T. J. Maher (1922–2002). Born in Boherlahan, Cashel, County Tipperary, he took over his family farm in 1948. Later he became the voice of the Irish farmer when Ireland was questioning the validity of joining the European Economic Community. In 1967 he was elected president of the National Farmer's Association (NFA), later known as the Irish Farmers Association (IFA). He was president of the IFA from 1967 to 1976. He successfully contested the European Parliament Elections in 1979 and served as an independent member for fifteen years. From 1976 to 1983 he was president of the Irish Co Operative Organization Society. From 1977 to 1979 he was the president general of the Committee for Agricultural Co Operation in the European Economic Community (EEC). Maher recognized that Ireland was first and foremost an agricultural society. He knew that hard work and heavy investment were needed to promote and develop the industry. In 1999 he was voted Farm Leader of the Century. In his later years T. J. Maher was a cofounder of Bothar, an Irish aid agency that provides livestock and agricultural aid to farmers in less-developed countries. While T. J. Maher represented the Irish farmers, his fellow clansman, Denis Meagher, was representing his home county and the homeland of the Mahers in North Tipperary.

Figure 22-2 Mae Meagher Quinn and Denis Meagher (courtesy of Mae Meagher Quinn)

Denis Meagher (1921–1998) was born in Shanakill, Roscrea. He lived most of his adult life in Killough, Killea, where his ancestors had lived for generations before. He served as a North Tipperary County councilor for seventeen years. Denis was first elected to the North Tipperary County Council in June 1974. He retired from politics in June 1991. During his years of service, he also served on a multitude of other boards, including the Agricultural Committee, the Drainage Committee, and as chairman of the County Council. His daughter Mae Meagher Quinn has followed in his footsteps and has been a member of both the County Council and the Urban District Council for the Thurles district.

This Land Is Ours

Gabrielle Ní Mheachair (1961)

This is our land, not yours,
Go take a hike and leave our shores.
Never more depress our mores,
We're free to spread our ancient lores.
The Celtic land is green again,
Not stained in the blood of our good men.
Its time to build and time to sow,
Let's plant the seeds and watch them grow.

I'd like a land that's truly Irish,
Not English beneath a silky veil
Finely decorated by a lonesome Gael.
Bring back the clans,
The Brehon laws,
The Irish dances,
And the Tara Halls.

Why do we fear liberty?
Isn't that what we fought and died to be;
A land that is totally free,
To do and choose our destiny?
So, where is the Irish,
The legends a score,

The dancing,
The singing,
The seanchaí go léir?
Where are they gone?
I'm confused,
I'm upset,
I don't get what is wrong!
The Irish I know are not Irish at all.
They have gone the ways of the agent and lord,
'Tis money, 'tis power and material hoards.
We fought and we died to get back our lands,
And now we have sold them to grease our own palms.

I am sick!
I am saddened!
I'm shamed by it all!
My land was once Irish,
And then it was stole,
We found it again
Though not in its whole.
The people have changed.
I don't know them at all.
It seems that dear Ireland
Has forgotten her goal.

The Killea/Drom Mahers

Throughout the Barony of Ikerrin, Maher families purchased their tiny farms, and in their lifetimes worked hard to enlarge their potato plots to substantial farms. The most prosperous Mahers of the Killea line were cousins Patrick Maher (1870–1961) of Ivy Hall, Templemore, and William Maher (1876–1943) of Knocka, Drom. Both increased their tiny holding to almost six hundred acres. After total dispossession by Cromwell, the O Meaghers were once again in possession of their land.

Figure 22-2 Patrick Maher (1870–1961)

When John Lloyd of Killea decided to sell his Lloydsboro estate and move back to England, Patrick Maher was determined to buy it. Patrick knew that Lloydsboro was, in fact, the old town lands of Gortruane and Barnaballynlegane from whence his ancestors came. These lands were the home of his great ancestors who had suffered eviction in every age and in every family, beginning with that first eviction by Lloyd in 1760. Patrick, himself, was a boy when his own father was evicted from Shanakill. The disposal of Lloydsboro was given over to the land commissioners who were determined to sell it in parcels to the tenants. Patrick Maher demanded, begged, bartered, and schemed to buy this property. Eventually the land commission allowed him to purchase one third of the property. This one third included the mansion house and the demesne grounds. The rest of the estate was divided among land commission tenants.

When Patrick assumed full ownership of the property, he renamed it Ikerrin Hall in honor of the ancient clan lands of his ancestors. In his lifetime, he accumulated six hundred acres and employed several laborers to help run his dairy, milk route, and farm. Laborers vied with each other to gain employment on his dairy farm. Patrick was also involved in local politics, and the townsfolk sought him out when in difficulty. Patrick Maher died in 1961, leaving his huge estate to his sons, John and Michael. John Maher (1913–1991) went to live at Ikerrin Hall and reared nine children there. Michael J. Maher (1915–1993) was given the Ivy Hall property. He reared thirteen children on this farm.

Michael J. Maher was to become the more famous son, because he followed the path of his father and entered local politics. Michael had been reared on the stories of his ancestors' turbulent past, the constant evictions, and the importance of land. He was party to family discussions, arguments, and meetings. His father, uncles, and cousins were active local politicians in Templemore, Borrisoleigh, Templetuohy, Loughmore, and Thurles. Hence, it is not surprising that he entered the political arena following in the forefather's footsteps.

Michael J. Maher happened to have lived through some of the most interesting times in Irish history: the 1916 rising, the land wars, Irish independence, the founding of the Saor Stát, the civil war, the founding of the two parties that would dominate Irish politics for the next century, the founding of the EEC, and two World Wars. He took up the political yoke with gusto and spent his adult life sincerely committed to the cause of the local population and their town. For thenext twenty years he worked tirelessly to improve Templemore and its environs. He helped with water schemes, housing schemes, employment, town planning and development, historical preservation, tourism, and conservation and environmental issues. He served as chairman of the Templemore Urban District Council (UDC) in 1970.

Figure 22-3 Michael J. Maher (1915–1993)

The fact that Michael was a great orator explains his popularity and guaranteed his selection as the town representative on many public boards, which included the Regional Development Association, Tipperary Joint Libraries Committee, North Tipperary Library Committee, Association of Municipal Authorities, and Irish Public Bodies Mutual Insurance's Limited. He was also a member of the Mid-Western Tourist Board, An Taisce, the Vocational Education Committee, and the Suir Drainage Committee and a director of the Shannon Side Tourist Board. He was selected to represent the Association of Municipal Authorities at the Social Conference of Europe during the founding of the EEC.

When Michael retired from active political work, he became a founding member of the Sister Aine Ó Cearbhaill Historical Association. He also took up the family tradition of beekeeping and was a member of the Beekeeping Association. In keeping with the many Mahers that came before him and the many who will follow, Michael J. Maher was dedicated to making his home town, his county, and his country a better place for all to live.

The Ó Meachair clan is unique among Irish clans. It is one of the few clans in Ireland that had the good fortune to live under the ancient Celtic system until the middle of the seventeenth century. In 1649 Cromwell's armies were responsible for the final dispersal of this ancient clan. Ironically, while the Ó Meachairs of the Barony of Ikerrin were among the last clans to be disposessed of their ancient clanlands, they were also among the last to regain proprietorship of their ancient lands. The tenants who populated those parts of the Barony of Ikerrin and Eliogarty owned by the Carden and Lloyd families were among the last tenants in Ireland to be given possession of their land. It was 1922 when Carden's tenants finally bought the rights to their land. As already mentioned, these Mahers got their land and their national freedom all at the same time! Theirs is a unique history.

Ó Meachair Nicknames

The tradition of family nicknames is more than three centuries old. When the Ó Meachair clan was dispersed, the clans people were no longer one large group with a common identity living under the protection of the Ó Meachair. They were now individual families fending for their personal livelihood. There were so many dispossessed individual Maher families living in the same localities that there was a need to distinguish among these families. Each family was given a new identity besides that of Maher. This new identity was the nickname. Those outside the family usually ascribed this nickname. Some were derogatory, and the family was ashamed of them. Such nicknames were never uttered in the presence of the bearer unless the desire was deliberate provocation and insult. Other family nicknames were honorable and a source of family pride. Some simply denoted place of birth or residence, while others listed paternal ancestors.

Nicknames have many origins, some tell of treachery done by the particular family (Maher Buisteirs). Some describe a physical trait (Maher Goss). Some depict the place of origin of a family (Maher Borrisbeg). Others denote occupation (Maher Smiths). Some even ascribe honor (Mahers of the Sword). Some denote lineage, the paternal grandfather (Maher Anthony), and many include three generations (Maher John William). Nicknaming is not unique to Mahers. It is common practice among all Irish clans.

Below is a smattering of nicknames from the Templemore, Roscrea, and Thurles areas in County Tipperary. It is certain that there are hundreds more in the greater County Tipperary and in County Waterford, where Maher is also a very common name.

Maher Abbey
Maher Andy
Maher Andrew
Maher Anthony
Maher Aughall
Big Jacks Maher

Big Jerry Maher
Big John Maher
Big Red Mick Maher
Maher Baker
Maher Balls
Maher Baltons
Maher Bannan
Maher Barber
Maher Baron
Maher Bás
Maher Bicycle
Maher of the Bog
Maher Big Jim
Maher of the Big Tree
Maher of Bigot
Maher Boaster
Maher Bog
Maher Bolton
Maher the Boot
Maher Breed
Maher of the Bridge
Maher Buck
Maher Bulls
Maher Buh
Maher Buisteár
Maher Cambie
Maher Caps
Maher Cill
Maher Citóg
Maher Conn
Maher Corr
Maher Costigan
Maher Count Van Knocka
Maher Craddock
Maher Crockes
Maher Crowe
Maher Curles
Maher Dan
Maher Danny
Maher Denis

Maher Dick
Maher Din
Maher Don
Maher Donkey
Maher Dowse
Maher of Dromard
Maher Eastwood
Maher Fields
Maher of the Ford
Maher of the Forge
Maher of the Furze
Maher the Gentleman
Maher of the Gate
Maher Grange
Maher Goss
Maher Hard Cabbage
Maher Hatched
Maher Herd
Maher Ikerrin
Maher Ivy Hall
Maher Jacks
Maher Jobber
Maher Joe
Maher Jos
Maher Jook
Maher Jude
Maher Kilcoke
Maher Kilduff
Maher Killough
Maher Knocka
Maher Kyle
Maher Lacks
Maher Lisanure
Little John Maher
Long Dinny Maher
Maher of the Lough
Little Pat Maher
Maher Mason
Maher Michael
Maher Micks

Maher Mike
Maher Miners
Maher Mixers
Maher Moores
Maher Mór
Maher Moyners
Maher Muca
Maher Mucknagh
Maher Musha
Maher Neds
Maher Nixers
Maher Oak
Maher of the Orchard
Maher Paddy
Maher Park
Maher Pollagh
Maher Puddles
Red Mick Maher
Red Dinny Maher
Maher Rabbit
Maher Ranglers
Maher Rattler
Maher Red Jerry
Maher Red Jim's
Maher Reed
Maher Red
Maher Pinch of Pepper
Maher of the River
Maher of the Road
Maher Rodgers
Maher Rodneys
Maher Rua
Maher of the Rue
Maher of the Trees
Maher Sadliers
Maher Scart
Maher Sceach
Scealie Maher
Maher Shanakill
Maher Shocks

Maher Skullys
Maher Smiths
Maher Sticks
Maher Suirside
Maher Suple
Maher Swine
Maher of the Sword
Maher Tailor
Maher Temple
Maher Theobald
Maher Tierney
Maher Tims
Toby Mahers
Maher Toher
Maher Toms
Maher Tulla
Maher Turf
Wedger Maher
Maher Waxies
Maher White
Maher Whitehead
Maher Wranglers
Maher of the Quarry
Maher Quarrels

References

Bassett, G. H. (1889 & 1991). County Tipperary One Hundred Years Ago, A Guide and Directory 1889, The Friar's Bush Press, Ireland.

Bateman, J. (Ed.). (1883). The Great Landowners of Great Britain and Ireland. Leicester University Press, New York.

Bluett, A. (1994). Things Irish, Mercier Press, Cork, Ireland.

Books of Survey and Distribution, (1641). (Vol. I–IV). Irish Manuscripts Commission, 1949–67, Dublin.

Burke, B. (1904). A Genealogical and Heraldic History of the Landed Gentry of Ireland, (Burke, Ashworth P. Ed.). 10 Edition, Harrison and Sons, London.

Burke, E. (1976). Irish Family Records, (5th ed.). Burke's Peerage Ltd. London.

Burke, E. (1994). The Irish Fiants of the Tudor Sovereigns 1521–1558, Edmund Burke, London.

Brewer, J. S. & Bullen, W. (1867). Calendar of Carew Manuscript, (Vol. I) Longmans, Green, Reader, & Dyer, London.

Callanan, M. (1995). Records of the Four Tipperary Septs, Jag Publishing, Tipperary, Ireland.

Carden, A. E. (2004). Carden of Barnane, private publication, West Sussex, England.

Carden, A. E. (2007). Carden of Templemore, Lulu, England.

Carney, J. (Ed.). (1942). Topographical Poems of Ó Dubhagáin and Ó hUidhrín, The Dublin Institute for Advanced Studies, Dublin.

Catholic Parish Registers, for Templemore, Roscrea, Drom, Clonmore, Killea, Loughmore-Castleiney, and Thurles, Co. Tipperary, Ireland.

Cavanagh, M. (1892). Memoirs of General Thomas Francis Meagher, Messenger Press, Massachusetts.

Census Returns of 1901 and 1911, Public Records Office, Four Courts Press, Dublin.

Christian Brothers, (1935). Flowers from Many Gardens, M. H. Gill and Son LTD., Dublin.

Christian Brothers, (1935). The Fifth Reader, M. H. Gill & Son LTD., Dublin.

Coffey, R. M. (1969). The American Dominicans, A History of Saint Joseph's Province, Saint Martin De Porres Guild, New York.

Colum, P. (Ed.). (1986). An Anthology of Irish Verse from Ancient Minstrels' Songs to Poems of the Modern Masters, Kilkenny Press, Kilkenny, Ireland.

Connolly, S. J. (1998). The Oxford Companion to Irish History, Edited by Oxford University Press, Oxford, England.

Cruise O Brien, C. & Cruise O Brien, M. (1985). A Concise History of Ireland, Thames & Hudson, London.

Cunningham, G. (Ed.). (1977,1983). Historic Roscrea Co. Tipperary, A Walking Tour, Shannon Side Tourism, Ireland.

Cunningham, G. (1976). Roscrea and District, Parkmore Press, Roscrea, Co. Tipperary, Ireland.

Cunningham, G. (Text). Monastic Roscrea, Roscrea People, Roscrea People, Roscrea, Co. Tipperary, Ireland.

Cunningham, G. (1987). The Anglo Norman Advance into the South West Midlands of Ireland 1185-1221, Parkmore Press, Roscrea, Co. Tipperary, Ireland.

Curtis, E. (1995). A History of Ireland, Routledge, London.

Curtis, E. (Ed.). (1932). Calendar of Ormond Deeds, 1172-1350, (Vol. I–VI). Oifig an tSoláthair for Coimisiún Láimhscríbhinní na hÉireann, Dublin.

Cusack, M. F. (1995). An Illustrated History of Ireland from AD 4000-1800, Bracken Books, London.

D'Alton, J. (Ed.). King James Irish Army List, (1698). (2nd ed.). (Vol. I & II.). Dublin.

De Breffny, B. (1977). Castles of Ireland, Thames and Hudson, London.

Delaney, F. (1986). The Celts, Grafton, London.

Dowling, A. (Ed.). (1981). Ancient Parish of Aghaboe Now Clough-Ballacolla, Wellbrook Press LTD, Co. Kilkenny, Ireland.

Down Survey Maps (1654). William Petty, England.

Duffy, S. (Ed.). (1997). The Macmillan Atlas of Irish History, Macmillan, New York.

Dunboyne, Lord, (1991). Butler Family History, (7th ed.). Modern Printers, Kilkenny, Ireland.

ÉILE, (1982, 1993, 2000). Journal of the Roscrea Heritage Society, Roscrea, Co. Tipperary, Ireland.

Fact and Fancy, (1963). Senior Text Book, Educational Company of Ireland.

Fogarty, P. (c.1970). A Short Historical Survey of Tipperary, PP. Templemore, Unpublished notes. Templemore, Co. Tipperary, Ireland.

Gleeson, D. & MacAirt, S. (Eds.). (1958). Annals of Roscrea, In Proceedings of the Royal Irish Academy, Dublin.

Gibbons, D. (Ed.) (1992). A Treasury of Irish Verse, Gill & Macmillan, Golden Bridge, Dublin.

Gleeson, D. F. (1947). Roscrea: Town and Parish, At The Sign of The Three Candles, Dublin.

Gleeson, J. (1915, 1982). History of the Ely O'Carroll territory, or ancient Ormond, situated in north Tipperary and northwestern King's County, Ireland, Dublin.

Griffith, R. (1851). General Valuation of Ratable Property in the Barony of Ikerrin, Valuation Office, Dublin.

Griffith M. C. (Ed.). (1966). Irish Patent Rolls of James I, Stationary Office for Irish Manuscripts Commission, Dublin, Ireland.

Hayes, G. (Ed.). (1993). A Garland of Irish Verse, Gramercy, Random House, New Jersey, U.S.A.

Hayes, Rev. W. J. (1970). Burials in Holy Cross Abbey, Holy Cross Abbey Restoration Committee, Holy Cross, Co. Tipperary, Ireland.

Hayes, W. J. (January 2, 9, 1993). The Mahers and their Ikerrin Homeland, Article by from Tipperary Star, Thurles, Co. Tipperary, Ireland.

Hayes, W. J. (1995). The Old Church and Graveyard Templemore, Sister Áine Historical Society, Templemore, J. F. Walsh, Roscrea, Co. Tipperary, Ireland.

Hayes, W. J. (1998). Tipperary in the Year of Rebellion 1798, Lisheen Publications, Roscrea, Co. Tipperary, Ireland.

Hayes, W. J. (2000). Thurles A Guide to the Cathedral Town, Lisheen Publications, Roscrea, Co. Tipperary, Ireland.

Hayes, W. J. (2001). Moyne-Templetuohy A Life of its Own: The Story of a Tipperary Parish, (Vol. I. II. III.). Moyne Templetuohy History Group, Thurles, Co. Tipperary, Ireland.

Hearth Money Rolls, (1665, 1666, 1667). Dublin.

Her, J. F. (1990). Streams, Arthur H. Stockwell Ltd., Devon, England.

Hewson, A. (1982). Clonakenny and Bourney, A Local History, J.F. Walsh, Roscrea, Co. Tipperary, Ireland.

Hussey De Burgh, U. H. (1878). The Landowners of Ireland, Hodges, Foster & Figgs, Dublin.

Hyde, D. (1980). A Literary History of Ireland, Ernest Benn Ltd. London.

Irish Families Historical Society, (1994). Meagher Maher O Meachair Clan Cian The Eberians of Ireland Lords of Ikerrin in Tipperary, New Jersey.

Kinsella, T. (Ed.). (1986). The New Oxford Book of Irish Verse, Oxford University Press, Oxford, England.

Land transactions of the Seventeenth century for the Barony of Ikerrin Tipperary

(Vol. 7 & 8). Can't find this anywhere.

Leask, H. G. (1964). Irish Castles and Castellated Houses, Dundalgan Press LTD.,

Dundalk, Ireland.

Lenihan. M. (1860). Book of Distribution of The County of Tipperary, manuscript County Library, Thurles, Co. Tipperary, Ireland.

Limerick Reporter, (February 23rd 1877). Hedge School, Washbin, Castleiney, Limerick, Ireland.

List of Popish Inhabitants of Half the Barony of Ikerrin 1750, Manuscript, National Library Ireland.

Loughmore-Castleiney Parish Newsletters, Legion of Mary, Loughmore, Co. Tipperary, Ireland

MacLysaght, E. (1973). The Surnames of Ireland, Irish University Press, Dublin.

MacManus, S. (1990). The Story of the Irish Race, Wings Books, Random House, New Jersey.

Maher, D. (1997). Medieval Grave Slabs of County Tipperary 1200-1600 AD, Volume 262 of BAR. British series, 262, John and Erica Hedges, University of Michigan,

Marnane, D. G. (1988). "Land and Violence in 19th Century Tipperary," Tipperary Historical Journal, Thurles, Co. Tipperary, Ireland.

McCarthy, Justin (1907). Irish Literature (vol. 7), John D. Morris & Company, Philadelphia. pp. 2871–2872

McGeoghegan and Mitchell (1884). The National History of Ireland, D & J Sadlier & Co., New York.

McMahon, A. (Ed.). (1976). Celtic Way of Life, Curriculum Development Unit,

O Brien Press, Cork, Ireland.

McMahon, S. (1987). Rich and Rare a Book of Ireland, Poolbeg Press, Dublin.

McMahon, S. (1990). The Poolbeg Book of Irish Placenames, Poolbeg Press, Dublin.

Mc Morran, R. (1977). History of Irish Art, Folens, Dublin.

Meagher, N. (1980). The Meaghers, Unpublished Notes, New York.

Moloughney, K. (1987). Roscrea Me Darling! J. F. Walsh, Roscrea, Co. Tipperary, Ireland.

Neubecker, O. (1979). A Guide to Heraldry, Casell LTD., Mc Grath-Hill, London.

North Tipperary County Council, (1983). Official Guide to North Tipperary, Condor Publishing Co. Ltd., Tipperary, Ireland.

Ó Cathaoir, B. (1999). Famine Diary, Irish Academic Press, Dublin.

O Cleary, M. (1644). Calendar of Irish Saints, Athlone, Manuscript Royal Irish Academy, Dublin.

Ó Comáin, M. (1991). The Poolbeg Book of Irish Heraldry, Poolbeg, Dublin.

Ó Corrain, D. & Maguire, F. (1981). Gaelic Personal Names, the Academy Press, Dublin.

O Daniel, V. F. (1855). The Dominican Province of Saint Joseph. Historical-Biographical Studies, National Headquarters of the Holy Name Society, New York.

O Donovan, J. (1838-1840). The Ordinance Survey Letters Co. Tipperary, (Vol. II). Unpublished, Dublin.

O Donovan, J. (Ed.). (1851). Annals of the Kingdom of Ireland by the Four Masters from the earliest periods to the year 1616, (Vols. 1-7). Hodges and Smith, Dublin.

O Dwyer, M. (1999). A Biographical Dictionary of Tipperary, Folk Village, Cashel, Co. Tipperary, Ireland.

O Hanlon, J. (Ed.). (1873). Lives of the Irish Saints, (Vol. I. II. III). James Duffy & Sons, Dublin.

O Hart, J. (1892). Irish Pedigrees, (5th ed.). (Vol. I). James Duffy & Co. Dublin.

Ó Meagher, J. C. (1890). Some Historical Notes of the O' Meaghers of Ikerrin, unknown, New York.

Ó hOgain, D. (1991). Myth, Legend and Romance, An Encyclopedia of The Irish Folk Traditions, Prentice Hall Press, New York

Ó Ríain, S. (1988). Dunkerrin A Parish in Ely O Carroll, Dunkerrin Historical Committee, Dunkerrin, Ireland.

Pender, S. (1939). A Census of Ireland circa 1659, Irish Manuscripts Commission, Dublin.

Prendergast, J. P. The Cromwellian Settlement of Ireland (1652-1660), Clearfield Publishing Company, 200 Eager Street, Baltimore.

Rate Books, (1971). Templemore and Drom Electoral Districts, County Library, Thurles, Co. Tipperary, Ireland.

Reeves, W. (Ed.). (1857). Adannan's Life of St. Columba, Irish Archaeological Society, Dublin.

Robertson, F. (Ed.). (1994). A Rich and Rare Land Irish Poetry and Paintings, Gill and Macmillan Ltd., Goldenbridge, Dublin.

Rolleston, T.W. (1985). Celtic Myths and Legends, Avenel Books, New York.

Ryan, S. (1960). Historical Account of the Parish of Loughmore, Unpublished Notes, Loughmore, Co. Tipperary, Ireland.

Saorstát Éireann (1932). Official Handbook, Hely's Ltd., Dublin.

Share, B. & Bolger, W. (Eds.). (1971). Irish Lives, Allen, Figgis, & Co. LTD., Ireland.

Sheehan, P. A. Glenanaar, The Phoenix Publishing Company Ltd., Dublin.

Simmington R. C., (Ed.). (1931). The Civil Survey of 1654-1656, (Vol. I). Irish Manuscripts Commission, Co. Tipperary, Dublin.

Skehan, W. G. (1993). Cashel & Emly Heritage, Abbey Books, Co. Tipperary, Ireland.

Somerset Fry, P. (1990). The Kings and Queens of England and Scotland, Grove Press, New York.

Soodlums, (1982). Irish Ballad Book, Oak Publications, London.

Stout, G. T. (1984). Archaeological Survey of the Barony of Ikerrin, Roscrea Heritage Society, Roscrea, Co. Tipperary, Ireland.

Taylor, G. & Skinner, A. (1778 & 1969). Maps of the Roads of Ireland, Irish University Press, Shannon, Ireland.

Trustees of Kilmainham, The Ghosts of Kilmainham, (1981). Elo Press, Dublin.

The Illustrated London News, August, September, October 1848, & December 1849, London, England.

The Students Treasury of English Verse Book III, Browne and Nolan Ltd. Ireland.

Tithe Applotment Books, (1814-1855). Public Records Office, Dublin.

Tipperary Historical Journal, (1990, 1993, 1988, 2000). Tipperary Historical Society, Thurles, Co. Tipperary, Ireland.

Von Volborth, C. A. (1981). Heraldry Customs Rules and Styles, Blandford Press, London.

"Whisperings," Templemore Parish Newsletters, Templemore, Co. Tipperary, Ireland.

Walsh, P. P. (1991). A History of Templemore and its Environs, J. F. Walsh, Roscrea, Co. Tipperary, Ireland.

www.ingramcontent.com/pod-product-compliance
Lightning Source LLC
Chambersburg PA
CBHW071658170426
43195CB00039B/2228